Andrew David Stedman teaches history at Newcastle University. He holds a PhD from Kingston University and was awarded the British International History Group Thesis Prize in 2008.

ALTERNATIVES TO APPEASEMENT

Neville Chamberlain and Hitler's Germany

ANDREW DAVID STEDMAN

I.B. TAURIS
LONDON · NEW YORK

New paperback edition published in 2015 by I.B.Tauris & Co. Ltd
www.ibtauris.com

Distributed worldwide by I.B.Tauris & Co Ltd
Registered office: 6 Salem Road, London W2 4BU

First published in hardback in 2011 by I.B.Tauris & Co. Ltd

ISBN: 978 1 78076 988 2
eISBN: 978 0 85773 628 4

A full CIP record for this book is available from the British Library
A full CIP record is available from the Library of Congress

Library of Congress Catalog Card Number: available

Printed and bound in Great Britain by CPI Antony Rowe, Chippenham

CONTENTS

PREFACE

When Britain declared war on Nazi Germany in September 1939, it marked the end of Prime Minister Neville Chamberlain's policy of appeasement, popularly viewed today as a cowardly and foolish venture, pursued by a misguided leader in a failed attempt to avert hostilities. The verdict of history on Chamberlain and appeasement began to be considered straight away, even during the war itself and in the emotional and recriminatory aftermath. Chamberlain's successor and the man who had defeated Hitler, Winston Churchill, looked back on 'the unnecessary war' and produced a damning appraisal of Chamberlain and appeasement in his memoirs, thereby opening the floodgates for a series of historical works reinforcing such negative interpretations. While the debate continues in academic circles today, it is clear which Prime Minister was the hero of the hour – and who was the villain of the piece – in the national memory of Britain's role in the onset of the war.

Though it has often been argued that it is not part of the historian's duty to say what *ought* to have been done, a large number of scholars writing about the Second World War have speculated about the various other paths not taken, and understandably asked whether the tragedy could have been avoided altogether. While counterfactual history in general has become increasingly popular and more specialised in recent years, most writing about alternatives to appeasement in specific remains vague, fragmentary and, ultimately, unsatisfying. A comprehensive, overarching synthesis has been long overdue.

In light of the significant gap in the literature, this study utilises a wide range of sources to systematically analyse the origins, nature and viability of the various alternatives to appeasement. Who suggested other policies, when and why? To what extent did the National Government consider the rival options it had available to it and how realistic were they perceived to be? Did Chamberlain have sound reasons for rejecting other paths and settling firmly on appeasement?

From isolationism, pacifism and accelerated economic and colonial appeasement, the League of Nations, collective security and various kinds of alliances, through to massive rearmament, the threat of war and, ultimately, war itself, this work seeks to explore whether or not Chamberlain could have done anything else that would have led to a better outcome. While we are able to enjoy hindsight unavailable to the actors in events themselves, such an analysis proves essential to the ongoing historical debate on Chamberlain and the origins of the Second World War. Meanwhile, appeasement more generally remains a provocative issue even today, still a relevant part of foreign policy discourse some seventy years later.

ACKNOWLEDGEMENTS

I would like to thank John Davis and Peter Beck at Kingston University for their guidance and encouragement in the preparation of my doctoral thesis and their continued interest in all I do. Peter Neville was an additional source of inspiration during my time at Kingston. Various colleagues at Newcastle University have offered advice as I worked on this book, not least Jakob Wisse, Fergus Campbell and Martin Farr. I would also like to thank David Dutton at the University of Liverpool and Angela Coss for their constant support and assistance. The former inspired my interest in Neville Chamberlain and appeasement during my undergraduate days, while the latter contributed in no small way to my enthusiasm for history in the first place.

Numerous Members of BISA's British International History Group are owed my deep gratitude for their continued interest in my work, particularly Gaynor Johnson of the University of Salford and Glyn Stone of UWE Bristol. Thanks are also due to the many postgraduate researchers who have provided feedback on my various papers and other publications, not least at the Institute of Historical Research, University of London. Joanna Godfrey and Rohini Krishnan, at I.B. Tauris and Newgen Imaging Systems respectively, have acted as invaluable guides through the process of producing this book, and are owed special thanks for their endeavours and enthusiasm. David Dutton, Peter Beck, John Davis, Suzanne Pink, Tim Paget and Lester

Freamon all commented on early drafts of this work and their input was invaluable to me. Finally, I would like to thank my friends and family for their love, encouragement and support. While I am grateful to all of the above for their varied contributions, the arguments in this work, and any errors in it, are mine alone.

INTRODUCTION

In none of the books and articles that I have read have I found a coherent answer to the question: given the circumstances of 1937 and 1938, what alternative was practicable?[1]

(Wilson, 1948)

A decade after Neville Chamberlain declared 'Peace for our time' following the signing of the Munich Agreement in September 1938, Sir Horace Wilson wrote to the Prime Minister's widow surveying the verdict of history so far reached in the years since the end of the war. It had not been kind. As Chief Industrial Adviser to Chamberlain's National Government and a close confidant of this most private of statesmen, Wilson was uniquely placed to comment on the many bitter and recriminatory assessments of Chamberlain's career in high office, produced in the emotional aftermath of the end of hostilities. Chamberlain's policy of appeasement during the late 1930s had provoked a wide range of deeply polarised responses from the British political elite and general public alike. Lauded as the saviour of the world at the time of Munich, he was heavily criticised from all directions when German tanks rolled into Prague just six months later.

In the immediate wake of Dunkirk in June 1940, a trio of left-wing journalists, Michael Foot, Peter Howard and Frank Owen, under the collective pseudonym of 'Cato', published their damning indictment of the *Guilty Men* who had brought the nation to this low ebb during a decade of political, military and moral decline. Chamberlain, who had been pushed out of the premiership just one month earlier, headed the opening cast list as the arrogant and foolish 'Umbrella Man', the naive leader who was duped by Hitler and failed to prepare his people sufficiently for the horrors now confronting them.[2] In turn, this best-selling polemic set the tone for the post-war debate apportioning blame for Britain's role in proceedings, most notably those articulated in the first 'orthodox' histories of the period, published in 1948 by Sir Lewis Namier, Sir John Wheeler-Bennett and Winston Churchill.[3] Though Chamberlain had died of cancer in November 1940 before he could dictate any memoir explaining his actions, his successor exerted greatest impact as the hero of the hour, the wartime leader who would never surrender to Hitler, the 'Greatest Living Englishman' as he had become affectionately known in some circles.[4] As one contemporary reviewer noted, 'no man alive has more right to tell the world "I told you so" ... than Winston Churchill'.[5] His book painted a picture of a decade in which his own repeated warnings of the looming threat of Nazism were ignored, first by Stanley Baldwin and then by Chamberlain, and of the years in which the British, 'through their unwisdom, carelessness and good nature allowed the wicked to rearm'.[6]

However, if it was easy to attack Chamberlain's policy from the sidelines, Wilson realised that it was far more difficult to suggest a viable alternative course of action. Nor was he alone in this view, as evidenced in 1952 when Sir John Simon, Chamberlain's loyal Chancellor of the Exchequer, asked 'Then what could Chamberlain do, other than what Chamberlain did?'.[7] We are still waiting for a definitive answer.

The ongoing historiographical debate about Chamberlain, appeasement and the origins of the Second World War has been as fierce as those occurring at the time. Although space does not permit an in-depth review of the literature – thankfully several works provide this already – a brief introductory discussion of the current state of play proves essential.[8] During recent decades, any writing on this subject has been heavily influenced by R.A.C. Parker's landmark 1993 study, *Chamberlain and Appeasement: British Policy and the Coming of the Second World War*. Championing the 'post-revisionist' school of thought on this Prime Minister and his policies, Parker resurrected many of the old *Guilty Men* charges voiced by Cato and Churchill, among others, against Chamberlain's National Government, thereby seeking to displace a wave of more generous 'revisionist' accounts emerging during the late 1960s as a result of the passing of time and the opening of archives. These more charitable analyses tried to explain Chamberlain's role rather than merely condemning it, as much of the historiographical orthodoxy had done. Acknowledging the near impossible hand he was dealt with – so often a central pillar of revisionist literature – Parker's Chamberlain was depicted as a capable but deluded leader, arrogantly assured that his own personal charm was able to induce Hitler to abandon the methods of war, even after the March 1939 Prague Coup, when German troops entered the Czech capital in violation of the Munich Agreement.[9]

Following Parker's lead and the opening up of previously untapped Russian archives, the Soviet dimension of the appeasement debate became a central focus as Keith Neilson, Hugh Ragsdale, Michael Jabara Carley, Geoffrey Roberts and Louise Grace Shaw, among others, offered striking new analyses of Anglo-Soviet relations in this period, frequently critical of British diplomacy.[10] Studies in the past few years by Robert Self and David Gillard highlight the active nature of the appeasement debate, the lack of an accepted consensus and the fact that historians today, though having access to the same evidence, still possess highly contrasting opinions of the wisdom of Chamberlain and the appeasers. For Self, Chamberlain 'remains a profoundly underrated, misjudged and misunderstood figure', whereas Gillard laments *Appeasement in Crisis* and condemns Chamberlain's guarantee of Poland as a foolish, strategically naive gambit making war all but inevitable.[11] Both David Dutton and Self recognise the significance of the issue of alternatives to the evolving debate and its importance for future research. Indeed, both concluded tentatively that there may have been no good, 'correct' or 'better' policies existing in this period, and that Chamberlain did quite well in view of the poor hand he had been dealt with.[12] But more depth is needed in this area of study. The time is now ripe for a comprehensive analysis of such questions in a single, detailed volume.

In Autumn 2008, a special issue of *Diplomacy and Statecraft*, published to mark the seventieth anniversary of the Munich Agreement, showed that the debate on appeasement and its most famous practitioner is far from over. Indeed, essays by Bruce Strang and Sydney

Aster offer exciting new pointers on where such literature might go next, advocating exploring the impact of issues such as ideology, ethnicity, gender, race and religion on the formation of policy. These areas are already bearing fruit.[13] Notwithstanding the vast and constantly expanding literature on Chamberlain and appeasement, there nevertheless remains a significant dearth of work regarding the other options available to him at the time. From this perspective, the challenges made by Wilson and Simon, as cited above, have largely gone unanswered, given the manner in which alternatives to appeasement have often been treated as a mere footnote by academics more interested in the wider debate surrounding Chamberlain's policies. Nor is there an informed critique investigating the origins, development and viability of the principal rival policies open to the government. The central topic of whether appeasement was 'good' or 'bad' has tended to dominate discussion and eclipse other lines of enquiry, or at least severely overshadow consideration of related questions.

There are, of course, several works examining specific alternatives, such as the League of Nations, alliances or rearmament, but these tend to treat any option in isolation. Any publication adopting a broader view does so only in a very sweeping or fragmentary manner. Indeed, there are only a handful of works that address the specific question of multiple alternatives in any depth. The obvious study to mention here would be *The Gathering Storm*. After all, Churchill asserted that 'there was never a war more easy to stop than that which has just wrecked what was left of the world from the previous struggle'.[14] Blessed with the hindsight that his predecessor was never able to enjoy, of course, Churchill speculated that various possible solutions to the Fascist menace had existed in the late 1930s, including the adoption of a tougher line in the Abyssinian, Rhineland and Czech crises in 1935, 1936 and 1938 respectively, and a committed League policy backed by massive rearmament. This was 'the unnecessary war', made sadly inevitable by a series of missed opportunities in the final years of peace, not least the possibility of a firm stand by Britain, France and Russia, united in a 'Grand Alliance' against Nazi Germany.[15] In 1966, the memoirs of another post-war Conservative Prime Minister, Harold Macmillan, cited 'sufficient force of arms' as the first essential in any credible foreign policy. Indeed, *The Winds of Change* stood out from the crowd in echoing Churchill at a time when revisionist literature on Chamberlain and appeasement was beginning to take off. He argued that a Grand Alliance during the Czech crisis would have succeeded in deterring Hitler, or, at worst, led to a war under more favourable circumstances than in 1939.[16]

In 1993, Parker's watershed study offered the best single contribution to the discussion of appeasement alternatives to date, devoting as he did an entire chapter to this question alone, outlining rival proposals and writing supportively about a Grand Alliance centred around Britain, France and Russia.[17] Even so, Parker's exposition of alternatives remained relatively limited, while his follow-up work, *Churchill and Appeasement*, largely confines itself merely to restating Churchill's argument.[18] Parker's provocative conclusions, alongside the ascendant post-revisionist trend, have encouraged historians to at last enter into long-overdue serious debate about appeasement alternatives, though they seldom put it in such terms. Doubtless they will frame further research in the area. Frequently, they have proved critical of Chamberlain, thereby reviving charges advanced by the orthodox school. For instance, Louise Grace Shaw claimed that in 1939 'Chamberlain alone', motivated by anti-Bolshevik prejudice, deliberately sabotaged the chance of an Anglo-Soviet alliance. This would have been a workable option at this time, discouraging or, if necessary, defeating Hitler.[19] Likewise, John Ruggiero attacked Chamberlain's 'baneful influence' on Britain's rearmament programme during the 1930s, whose course, he contends, would have taken a 'vastly different turn' without him – and possibly even deterred Hitler from war.[20] Redressing the balance somewhat, James Levy has rejected Ruggiero's alternative, countering that an early, mass rearmament drive might only have been counterproductive, freezing in place the manufacture of weapons that were largely obsolete by the middle to later stages of the war.[21]

* * *

Frustratingly for the appeasement historian, no record exists of a Cabinet or Foreign Policy Committee meeting where Chamberlain and his senior colleagues openly discussed the pros and cons of all the

possible options available to them. As a result, the issue of government consideration of alternatives has remained shrouded in mystery
and the archives must be searched far and wide to find enlightening
references to this question. And yet, in order fully to understand why
Chamberlain pursued appeasement, it is necessary to consider which
alternatives he rejected and why. In making any decision, all humans
consider the likely outcomes of their choices and these conclusions give
impetus to their actions. Implicit in this study, therefore, is a degree
of what has been termed 'counterfactual history' – assessing the likely
outcomes of paths not taken.

Variously discredited as an 'idle parlour game', or even, less elo-
quently, as 'unhistorical shit', counterfactual history is often frowned
upon by academics as being too simplistic and fanciful a pursuit,
overplaying the importance of chance and contingency.[22] Conducted
responsibly, 'what if?' speculation can, in fact, prove very useful
indeed, by allowing the historian to step into the shoes of key historical actors, in this case suggesting what drove Chamberlain to act in
the way he did. The rationale for his appeasement policy can only be
understood when the strengths and weaknesses of the other options he
considered are analysed, and this can be aided by informed conjecture
about the likely results. While this study is perhaps more concerned
with the viability of alternatives to appeasement as perceived by the
policy makers at the time – rather than how successful they might
have been if pursued – there will be some brief counterfactual speculation towards the end of each chapter.

Further justification for embarking on a study of this kind lies in
the fact that appeasement is still very much present in the political,
media and cultural vocabulary of our own day. The so-called 'lessons of appeasement' have been regularly cited by politicians like
Tony Blair, Gordon Brown, George W. Bush and Barack Obama to
justify their foreign policy initiatives to the general public, just as
their critics have accused them of being 'appeasers' when adopting
what was seen as a weak policy towards another state.[23] For example,
the Foreign Secretary David Milliband faced such charges in July
2009, over his widely mooted plan to sit down with Taliban representatives in Afghanistan. Sensitive to potential criticism, he claimed

when interviewed that the intent was to deal with the terrorist threat 'and not to appease it'.[24] However erroneous some of these historical comparisons may be, the issue of appeasement clearly remains a live and contentious one. Even a recent Stephen Poliakoff thriller directly implicates Chamberlain's government in a sinister plot to murder anti-appeasers during the summer of 1939.[25]

Against this background, this study, centred upon the British government during the period 1936–1939, has three main aims:

1. to chart the origins, nature and development of the main suggested alternatives to appeasement, with reference to who advocated these options, when, why, and how;
2. to assess how far these alternatives were considered by the leading policy makers within the National Government, broadly defined here as the Prime Minister, his Cabinet colleagues and senior Foreign Office, Treasury and military personnel; their perceived viability, and why they were rejected;
3. to offer some tentative conclusions about the likely success of these alternatives if actually adopted, thereby responding to Wilson's challenge, above. Did Chamberlain have any other realistic options? More importantly, could the Second World War have been avoided?

It is the most commonly advocated alternatives, as offered by contemporary appeasement detractors and revisited later by historians, and which were *also* considered by Chamberlain himself, that are the main focus of this work. Thus, bigger, more radical alternatives requiring a wholesale change to the character of the nation in general – some critics advocated a Socialist world revolution or the formation of a British Popular Front – let alone a change of government and Prime Minister will be addressed only in passing. Similarly, other very extreme policies such as assassinating Hitler or even joining with him, suggested on occasion in throw-away comments by government figures but never seriously contemplated, will be ignored.[26]

It is the author's contention that each chapter of this book could encompass a study of its own. Thus, it is only a general summary of each alternative that can be made in a work of this length. Word limitations do not permit a detailed chronological narrative or explanation of the 'story' of Chamberlain, appeasement and the origins of the Second World War, though there is a basic chronology of key events at the end of this book.

What, then, were the various other options? The six main alternatives discussed here are as follows:

1. Isolation and Absolute Pacifism.
2. Economic and Colonial Appeasement.
3. League of Nations.
4. Alliances.
5. Armaments and Defences.
6. War and the Threat of War.

The main, but not exclusive, focus of this work is British policy towards Hitler's Germany, whose threat weighed more heavily than the danger posed by Italy or Japan in the minds of the British policy making elite. The combined menace was most troubling, however. The Committee of Imperial Defence had stated in December 1937: 'We cannot foresee the time when our defensive forces will be strong enough to safeguard our territory, trade and vital interests against Germany, Italy and Japan simultaneously.'[27] Chamberlain's throwaway remark that 'if only we could get on terms with the Germans I would not care a rap for Musso', however, while oversimplifying the picture somewhat, nevertheless reaffirms the centrality of Hitler in British thinking.[28]

The precise order of chapters reflects two main factors; first, each alternative differs in its level of aggression towards Nazi Germany and the other Fascist states, Italy and Japan. For the purposes of simplicity and consistency, Japan is loosely considered here to be a 'Fascist' power in the late 1930s, even if such a descriptor remains debatable. Each alternative becomes more extreme, confrontational and removed from Chamberlain's original conception of appeasement as this study progresses, through options seeking to work with, 'manage' or contain the Fascist threat, culminating in the full-scale attack envisaged in the final chapter. Thus, Chapter One effectively considers aspects of retreat in face of the German menace, whereas Chapter Six contemplates an assault; second, certain alternatives have links lending themselves to treatment in close proximity, as evidenced by the way in which the chapter on alliances follows that on the League of Nations, or the analysis of war succeeds that of armaments and defences.

It could be argued that Chamberlain's own policy often contained aspects of each of the so-called alternatives to appeasement as identified so far. Was not appeasement, at its core, essentially an isolationist and pacific policy? Did not Chamberlain offer Hitler loans and colonies in return for assurances of peace? Did not Britain, at one time or another, act through the machinery of the League of Nations, pursue alliances with other countries, and begin a vast rearmament programme in face of the growing threat? And the ultimate resort to war was indeed taken by Chamberlain in September 1939. The central questions here are those of timing and extent, given that frequently anti-appeasers advocated some of the actions taken by Chamberlain himself, though often much earlier and in far greater measure. It may be more accurate, therefore, to talk less of alternatives to appeasement *per se*, than of radically different conceptions of how Chamberlain's appeasement policy should have been carried out. This strategy, as practised by the Chamberlain government, was a much more complex and ambiguous phenomenon than is often understood, operating at many levels and frequently encompassing seemingly contradictory strands within its broad framework.

* * *

Before we can consider the alternatives to appeasement, we must first try to define what appeasement actually was. To the layman, the policy is almost always associated with Chamberlain, the man with the umbrella and the piece of paper, and perhaps also the phrase 'Peace for our time'. Chamberlain has become the personification of a policy widely perceived as cowardly and dishonourable, with its nadir being the 1938 Munich Conference, when the starry-eyed Prime Minister was allegedly fooled by Hitler and threw Czechoslovakia to the wolves.

Such oversimplifications and myths hold firm. However, in reality, as stressed by Martin Gilbert, this strategy had been a central pillar of British foreign policy throughout the entire interwar period, as successive administrations from different sides of the political spectrum sought to avoid a repeat of the calamity of the Great War by redressing the enduring injustices of the 1919 peace settlement.[29] Indeed, for some commentators, the policy can be traced even further back into the nineteenth century, when Gladstone pursued better relations with Germany by attempting to satisfy Bismarck's colonial ambitions.[30]

In brief, appeasement, though often perceived as an almost 'dirty' word, was, in its various forms, widely supported in comments on British foreign policy over long periods of time. Indeed, it was frequently viewed as a positive and noble practice. Speaking in July 1921 as Colonial Secretary, even Churchill, the archetypal anti-appeaser, asserted that 'the aim is to get an appeasement of the fearful hatreds and antagonisms which exist in Europe and to enable the world to settle down. I have no other object in view'.[31] Likewise, in June 1936, Anthony Eden, another supposed anti-appeaser, asserted that 'European settlement and appeasement should be our aim'.[32] From this perspective, much of the opposition to appeasement in the years before the Second World War might, therefore, be more accurately described as opposition to Chamberlain's conception of the policy, rather than to the general ideal.

It is another of this work's contentions that Chamberlain's policy was fluid and multifaceted, rather than uniform and rigid. 'Appeasement' is often used as a lazy umbrella term to describe a policy Chamberlain pursued consistently from assuming the premiership until the outbreak of war, particularly with regard to making concessions to Nazi Germany. However, this is greatly to oversimplify the picture and warrants a brief discussion here. To borrow a term from Paul Kennedy, Chamberlain's appeasement was actually 'a very hybrid creature indeed', made up of several distinct phases, each with differing aims and a specific agenda.[33] To put it somewhat crudely, before the *Anschluss* between Germany and Austria in March 1938, Chamberlain's policy was aimed primarily at Mussolini rather than Hitler, in an attempt to detach Italy from the chief threat and explore a reinvigoration of the 1935 Stresa Front – Britain, France and Italy united.[34] The *Anschluss* shook British faith in the words of Dictators and brought the issue of Czechoslovakia suddenly on to the table. Hereafter, Germany became the central focus and Italy was now perceived of primarily as a tool with which Chamberlain, through the personal influence of Mussolini, might moderate Hitler's behaviour.[35] Japan was an even lesser consideration, though still a complicating factor. The period of 'classic' Chamberlainite appeasement occurred between the *Anschluss* and the Prague Coup one year later. When people talk of 'appeasement', it is the concessionary policy of Britain during this single year that most are thinking of, the zenith being the Munich Agreement in September 1938.

After events in Prague, this phase of appeasement was effectively abandoned and Chamberlain signalled a significant reorientation of his policy during a speech in Birmingham on 17 March 1939. Here he asked of Germany, 'is this the end of an old adventure, or the beginning of a new?'[36] Hereafter, the pursuit of peace through major concessions was all but over and Chamberlain sought to establish peace through deterrence. While the Prime Minister never gave up his hopes for a lasting general settlement, and continued to regard appeasement as the ultimate best means to avoid war, the Prague Coup had shattered his illusions about Hitler's promises once and for all. Indeed, Chamberlain now turned to one of the alternatives so often advocated by his critics and began to build a 'Peace Front' bloc of alliances in a last, desperate to attempt to avert war.

Although Chamberlain did not become Prime Minister until 28 May 1937, there are several reasons for beginning this study earlier, not least given the way in which he confided to his sister in March 1935, 'I have become a sort of acting PM – only without the actual power of the PM'.[37] In view of Baldwin's declining health, he proved the driving force of government policy, as evidenced by his leading role in drafting the National Government's 1935 election manifesto. Furthermore, 1936 also witnessed key events in the drift to war, such as the culmination of the Abyssinian affair, Germany's remilitarization of the Rhineland – often viewed as a last, missed opportunity to check Hitler's ambitions without resort to conflict – and the outbreak

of the Spanish Civil War. This struggle fanned the flames of tension between Right and Left in Europe and fused the bonds between
the two leading Dictator powers, Germany and Italy. Similarly, the
National Government's Foreign Policy Committee was established in
1936, a body which superseded Cabinet as the most important government forum for the discussion of pre-war foreign affairs.

In what follows, repeated references to apparently simplistic terms
such as 'Chamberlain's policy' or 'Chamberlain's appeasement' and so
on highlight the fact that the Prime Minister was by far the most dom-
inant figure within the British foreign policy making elite. Although
this is unsurprising, Chamberlain proved a particularly autocratic
leader, single-handedly dictating foreign policy, interfering in areas
beyond his expert knowledge and surrounded by a Cabinet packed
increasingly with toadies.[38] Chamberlain's first Foreign Secretary,
Anthony Eden, famously asserted in his memoirs that the Prime
Minister 'deliberately withheld' information from him and routinely
misled the Foreign Office about his plans, lest the experts there would
disagree with him.[39] By contrast, Chamberlain's Home Secretary,
Sir Samuel Hoare, countered that 'if, nine times out of ten, he had
his way, it was because his way was also the Cabinet's way'. Even so,
Chamberlain, blessed with keen management skills and an impressive
command of detail, was clearly obstinate, strong-willed, and the front
seat driver of British foreign policy.[40]

The primary source that all appeasement scholars would like to
have access to unfortunately does not exist. Chamberlain's death just
six months after the end of his premiership has robbed us of any memoir he might have published and which would have been invaluable
in illuminating his motives and innermost thoughts on policy at this
time. The private letters frequently written to his sisters, in which
Chamberlain expanded upon events and decisions, are the next best
thing available, and have been consulted extensively. Hitherto, parliament has been covered sparingly in the existing literature, except
to discuss the way in which a massive Commons majority allowed a
single-minded Prime Minister to take control of foreign policy, acting
with – to quote one observer – 'extreme secrecy, and even irascibil-
ity' towards the House, deliberately starving members of information

and riding roughshod over traditional procedures.[41] Providing a diverse mix of viewpoints and ideas articulated by MPs and peers about rival foreign policy strategies, *Hansard* proves an equally useful source, notably upon the riotous scenes at the announcement of the Munich Conference or Chamberlain's fall from power, to give just two examples. Notwithstanding the prime focus upon the House of Commons, the House of Lords assumed extra importance during a period when Lord Halifax was Foreign Secretary, succeeding Eden in February 1938. Giving birth to National Labour, Independent Labour, Liberal National and so on, party rivalries in this chaotic period escalated tensions further, as did events like the Spanish Civil War and the Abyssinian crisis. Parliamentary exchanges, therefore, provide a flavour of the fluidity, complexity and passion of policy debates at this time which few other sources can match. As another scholar of British politics and foreign affairs has astutely remarked, parliament was 'the forum in which tensions within particular traditions of approaching foreign policy were noted and shifts marked'.[42] Its importance to this study is considerable.

1

ISOLATION AND ABSOLUTE PACIFISM

I believe that we should gradually and honourably detach ourselves from all these commitments which we have. I believe that
by our own strong arm, and by that alone, we shall win through
and be a power for peace in the world.[1]

(Sir Rupert de la Bere, House of Commons, June 1936)

Introduction

It has been argued by some of Chamberlain's many detractors,
amongst contemporaries and historians alike, that the National
Government should have pursued a policy of isolation as an alternative to appeasement in the late 1930s. Unlike the Prime Minister,
these critics envisaged a country that deliberately chose to have no
ties in Europe, withdrawing almost entirely from continental affairs.
'Splendid Isolation' had, of course, been a traditional foreign policy
strategy for Britain, an island nation separated from Europe by the
channel and its formidable navy, for hundreds of years.[2] Even in the
late 1930s, however, the belief that the best way to secure peace
would be an armed detachment from Europe remained the avowed
preference of a small number of staunch advocates, with figures such
as press baron Lord Beaverbrook and MP Leo Amery among its most
committed supporters.

This chapter will examine the origins and viability of the strategies of isolation and, later, absolute pacifism as alternatives to appeasement. The latter is defined here as the organised non-violent resistance policies of the small number of ultra-committed diehards among the general pacifist community, as well as demands for appeasing Hitler long after Chamberlain had effectively abandoned this approach. Advocates of both isolation and pacifism were determined and vocal critics of the National Government in the years before war, convinced that theirs was the only course that could avert catastrophe.

The few references to isolation and pacifism in the orthodox period of writing on Chamberlain and appeasement do not seem to regard them as realistic options. Historical memoirs from political figures who had played a leading role in events form a substantial portion of this literature. Sir Robert Vansittart, Permanent Under-Secretary at the Foreign Office between 1930 and 1938, and no great admirer of the Prime Minister who had removed him from this post, addressed both strategies. Looking back on the origins of the Second World War, Vansittart deemed pacifism to be an unobtainable ideal and argued that isolation actually brought war closer: 'Nothing is more certain to provide the eventual cataclysm than the policy of implied, let alone proclaimed, isolation advocated by such people as Lord Beaverbrook.'[3] Harold Macmillan offered a similar perspective, asserting that the actions of leading pacifists in the 1930s helped create the conditions for war, undermining British defence preparations and hamstringing efforts at deterrence.[4]

It was not until some time later, however, in the revisionist and post-revisionist periods of appeasement historiography, that works of real depth on isolation and pacifism in the late 1930s were produced. A.J.P. Taylor's 1972 biography of Beaverbrook offered a stoic defence of his friend's devotion to the isolationist cause and asserted that it was probably the most sensible option available at the time. Did not appeasement and policies such as collective security fail? Had not Britain been forced into isolation by the summer of 1940, and did not the country yet emerge victorious? Such were the provocative questions Taylor posed.[5]

Most recent work on isolation and pacifism has failed to add to our knowledge on the question of viability. Historians such as Martin

Ceadel and Parker discuss the pacifist and isolationist movements at this time without taking up the question of whether either offered a realistic alternative to the policies of the National Government.[6] However, following John Charmley's provocative suggestion that a strategy of peaceful coexistence with Nazi Germany might have offered a better outcome for Britain and its Empire than the events that actually unfolded, Roy Denman produced *Missed Chances* in 1996.[7] Drawing heavily upon hindsight and counterfactual speculation, this work resurrects some of Taylor's earlier claims about the likely success of isolation. Denman claims that Chamberlain would have been able to gain parliamentary support for a policy of this kind during the 1938 Czech crisis and that this would have resulted in Germany turning on Russia, rather than France and Britain, after the fall of Czechoslovakia.[8] These assertions are impossible to prove, however, and Denman adds little to Taylor's original thesis.

There are links between isolation and pacifism and their many contemporary advocates which justify the two policies being considered together here. Many pacifists were also isolationists, and *vice versa*, while the two strategies shared conceptual links, in that they both considered standing aside from European troubles and disengaging from the Fascist threat in a way that none of the other alternatives in this study quite match. The absolute pacifist policy of regimented non-violent resistance, covered below, can even be said to have constituted a very particular form of the wider isolationist approach.

Origins and Nature of the Alternative

While the policy of isolation was largely discredited in Britain by the mid-1930s as a relic of the pre-Great War era, echoes still resounded from time to time. British policy was to remain aloof from the Manchurian and Abyssinian hostilities. The government's strategy of non-intervention during the Spanish Civil War ensured that the issue remained relevant and a point of discussion over the next few years. The German reoccupation of the Rhineland in March 1936 served to crystallize foreign policy debate in Britain further, prompting a reconsideration of the country's role on the continent by the political elite.

Liberal peer Lord Lothian, for example, speaking in parliament on 24 March, asked, 'is there any necessity for us to be scared into further military commitments in Europe? Europe has immense reserves for the defence of the *status quo* if it likes to organise them without calling on us at all'.[9]

Advocates of isolation tended to promote their cause with greater force in the earlier part of Chamberlain's premiership, before events such as the Czech crisis and the Prague Coup suggested that worst fears about Hitler might soon be realised. Calls for isolation peaked throughout 1937 and early 1938, fading away in the latter part of that year following the Munich Conference – although a few diehards were still enthusiastically promoting the cause in the wake of the agreement. Supporters of this policy also tended to be Conservatives or from the Right of the political spectrum, usually old enough to recall the glorious days of British Imperial grandeur in the late Victorian period. Harold Macmillan, recounting foreign policy opinion across the political spectrum during the decade, confirms that it was mainly 'the Right' who would have preferred 'a policy of semi isolation, relying on the reserve power of the still potent Empire'.[10] Indeed, almost all isolation supporters were also passionate advocates of strengthening Imperial ties, rather than those with the League of Nations, which was predominantly supported by the political Left. In January 1937, when Tory MP Sir Arnold Wilson addressed the British Universities League of Nations Society meeting in Oxford, he controversially urged that the League be sidelined and the way 'of isolation' studied, 'not merely as a practicable policy for Great Britain, but for all great powers'.[11] This did not go down well with his audience.

Two of the most prominent advocates of isolation during the Chamberlain period demonstrate these characteristics, being both right-wing and committed supporters of Empire. Conservative MP and former Colonial Secretary Leo Amery was never short of an opinion on government policy and, amongst several proffered solutions to the crises of the era, championed isolation during much of Chamberlain's premiership. In his 1935 work, *The Forward View*, Amery summed up his continental policy in one sentence: 'Detachment from European affairs; subject only to the proviso, embodied in our Belgium and Locarno undertakings, that we will not look with unconcern upon purely aggressive military operations within short air range of Dover.'[12]

In November 1937, Amery lectured Chamberlain in a letter calling for Britain to concede parts of Europe to German domination and withdraw from affairs therein.[13] Even as late as 10 October 1938, shortly after the Munich Conference, he expressed similar views in a note to the former Foreign Secretary, Anthony Eden:

> There is much to be said for the policy of deliberately withdrawing both France and ourselves from Central Europe. Germany will undoubtedly be much stronger materially, but psychologically and strategically, France and ourselves will now be in a much simpler defensive position.[14]

It is evident that Amery, in common with many other isolationists, was not calling for Britain to distance itself from every nation on the continent. The traditional close relationship with France and the strategic importance of the Low Countries were usually regarded as sacrosanct, for obvious geographical reasons, as likely staging-posts for an invasion of Britain from the continent. Isolation, therefore, rarely meant the wholesale abandonment of all Europe, even for the most ardent supporters of the cause. Instead, an element of strategic retreat tended to be linked to a limiting of commitments, and a Gallic shield was taken for granted.

The other most noteworthy advocate of isolation was the Tory press baron Lord Beaverbrook, owner of the *Daily Express*, then Britain's most widely read newspaper.[15] In the most vocal, comprehensive and long-running campaign for isolation during this decade, the *Express* had been preaching this particular gospel for years. An extract from 15 July 1935 is typical and underlines the Imperial preoccupation of many isolation supporters:

> Interference in Europe means war for certain ... If we stand out of European commitments, we are given the hope and expectation

that there will be no war for Britain ... Interference in Europe divides us from the Dominions. It is a policy which means the break-up of the British Empire.[16]

Hitler's remilitarisation of the Rhineland in March 1936 was met in the *Express* with an appeal for Britain to 'Keep Calm!' It continued: 'We should stand aside. There is no need whatever, *no British need*, to take a part. No interest of ours will be challenged.'[17] Beaverbrook underlined that domestic concerns were his priority just a day later: 'Leave the French and Germans to keep watch over the Rhine. Our watch should be along the Tyne. Better days are coming there; we could make them better still.'[18] Two years on, in response to the March 1938 *Anschluss* and the elevation of Czechoslovakia as the issue of that summer, the *Express* was still calling for Britain to 'Mind Our Own Business!' Czechoslovakia, it proclaimed, 'is not our business. If we tie ourselves up there we may one day have to cut our losses as hurriedly as we are doing now in Austria'.[19]

As old friends and colleagues, and two of the most vocal advocates of the isolation alternative, Amery and Beaverbrook corresponded at length. Their exchanges shed light on the limited nature of wider support for the cause, suggesting that isolationists lacked coherence and leadership even before Chamberlain became Prime Minister. As Beaverbrook wrote in November 1936,

> One great advantage of Isolation is, of course, that it is the only means of bringing our foreign policy in line with that of the United States. I say nothing about the Empire, because it is most obvious to most people that Isolation is the only policy on which we can hope to maintain unity with the Dominions.
>
> Why don't you lead the movement? There is nobody in politics more competent to do it than you are.[20]

Two days later Amery replied:

> I appreciate the compliment you pay me when you suggest that I should lead a movement for which you regard yourself already

too old! The trouble is, one cannot simply step out one day and say "I am going to lead". Leading requires a devil of a lot of spade work and presupposes both a band of followers and support in the press and elsewhere ... Tell me, my dear Max, what more I could have done in the way of leading, or establishing my claim to lead? What I want is more support. You can do a lot in your Press for our campaign.[21]

Beaverbrook's repeated references to the Empire – and also in this instance the United States – is further evidence that isolationists often reinforced separation from Europe by emphasising bonds of friendship away from the continent. America, of course, as well as being an old English-speaking ally, had its own strong isolationist agenda in the late 1930s and was often held as a yardstick to which Britain should aspire.

Beaverbrook estimated that around 60 per cent of the British public were keen isolation supporters at the close of 1936.[22] Such a figure was clearly wishful thinking on his part – the number of letters published by the *Express* backing this policy suggested a much lower figure – or else was based upon the paper's rather dubious estimations of wider opinion. For example, it confidently proclaimed that 'Business Leaders Want Detachment' in March of that year, when the accompanying survey asked only four industrialists the particularly tendentious question of whether or not they backed the 'watchful and sympathetic' isolation of Britain from the 'disputes of Europe'.[23] Gallup Polls and Mass Observation data from the period are no more illuminating on this issue, with the former source not even deeming the topic worthy of investigation. The latter, as vague and unscientific a measure of public opinion as this was, yielded merely one or two relevant statements. Here, a survey of the citizens of 'Metrop', an unnamed London borough, produced just one individual who called for Britain to 'keep out of entanglements' in the troubled weeks before Munich.[24] The claim of wide-scale popular support for isolation seems highly questionable therefore. Moreover, few other political groups actively promoted the cause. The extreme Right sometimes backed isolation as it suited the pro-Fascist leanings of a select few to acquiesce in the activities of the European Dictators. Oswald Mosley's British Union of Fascists ran a campaign during the Abyssinian conflict under the banner 'Mind Britain's Business', which urged no involvement in the dispute, and was sympathetic to the Italian cause.[25]

The promotion of isolation as an alternative to the National Government's policy continued well into the Chamberlain premiership. The Prime Minister's conversations with Mussolini at the beginning of 1938 and close consultation with France and Germany throughout that difficult summer were interpreted by many isolationists as a foolish attempt to draw closer to powers on the continent and entangle Britain in dangerous European affairs. The March 1938 *Anschluss* brought Czechoslovakia on to the table as the likely next target for Nazi expansion and discussion was rife over whether or not a guarantee should be offered to ward off a possible German advance. Fears were so high that even some non-Conservatives now spoke up in support of isolation. Liberal National MP George Lambert addressed Commons on 24 March:

> I do not want commitments on the continent. I want to keep out of them. I believe in being strong and being a good neighbour. Good neighbours are not always interfering in the affairs of their neighbours ... I would far rather be left alone than to have to stand for other people's commitments.[26]

When Britain guaranteed rump Czechoslovakia as part of the Munich Agreement later that year, there followed the last really widespread calls for isolation. Invoking a powerful literary metaphor, Tory peer Lord Saltoun bitterly attacked the Prime Minister's policy:

> Our government is not a Sancho Panza, to stretch its arm and say that, after all, it is a fine thing to ride about the world righting wrongs, and to go out and take counsel with its donkey ... Let us right the wrongs at our doors, and learn from the Bible who is our neighbour.[27]

That Munich marked the beginning of the end for the isolationist cause may be explained by two factors; first, international events now drifted through the 'Munich winter' to the Prague Coup in March 1939, a watershed event that convinced even the most ardent isolationists that the time was ripe for commitments on the continent. The Nazi orchestrated pogrom of *Kristallnacht* in November 1938 also demonstrated to the world some of the hitherto under-recognised characteristics of the regime; second, in excluding the League of Nations from his foremost act in foreign policy to date, and in signing the accompanying Anglo-German declaration, Chamberlain seemed to many to want to draw a line, of sorts, under European affairs. He had rejected other types of alliances, after all. This confirmed in the minds of some isolationists what one or two already suspected – that the Prime Minister had himself adopted the policy of isolation. Even before the Munich Agreement was concluded, Beaverbrook had confided to Tory MP Edward Grigg: 'As we have isolation in fact, although not in name, I have not much to complain about. Later on, if the government tries to change its policy, then I must try to do something.'[28]

*　*　*

If advocates of isolation can be said to have favoured turning a blind eye to the march of Fascism, there were also those who recommended turning the other cheek. Together with the policy of isolation must go a brief discussion of pacifism, not least because many campaigners for the former were also committed supporters of the latter. Both philosophies essentially involved stepping aside from the troubles of Europe, rather than attempting to confront them as the other alternatives in this study might have envisaged. As one of the leading historians on the subject observes, 'the more optimistic pacifists believed that avoiding provocation would also encourage a positive response ... And even those more pessimistic about European passions could hope for isolationism at least'.[29] Lord Lothian, for example, has variously been labelled as an isolationist *and* a pacifist, and it was common for membership of both groups to merge in this era.

Pacifist thinkers often regarded isolation as the best available option to keep the peace, on the straightforward assumption that the less Britain meddled, the more likely it was to avoid war. Bertrand Russell, a popular writer on such matters in this period, considered the merits of isolation in some depth in his 1936 work *Which Way to Peace?*[30] One-time Labour MP Wilfred Wellock also illustrates the regular convergence of the two strategies at this time. Contributing to the leading pacifist journal of the era, *Peace News*, he wrote in the wake of the Rhineland affair: 'It may be that the catastrophe of a Second World War is unavoidable, but should it occur I think it is supremely important that this country should not be involved in it.'[31] This is not to say that isolation and pacifism were the same thing, of course, and there are areas where huge cleavage existed between the two policies and their supporters. For example, if it can be broadly argued that isolation was favoured by many on the Right, especially enthusiasts for Empire, then it must be acknowledged that pacifism appealed to the left-wing of the political spectrum more often than not. However, it is undeniable that wider links existed.

A full discussion of British pacifism in the late 1930s, in all its many guises, could well constitute an in-depth study of its own – and, indeed, there exist a number of such works.[32] Thus, it is only a very particular brand of what might be termed absolute or 'pure' pacifism that shall be considered here – the policies of the most ardent, proactive, well-organised and passionate exponents of the cause. As Ceadel has observed, pacifism in the Chamberlain period is a vague and ambiguous phenomenon, a catch-all label applied to a great many different people who might more accurately be described as being part of a larger, more general peace movement. He draws particular distinction between what he terms 'pacifists' – diehard advocates, who argued that all war was always wrong – and 'pacificists', who took the view that war, while generally irrational, was sometimes necessary but always best avoided.[33] As this latter, much larger body encompassed many people from numerous different groups, across all shades of political opinion, they will not be addressed in any detail here. Rather, the focus is on the committed hard-core of 'pure' or absolute pacifists who loudly promoted a policy of organised, non-violent resistance to any potential aggressor aiming to occupy Britain.[34]

Such a strategy was the favoured line of many of the leading members of the largest pacifist movement of the day, the Peace Pledge

Union (PPU). This body was formed by Canon Dick Sheppard in May 1936, following the wave of support he had received for his 'Peace Letter', published in the national press some 18 months earlier. The PPU was responsible for some of the other major expressions of anti-war sentiment in the early to mid-1930s, such as the 'Peace Ballot' in 1935, in which over 11 million people voiced strong anti-war senti-ment and reaffirmed their commitment to unilateral disarmament and the methods of the League. After Sheppard's sudden death in October 1937, figures such as George Lansbury, former Labour Party leader, took on the management of the PPU and tried to spread the mes-sage of peace through more mainstream political channels including parliament.

Founding Union members such as Labour peer Lord Ponsonby or the writer Aldous Huxley were among the most committed exponents of strictly regimented, non-violent resistance. Interviewed by a fellow pacifist during the 1935 Abyssinian crisis, Huxley asserted that 'the only practical way of dealing with the problems of war is the organ-isation of what Gregg in his recent book on the subject calls Non-Violent Coercion – the method of Gandhi and so many others'.[35] This policy sometimes became known as 'Greggism', after the influential American pacifist Richard Gregg who had studied figures such as Gandhi for many years, and it continued to be advocated by many leading members of the Union even after Chamberlain became Prime Minister. While he preached reconciliation with the Fascist powers, supporters of Greggism called for the formation of crack pacifist cells throughout the country to organise the peaceful resistance of the British people to any future invader.

Unsurprisingly, absolute pacifism began to decline as Sheppard's death and the approach of war took their toll on the movement. Greggism became discredited even within the PPU's own ranks, and the majority of pacifists fell in behind Chamberlain's appeasement strategy as the best means to avoid war.[36] By mid-1938 the official policy of the PPU *was* appeasement, though it heavily emphasised the economic dimension, as expressed by personalities such as Lansbury and Ponsonby in parliament throughout the remainder of the year. Many pacifists also supported unilateral disarmament, of course, another area of divergence with most isolationists, and Lansbury regularly spoke in favour of this throughout the earlier part of the decade.[37] Disarmament also declined in popularity, however, as the government was forced to rearm substantially in view of the darkening skies. Nevertheless, Ponsonby still felt compelled to call for a fresh disarmament drive in his stinging attack on Chamberlain's part in the Munich settlement:

> You say 'Trust Hitler', and yet you come home and say you must go on with rearming. I do not think those two things really stand side by side ... I believe the reduction of armaments must be the very first question that is tackled between the nations of the world.[38]

Following the Prague Coup, when Chamberlain effectively abandoned his pursuit of major concessions in favour of deterrence and alliances, there were still one or two demands for ultra-pacifist alternatives. Such calls can be seen as the product of a last, desperate attempt to avoid war. On these lines, during a speech in the Lords, the Archbishop of Canterbury, Cosmo Lang, twinned his support for alliances with a plea to all the leading members of the European Christian community to issue simultaneous peace declarations.[39] For others, it was a case of advocating appeasement after the Prime Minister himself had all but rejected it – what some contemporary critics would have derided as a 'peace at any price' policy. For example, in the same debate, Liberal peer Lord Arnold asserted: 'I know it is the custom nowadays to sneer at pacifists [but] ... in my view pacifists are much more in touch with realities than those who are urging the nations on to another war.'[40]

Less than a month before the outbreak of that war, the PPU Chairman, Stuart Morris, gave an interview to the *News Chronicle* in which he controversially proclaimed that Chamberlain had not gone far enough: 'I am all for giving a great deal more away. I don't think that Mr Chamberlain has really started yet on any serious appeasement.'[41] Many absolute pacifists of this type were even unaffected by the beginning of hostilities and urged peace negotiations with Hitler well on into 1940, with some becoming conscientious objectors. It should be noted, however, that not all 'arch-appeasers' were pacifists and *vice versa*. Some people called for a return to appeasement in late 1939 because of a devotion to the moral sanctity of diplomatic methods, or even outright pro-Nazism and extreme right-wing convictions.[42]

While such forms of absolute pacifism were not really alternatives to appeasement as such, they clearly marked a rival conception of how the Prime Minister ought to have carried out his policy and, therefore, warrant discussion here. It could also be argued that those who called for Greggism in Britain, preferring to wait for the invasion to come and then resisting it through squads of non-violent activists, offered a very particular take on the isolationist cause.

Consideration of the Alternative

How viable were isolation and absolute pacifism considered to be as alternatives to appeasement during the late 1930s? To what extent did Chamberlain and his government view these policies as realistic options? First, we must consider whether isolation and pacifism were actually related to, or even facets of, Chamberlain's own policy. In the months after Munich, for example, many members of the opposition scolded Chamberlain for cowardice and implied that the National Government was ardently pacifist, pursuing a 'peace at any price' strategy. Labour leader Clement Attlee's attack on the Munich Agreement in the Commons on 3 October 1938 was typical of this sort of charge. Here he expressed a certain admiration for the 'complete pacifist' stance of figures such as Lansbury, but inferred that Chamberlain, his government and other appeasers were only 'the pleasure-loving people, who are pacifists because they will not take up any reasonable position'.[43] While Attlee sympathised with the general ideal then, this illustrates how pacifism could be tagged with charges of self-interest, laziness and even hedonism by critics, as if devotees were letting down their fellow countrymen and shirking responsibilities.

As previously shown, some supporters of isolation also came to believe that Chamberlain's policy was increasingly moving towards their own as 1938 progressed, and opponents often tried to paint appeasement in this light in order to win popular support in condemnation of the government. As early as February 1937, before Chamberlain even assumed the premiership, Labour MP Sir Stafford Cripps claimed to have 'no doubts in my own mind as to what the foreign policy of the government is. It is a policy of remaining in loose isolation'.[44] Little over a year later, Liberal Party leader Sir Archibald Sinclair echoed this charge, accusing the government of 'swinging towards it' during a Commons debate in July 1938.[45] Though the exact validity of such accusations are dubious, and many opposition figures knew it, they nevertheless illustrate some of the tactics adopted in policy debate at this time, and the wider unpopularity of the isolation cause.

At first appearance, there are many similarities between appeasement and isolation, and Chamberlain's policy did indeed have elements of the latter strategy within it. The Prime Minister, for the most part, sought to avoid alliances, at least before the Prague Coup, and to reduce Britain's commitments on the continent and further afield. Similarly, his strategy aimed at the rejection of multilateral approaches such as the League of Nations – which, of course, infuriated the opposition further – in favour of direct contact with the Dictators and the pursuit of bilateral deals. British policy in the Spanish Civil War remained one of non-intervention, whilst commitment to the Empire, so adored by many supporters of isolation, seemed relatively undiminished. However, Chamberlain's appeasement differed from isolation in several key respects. Seeking to limit military commitments on the continent should not be confused with the isolationist's favoured strategy of withdrawing from Europe altogether. The strategy of 'limited liability' – reducing forces on the continent due to the vulnerability of Britain in face of the convergence of Germany, Italy and Japan – became a central pillar of Chamberlain's policy. Sir Alexander Cadogan, who succeeded Vansittart as Permanent Under-Secretary at the Foreign Office in early 1938, even outlined how a similar mindset could be applied to the Empire as a whole, in a policy memorandum from that period:

We have inherited responsibilities all over the world, which have become onerous with the rise to power of other nations such

as Japan ... [The] Dominions make some contribution towards
their own defence, but it is very much to be hoped that ... they
may find it possible to take a rather larger share, and to that
extent leave us with a freer hand to deal with the menace nearer
home.[46]

Limited liability was more specifically concerned with the defence of
mainland Europe, and this strategy was reinforced by many within the
government conceding that Germany should enjoy a 'natural' position
of dominance at the heart of continental affairs. Lord Halifax confided
to his Private Secretary on 19 March 1938 that he had 'no objection
to Germany having economic hegemony in Central Europe. What he
objected to was the methods employed'.[47]

On the basis of a harsh, almost *Realpolitik* assessment of the strategic position, limited liability sought to cut losses and concede
areas of the globe to Fascist domination, but it did not envisage the
wholesale abandonment of all of Europe to Nazi rule.[48] The same
was true of Britain's non-intervention during the Spanish Civil War,
as Halifax's predecessor, Eden, was keen to point out. In a speech in
Llandudno on 15 October 1937, the Foreign Secretary stressed that
there was 'a clear distinction between non-intervention and indifference. We are not', he claimed, 'indifferent to the maintenance of the
territorial integrity of Spain ... We are not indifferent to vital British
interests in the Mediterranean'.[49] Removing a foot from the water
did not mean that Albion was stepping out of the ocean entirely,
and both isolation supporters and the opposition parties knew this.
Indeed, limited liability represented a sort of halfway house between
full isolation and Chamberlain's preferred strategy of dialogue and
arbitration. It allowed aspects of retreat from Britain's unwieldy and
burdensome commitments, something many isolation supporters
would approve of, while avoiding tying the Prime Minister down in
total seclusion and still affording him the means to exert influence
on European affairs.

Chamberlain's appeasement also differed from isolation in an important theoretical sense. Whereas the majority of advocates of the latter
envisaged a bolting of the doors, turning their backs on Europe and

ending all diplomacy with the Fascist powers, Chamberlain most certainly did not. Furthermore, isolation often implied a measure of drift, of 'wait and see', even of indifference or apathy to European issues and this, again, was a characteristic that appeasement did not share. Chamberlain was a proactive and dynamic figure – some thought overly so – and watching affairs go by was simply not in his nature. 'Lasting peace is not to be obtained by sitting still and waiting for it to come,' he asserted after Munich. 'It requires active, positive efforts to achieve it.'[50] Others shared this view. A month before Chamberlain assumed power, Cadogan pondered British policy options. 'It's no use', he asserted, 'shutting our eyes and hiding our heads in the sand and doing nothing'.[51] Allowing events to progress in Europe while watching from the sidelines was not to be a feature of this government's policy. In many ways, Chamberlain's appeasement was a meddlesome strategy, a bold and even brave policy, given how the League of Nations had sought to write the rules of international diplomacy over the past 20 years. Chamberlain imposed himself upon Hitler at Berchtesgaden in September 1938 and went directly one-on-one with the Fascist leaders in a very new style of summit diplomacy.[52] To return to Lambert's 'good neighbour' metaphor, it is clear that Chamberlain would have been among the worst kind, inviting himself for tea with the man next door.

Where pacifism was concerned, the shared characteristics with appeasement are even more obvious. The whole *raison d'être* of Chamberlain's policy was to maintain a lasting peace. But such policies as Greggism and organised, non-violent resistance would have been repugnant to the Prime Minister and he was always ready, however reluctantly, to fight in order to resist an attack upon any of Britain's vital interests. In Ceadel's terminology, Chamberlain and his policy of appeasement might be described as 'pacificist', but not pacifist, despite the claims of some contemporary opponents.

It is also telling that many of those who most fiercely supported appeasement were keen to draw distinctions between that policy and either isolation or pacifism. It suited advocates of these strategies to align themselves with government policy more than it suited the government to be linked with them. Conservative peer Lord Londonderry was at pains to declare that he was 'not for an isolationist policy' in the Lords, shortly after the *Anschluss*.[53] His colleague the Earl of Darnley, who was similarly passionate about Chamberlain's strategy, was moved to comment that 'the policy I am advocating is not a policy of pacifism or idealism, nor is it a vision of Utopia', when he addressed the upper chamber following the Prague Coup.[54] The reference to 'Utopia' again underlines some of the negative connotations pacifism was tagged with by many critics – the notion that it was a fantasy policy for idealists, the ultra-religious, literati, or others with their heads in the clouds.

*   *   *

Given that Chamberlain's appeasement policy, while embodying some of the characteristics of isolation and pacifism, can be seen as distinct and separate from them, is it possible to make an assessment of how far his government considered either as viable options to pursue? Isolation had been a policy debated by Baldwin, Chamberlain and their senior Cabinet colleagues throughout the summer of 1936, when the Foreign Policy Committee discussed reform of the League of Nations. The Abyssinian affair was progressing so badly at this time that the government secretly contemplated effective withdrawal from the League – by abandoning some of the binding articles of the Covenant – and was considering possible strategies in such an event. In this case, however, isolation was posed as one possible course of action, rather than a cut and dried solution to the problem. A Foreign Office memorandum prepared on 13 July 1936, and circulated in the Cabinet and Foreign Policy Committee, asked: 'Is it not best that nations should know exactly where they stand and should make their own arrangements for self-defence in accordance with their national interests, either in isolation or in conjunction with others?'[55] In the end, of course, Britain remained a member of the League. Such a document is, however, evidence that isolation was still up for consideration as a serious policy option and that it was often seen in a favourable light. A Foreign Office memorandum from August, discussing Cabinet views on Britain's role in the League, echoed this point. Here Cabinet Secretary Maurice Hankey recommended that 'the greater our detachment from European entanglements the better'.[56]

On 2 October of that year, in a speech to the Annual Party Conference, Chamberlain explained government policy in Spain and more generally:

> We covet no one else's territory and we have no wish or intention to interfere with the internal affairs of any other nation ... The dangers of interventions could not be more forcibly illustrated than by recent incidents in connection with the deplorable struggle now going on in Spain.[57]

Just four days later, in response to being sent a copy of *The Forward View* by Amery, Chamberlain penned in reply: 'I think you know that limitation of commitments in Europe is the policy which commends itself to me.'[58] Before Chamberlain had even assumed the premiership, then, he and many of the senior figures in the government had given consideration to isolation, or at least some degree of it, as a live foreign policy option. Even at this early stage, the Prime Minister in waiting clearly recognised that limiting commitments would have to be a part of any future strategy he would drive. In the very month he became Prime Minister, Orme Sargent, Assistant Under-Secretary in the Foreign Office, reiterated that Britain still might have to 'abdicate our position and go into isolation' in response to events on the continent.[59]

However, accepting that a degree of isolation would be a feature of his foreign policy did not mean that Chamberlain wanted to go the whole way when power eventually came to him. On the contrary, the evidence suggests that he and his colleagues deemed both isolation and pacifism as largely unrealistic strategies, given the condition of the world they inherited. The crux of the question is well illustrated in a letter Chamberlain wrote to a distant relative in January 1938. Here the Prime Minister discussed American isolation and outlined his wider views on the issue:

> I can well understand this frame of mind ... Indeed we have a similar school of thought here ... Yet, though my people are haunted by a constantly recurring fear of war, we are too close to

the danger spots for any but a few cranks to hope that we could remain safe in isolation. We are a very rich and a very vulnerable Empire, and there are plenty of poor adventurers not very far away who look on us with hungry eyes.[60]

While expressing a certain sympathy with the general ideal, then, Chamberlain's fear of the Dictator powers being able to take advantage of Britain's far-flung Imperial commitments and proximity to mainland Europe seemed to render isolation impractical from the outset. The world was now a much smaller place. This was, after all, the beginning of the age of much feared bomber aircraft and the English Channel now offered scant protection against attack. 'The bomber will always get through', stated Baldwin in the Commons as far back as 1932, and the fear of aerial bombardment in Britain during this decade was widespread and profound.[61]

That Chamberlain's new direction also considered pacifism as derisory and unrealistic is strongly implied in a Conservative Research Department paper from the summer of 1938. In the 'Points for Propaganda' files, which essentially encompassed documents and evidence collected by the Tories for use against political opponents, a newspaper article was included that illustrated the impracticality of the cause in the face of the pressing need to rearm. On 5 July, the *Daily Telegraph* had reported how Socialist MP Ernest Thurtle, a noted pacifist, was reconsidering his views:

> He said that he used to cry, 'No more war'. The world had changed, and we now had no alternative but to take precautions to preserve our liberties from would-be tyrants in Europe. 'You can be the finest pacifist in the world and still take part in Air Raid Precautions with a clear conscience,' Mr Thurtle said.
>
> 'It is purely humanitarian, in the same category as the St John Ambulance Brigade and the Red Cross.'[62]

Storing of this article in this particular file is evidence enough for the fact that mainstream Conservatives saw pacifism as unsuited to the essential needs of the day, such as rearmament and improving defences.

Unsurprisingly, therefore, unilateral disarmament was also afforded little serious consideration by the government, despite the hand-wringing
and lip-service which frequently accompanied rearmament announce-
ments, especially in the earlier part of our period. In February 1936,
Eden told the Commons that 'I deeply regret that increased expenditure
upon armaments by this country should have become inevitable ... but
there is a measure of comfort that rearmament to strengthen collective
security is the cheapest form of rearmament'.[63]

More concrete discussions came on measures of arms limitation,
but, again, these were largely hazy proposals for some distant point
in the future and yielded few tangible results. The pursuit of an air
deal with Germany was a regularly occurring feature of Foreign Policy
Committee debate throughout early 1938, with Halifax stressing the
importance of 'some substantial measure of air disarmament' to any
general settlement. Chamberlain himself thought that the abolition of
all bomber aircraft 'would be an enormous advance and of incalculable
value to all concerned'.[64] However, he also acknowledged that 'this was
a matter which must in the most favourable conditions take a very long
time to arrange'.[65] Indeed, by October 1938, despite the new spirit of
cooperation emanating from the Munich Agreement, a Foreign Office
memorandum still argued that, while 'an offer of limitation of armaments or restriction of air warfare should be sympathetically received
and carefully considered ... no agreement should preclude us from
reaching substantial air parity with Germany if we can'.[66]

There was still some support for isolation during the Chamberlain
period from military planners and strategists. Admirals, in particular, readily favoured isolation. Parker cites both the First Sea Lord,
Ernle Chatfield, and retired Admiral, Sir Barry Domvile, as committed supporters. The latter, once President of the Royal Naval College
but imprisoned in 1940 as a collaborator with the Nazis, remarked in
1937 that it was 'quite certain that the man in the street is not going
to be led into any wild business in which his own country's interests
are not directly concerned'.[67] Admiral Reginald Drax, who came to
prominence during the 1939 mission to Moscow, was no exception to
this rule. In a 1936 Admiralty paper, written shortly after the remilitarization of the Rhineland, he called for Britain to 'withdraw from the

muddle to the fullest extent that we can ... Make pacts and alliances with none, merely using our utmost diplomatic influence in favour of all who are supporting Right against the use of Might'.[68] By October 1937, he had come out in favour of a strategy he entitled 'Modified Isolation ... the policy of America', in which Britain would remain aloof from European affairs but stand by the general principles of international cooperation and League sanctions against any nation pursuing 'unjustifiable' policies on the continent.[69]

It is clear that Chamberlain's government had to perform a delicate balancing act. The limited liability dimension of appeasement emerged almost as a concession to the strategic needs of the day. Britain, the defence Ministers and Chiefs of Staff constantly warned, had to reduce its commitments in Europe and decrease liabilities around the world. At the same time, Chamberlain and his senior colleagues recognised that total isolation was a dangerous policy – for the 'cranks' – given these numerous responsibilities and the nation's vulnerability to attack. Appeasement can be seen, in part, as an attempt to tackle this dilemma and make the best of a bad lot.

* * *

A brief survey of wider opinion seems to support Chamberlain's decision to reject both isolation and pacifism in the years before war. The vast majority of speakers on either policy, from all sides of both Houses, were overwhelmingly hostile. These were largely seen as outdated strategies, given the escalating threat to Europe and the Dominions. The Under-Secretary for Foreign Affairs, Viscount Cranborne's assertion that 'until somebody can find a method of detaching this island from its foundations and towing it away to a less vulnerable position, it seems to me that the policy of isolation is the policy of an ostrich', was variously echoed by the leaders of the opposition ranks.[70] Sinclair's claim on 23 June 1936 that isolation is 'not to reduce our liabilities. It is greatly to increase them' was accompanied by Attlee's apparent attack on both isolation *and* pacifism on the same day.[71] The former, he asserted, gave no security; the latter he just could not understand.[72] Even Churchill, by no means an enthusiast for government policy at this time, seemingly defended Chamberlain's more realistic outlook when, in late 1937, he derided Lansbury for putting on his 'rose coloured spectacles' whenever he looked at the world's problems.[73]

Press and public opinion offered limited support for these policies and were frequently outrightly critical. The *Daily Herald*, a strong supporter of the Labour Party, wrote of the 'blank reasonable futility of pacifism' witnessed in the days before Munich.[74] At the time of the *Anschluss*, it had asserted that isolation would bring 'no permanent peace, either for ourselves or the world'.[75] The *News Chronicle* concurred:

> How can Lord Beaverbrook talk in the same breath of preserving the Empire and isolating Britain from Europe? If Lord Beaverbrook glances at a map he will see that the Mediterranean is part of Europe. And the Mediterranean happens to be a vital artery to a large part of the Empire, the peace of which he hopes to secure.[76]

A letter to the *Manchester Guardian* from Harold Picton of Hertfordshire a few days earlier offers an example of how public opinion was generally in accord: 'There are both voices and silences luring us towards isolation... The man who says, "I will never fight to defend anyone but myself" is not admirable.'[77] A year later, following events in Prague, pacifism received a similarly damning verdict from one *News Chronicle* reader, Archie Robertson of Bournemouth: 'It is hard to follow the logic of pacifists. They think it wicked to resist aggression, and yet they seem to be never tired of making excuses for the aggressor! ... Pacifism is a dirtier creed than I supposed.'[78]

Contemporary support for the rejection of isolation and pacifism can also be found further afield. It is perhaps surprising that Gilbert Murray, Chairman of the League of Nations Union (LNU) – which Ceadel would term a 'pacificist' organisation – came out so strongly for rejecting the absolute pacifist option. Reasserting his belief in collective security during May 1938, he also poured scorn on isolationism:

> How, then, can security be attained?
> If we rule out a policy of absolute Non-resistance as neither practicable, nor likely to discourage an aggressor, nor compatible

with the obligations of human brotherhood, there remain two possibilities, Isolationism and Collective Defence.

Isolationism has immense attractions to conventional and unpractical minds. It enables a nation to indulge its prejudices, to ignore foreign complications, and to pursue a purely selfish policy. But clearly it cannot bring security to any European nation weaker than Germany, nor yet to an Empire so vulnerable and so tempting to the spoiler as the British.[79]

Conclusion

Isolation and absolute pacifism were clearly-stated policies advocated in the Chamberlain period by a small but devoted band of enthusiastic supporters. The Prime Minister's policy contained elements of both rival strategies, but can also been seen as a distinct entity, separate from them, incorporating elements that the other two did not share. While Chamberlain and his government considered isolation briefly, both alternatives were eventually rejected as unrealistic strategies given the actions of the Fascist powers in the late 1930s. Ironically, it was the cherished gem of so many isolation supporters – the British Empire – which was the decisive factor in the demise of isolation. The fact that bomber aircraft had severely undermined the defensive capability of the English Channel also played an important role.

Moreover, it was very difficult to be indifferent to the affairs of Europe in this period. Indeed, some have argued that Europe as a whole was engaged in a civil war during this decade. Given that social and political movements often transcended national borders, would public opinion have tolerated isolation or absolute pacifism indefinitely?[80] When war eventually came, the mood of the nation and Commonwealth was determined and united. In the age of Hitler and Fascism, the shelf-life of isolation and pacifism was always going to be limited.

Pursuit of either strategy by Chamberlain would have been extremely unpopular and seen as highly risky, and it is understandable why he eventually rejected these alternatives. Britain could not have won the Second World War acting alone. The country found itself in virtual isolation during the conflict because of the lottery of events; Chamberlain did not consciously choose that path, as A.J.P. Taylor suggested he could have done. Furthermore, neither Taylor nor Denman, enjoying the luxury of hindsight, ever contend that isolation would have averted war and the central aim of appeasement was to do just that. Indeed, it could even be argued that isolation or pacifism, pursued vigorously by the National Government, might have only brought war earlier. Chamberlain's key role in securing the Munich Conference avoided this war in late 1938, hostilities looking all but certain had his personal interference not induced Hitler to come to the table and settle matters peacefully.

What, then, might have happened in the late 1930s had Chamberlain tried to steer Britain towards either isolation or pacifism, as highly unlikely though this was given the state of wider opinion? Fascist militarism in Europe would not have been diminished and would very probably have been emboldened. Events, therefore, might have taken a roughly similar course through 1937 and much of the following year. Had Chamberlain stayed at home during September 1938, however, it is probable that a war would have erupted. Hitler famously asserted shortly after the Munich Conference that he had been 'cheated' by Chamberlain out of his desired small, local conflict.[81] In Britain's absence, France might have been forced to take a more prominent role in events, but it is difficult to believe that that country alone could have deterred Hitler from marching into the Sudetenland, or convinced him to hold a conference and settle the matter peacefully, as Chamberlain eventually did. Indeed, French Premier Edouard Daladier might have acted even more timidly than he did in September 1938, notwithstanding his country's direct commitment to the Czechs. If Britain and France appeased together at Munich, it is unlikely that France would have fought alone. Moreover, the chances of Russia joining France and Czechoslovakia in some stand against Germany in 1938 – which are far from certain as it is – would have been even lower without British assistance.

Had Britain remained aloof, it is possible that Hitler might have attempted to secure an Anglo-German alliance at some stage. It is known from the pages of *Mein Kampf* that this was considered favourably by him at one time and the Anglo-German Naval Agreement of 1935 seemed to suggest that such a deal might not be rejected out of hand.[82] However, unless Britain was prepared to pursue an utterly cynical policy and acquiesce in Nazi Germany's attempt to subvert the continent, then this could not have been accepted by the time of Chamberlain's premiership. Despite widespread sympathy for Germany in the earlier 1930s, and a mutual fear of the Soviet Union, outright pro-Nazism in Britain was reserved for a tiny few – the so-called 'Fellow Travellers' within the BUF and anti-Semitic groups such as The Link. Would Hitler have left Britain alone during any resulting war? Once France had fallen, which might have occurred even more quickly without British assistance, it is likely that the *Führer* would have attempted an invasion of Britain given his treatment of other neutral states during the war itself, and how he turned against his Soviet ally in 1941. Even more likely, some vital interest of Britain's – perhaps a colony or Dominion – would have been menaced by one of the Axis powers and Britain would then have had to join in the struggle or take the non-violent resistance approach of the absolute pacifists.

Would the resulting war have been 'better' or 'worse' for Britain than events as they occurred? On a purely selfish basis, it may have been possible for Britain to have survived invasion during some hypothetical 'other' war, as actual proceedings during 1940 would suggest. Conversely, Charmley's notion of peaceful coexistence with Hitler might well have been more beneficial for the British Empire than real events as they unfolded.[83] However, the moral basis for such a line would have been non-existent and the Charmley thesis takes little account of wider factors undermining Empire at this time. It is doubtful, however, that the country could have been induced to rearm sufficiently to survive conflict, had appeasement not been tried and failed – and, therefore, demonstrated the *need* to prepare for war more vigorously. The year's grace secured at Munich, in which most of the Hurricanes and Spitfires that won the Battle of Britain were built, might not have come about without Munich itself, and the betrayal of this agreement by Hitler at Prague.

Finally, it is doubtful whether an isolationist Britain would have gained the sympathy and eventual assistance of later allies such as the USA, whose own isolationist tendencies might have been reinforced by Britain's detachment from Europe, rather than being eroded by the efforts of Chamberlain and Churchill to appease and then resist Nazi Germany. It is difficult to believe that war would have been averted, or that the eventual outcome would have been any more favourable, had isolation or absolute pacifism been pursued by this country. Chamberlain's scepticism was well-founded.

2

ECONOMIC AND COLONIAL APPEASEMENT

Economic questions should be thoroughly and systematically studied with a view to large changes in what I may call the economic and colonial layout of the world ... It may well be, in the course of these discussions, that a large number of special British privileges will have to be surrendered for the sake of the peaceful and prosperous future of the world as a whole.[1]

(Hugh Dalton, House of Commons, March 1936)

Introduction

Many of Chamberlain's contemporary critics asserted that the National Government should have pursued the economic and colonial aspects of appeasement with far more energy and to a far greater extent than it ever did. Some political opponents held that such a strategy might have secured a lasting peace by removing a major grievance of the Fascist powers. Many commentators, still suffering from the effects of the Great Depression and recently introduced to Marxist-Leninist doctrine, held that economic strangulation bred global resentment and fostered the causes of war.[2] They argued that by removing trade restrictions, reducing commercial barriers and increasing access to colonies, raw materials and living space, certain 'Have-Not' powers could be satisfied and Britain would be making a vital contribution to world peace. Others felt that Chamberlain, although periodically undertaking forays into economic and colonial appeasement himself, did not go far enough.

This chapter will examine the origins and viability of the closely related strategies of economic and colonial appeasement as alternatives to the policy Chamberlain pursued in the late 1930s. Colonial appeasement was one specific aspect of the wider economic policy, principally concerned with Hitler's demands for the return of the former German territories in Africa, confiscated as part of the 1919 peace settlement and placed under a League of Nations mandate. Areas like Tanganyika, Togoland and the Cameroons, entrusted in part to British administration by the League after the Great War, were particularly contentious. Mussolini, too, had colonial grievances and the successive Japanese regimes of the period also had ambitions in this field, but the colonies were essentially an Anglo-German facet of the economic question. After all, this was an issue in which Hitler's complaints were levelled primarily at Britain, rather than to the victor states in general, because that country was still the world's foremost Imperial power and was best placed to affect colonial readjustment.

References to economic and colonial appeasement are few and far between in the diaries and memoirs of Chamberlain's contemporaries, which comprise a large part of the orthodox historiography. Robert Boothby claimed that wide-scale economic appeasement was a missed opportunity that should have been pursued much further and might have averted war. This is somewhat surprising, given that Boothby was one of the most consistent Tory rebels of the period and a vehement anti-appeaser. Assessing the main turning points leading to the Second World War, Boothby asserted that the failure of Britain and the USA to cultivate greater equality throughout the world economy was a major contributing factor. European tensions over these matters were particularly important.[3]

It is ironic that while an ardent anti-appeaser like Boothby came to believe that economic appeasement should have been pursued to a much greater extent, Clement Attlee, one of the most fervent advocates of such a policy at the time, later came to view it as a misguided cause. His retrospective interview in Francis Williams' *A Prime Minister Remembers* was particularly illuminating. Here Attlee undermined the claims of figures like Boothby by admitting that the Labour Party was wrong to have thought such measures could have saved peace:

(Williams):   Do you still feel, as you suggested then, that offers of economic cooperation or development in the colonies, or anything of that kind, might have kept Hitler from war?
(Attlee):   No, I don't think so. I think he would have had to show something worthwhile.[4]

It is in the revisionist period of appeasement literature that such questions began to be analysed in depth, as a series of historians produced works closely examining the importance of the financial dimensions of Chamberlain's policy. Chief amongst these were the studies of Berndt Wendt, Gustav Schmidt and Andrew Crozier. Though each had differing aims and agendas, all three historians agreed on several main points that suggest that economic and colonial appeasement were unworkable alternatives for the government to have explored in depth; first, they asserted that economic appeasement had hitherto been an overplayed aspect of Chamberlain's policy and that it should be seen as just one small part of the Prime Minister's wider strategy. Crozier, for example, claimed that the government 'had no intention of allowing the colonial question to become a serious issue';[5] second, they argued that radical economic approaches would have failed because of a flawed belief in British policy making circles that there existed so-called 'moderates' in the upper echelons of the Nazi Party – Economics Minister Hjalmar Schacht, for example, or Hermann Göring – who could influence Hitler to look favourably upon such approaches. As Wendt argued, Hitler was not really interested in economic and colonial questions, despite his frequent rhetoric on the subject, and could not be persuaded otherwise.[6]

Schmidt concurred with this general line but was also keen to play up wider domestic factors in his assessment of why economic appeasement never really took off in the way government critics demanded. He believed that the absence of a cross-party alliance in trying to make such measures workable hamstrung these initiatives from the outset.[7] This was, after all, a policy favoured by the political Left much more than the Right. A conflict of interests and ideas within the government, between those arguing for the pre-eminence of political measures over economic ones, and a smaller group backing the financial dimension as the best way forward also meant that the latter approach was usually downplayed.[8]

Post-revisionist literature on economic and colonial appeasement has merely tended to reinforce, rather than undermine, such arguments. Neil Forbes echoed Schmidt's concern that domestic political factors should not be underplayed when assessing why radical economic initiatives were not viable:

> The Board of Trade was highly suspicious of the activities of the Foreign Office, while the extreme hostility the latter showed to the attitudes of the Bank of England ... has been underestimated ... The paper schemes of the economic appeasers counted for nothing against the harsh realities of the commercial world.[9]

Similarly, Scott Newton echoed Wendt in claiming that Hitler was the main reason why such approaches did not get very far:

> The hopes of a settlement based on colonial appeasement were dashed. Indeed, they never really existed outside the minds of British Ministers and civil servants and, perhaps, Hjalmar Schacht. The fundamental difficulty was Hitler ... There is no reason to believe he ever believed their restoration, in whatever form, would be acceptable as part of a general settlement.[10]

Even more recently, in 2006, Richard Grayson has addressed the argument that conceding spheres of economic influence to Germany in Central and Eastern Europe might have diminished the chances of war. While admitting that such a gesture would have been attractive to Hitler, and might have reduced the need for German expansion, he asserts that it would have had 'little impact' on the *Führer's* ultimate aim of aggressive territorial aggrandisement. After all, his goals were not just economic in their origins.[11] It is clear, then, that the main historiography on economic and colonial appeasement views such approaches as only ever piecemeal and subservient to wider political measures in the government's eyes. Moreover, the likely results would have been very questionable. This chapter will address these claims.

Significantly, the 'alternatives' to appeasement discussed within this chapter were actually, to an extent, carried out by Chamberlain's government. Advocates of economic and colonial appeasement were as likely to be found in the Cabinet as they were across the chamber of the House of Commons. But those within the policy making elite usually saw economic appeasement as only one small aspect of – and complementary to – the central political strategy; as a means rather than an end. Timing and extent emerge as important factors, with government opponents regularly arguing that it should have gone much further. As will become clear, there were also differing conceptions of what 'economic appeasement' actually meant – and how it should be carried out – depending largely on which side of the political spectrum the advocates occupied.

Economic and colonial appeasement were complex phenomena with many facets, often encompassing numerous and seemingly contradictory characteristics. Schmidt, in particular, is keen to stress the difficulties of defining exactly what 'economic appeasement' towards Germany was. Indeed, he identifies nine separate facets of the policy existing in British government minds at the time. These are as follows: (1) granting of economic concessions to Germany in order to foster closer cooperation and remove grievances; (2) encouraging Germany to return to a global system of trade; (3) attempting to win Germany over towards the economic systems of Western Europe as opposed to the Soviet sphere, where Russo-German cooperation was greatly feared; (4) recognising that certain areas of Central and Eastern Europe were to be left to German economic domination; (5) settling of debts and potential exchange of loans, colonies or raw materials between Britain and Germany; (6) creating a unique Anglo-German economic partnership to shield their mutual recovery from the Depression; (7) revising any British economic practices that were disadvantageous to Germany; (8) promoting peaceful ways in which Germany could alleviate its most serious economic problems; and (9) fostering closer relations between British and German industrialists.[12]

Though Schmidt's definition is already quite broad, it is by no means comprehensive and merits further consideration today.[13] For example, what most people at the time simply termed 'economic appeasement' can, in fact, be seen as a sort of two-headed beast, encompassing concessionary and pacific characteristics alongside aggressive and restrictive ones. Thus, while Chamberlain's government at various times during the late 1930s offered to provide Germany with loans and trade deals so that it would behave more amicably, it also tried to pump resources into Germany's neighbours, thereby building a bloc of economic dependents to encircle the Nazi regime. In short, many advocates of economic appeasement, both inside government and outside, periodically aimed to financially strangle one region or power as a by-product of economically appeasing another. A blurring of the lines between economic appeasement in its traditional sense and naked economic warfare is often apparent, particularly after the March 1939 Prague Coup, though the two contrasting strands of this single strategy were not always clearly distinguished. This has resulted in an overly-simplistic understanding of the policy. These subtle nuances are important to recognise and will be discussed in greater detail below.

Origins and Nature of the Alternative

Economic and colonial appeasement had been considered in Britain and the wider world long before Chamberlain assumed the premiership. Discontent with the 1919 peace settlement was rife and it was not long before both victors and vanquished expressed a desire to revise many of its terms. At the Locarno negotiations in 1925, economic discussions were important factors and German Chancellor Gustav Stresemann enquired into the possibility of having a colonial mandate awarded to Germany. He was unsuccessful. Colonial claims were at the heart of more general economic questions during the 1930s through the issues of raw materials, minerals, living space and territories for commercial exploitation. Discussion of colonies also opened up the bigger issues of Empire and Imperial trade, with many amongst both the winners and losers in the Great War convinced that Britain's place at the heart of a huge Commonwealth trade monopoly was grossly unjust. At a time when most of the globe was suffering from unparalleled economic hardships born of the Wall Street Crash, the system of British Imperial Preference was a bitter pill for many to swallow.

After the Great Depression had given the Nazis a platform to gain power in Germany, it was not long before Hitler began to tie up economic issues like these with more general aspirations of dismantling the Versailles system and securing German national resurgence. He linked his March 1936 offer to rejoin the League of Nations – a 'peace gesture' following the reoccupation of the Rhineland – with a vague *quid pro quo* insistence that 'within a reasonable time, and by means of friendly negotiations, the question of colonial equality of rights will be cleared up'.[14]

Concrete proposals for economic and colonial appeasement began to surface in Britain at this time. Former Liberal Prime Minister David Lloyd George was one of the first to raise the issue of a new colonial deal with Germany in February 1936. He cited the injustice of that country having no colonial territories in Africa to exploit, while smaller European powers like Belgium, Holland and Portugal did. He also pointed out that the territories which passed into British administration under the Treaty of Versailles were not its possessions to plunder in the way of the old Empire, but belonged instead to the League of Nations – and that this system, in turn, should be addressed: 'I do not believe that you will have peace in the world until you reconsider the mandates,' he concluded.[15] A few weeks later, the Liberal leader Archibald Sinclair broadened the discussion. The economic adjustments he favoured were bigger than colonies alone:

> Markets are as important as raw materials, and if we are to solve the great question of migration and the economic suffocation from which many countries are suffering, we shall have to take a wider view of the task than merely facilitating access to raw materials.[16]

As the Rhineland crisis broke in March, former Labour leader George Lansbury developed this line further:

I want the government led by the Prime Minister to go to the world, even in the midst of this terrible upheaval with Germany and France, and say that for our part we are willing to make whatever sacrifices are necessary; not to share out bits of land here and there, but to find a means of pooling the resources of the world, sharing the markets and the territories of the world for the service of mankind. It is the only way to peace. No other way is possible.[17]

Even the earliest calls for wide-scale measures such as these demonstrate that the policy was backed mostly by the Left or Centre-Left of the political spectrum. Lord Lothian wrote a letter to *The Times* on 11 February 1936, for example, extolling the virtues of removing trade barriers and increasing access to raw materials.[18] Indeed, apart from the League of Nations route, economic and colonial appeasement was the most consistently advocated alternative to government policy as suggested by Labour and the Liberals during the late 1930s.

Calls for economic and colonial appeasement gathered momentum in parliament throughout the remainder of the year with one or two Conservatives also expressing sympathy for the cause. Sir Rupert de la Bere favoured reorganisation of the League in order to make it a 'vast chamber of commerce'. Its central purpose, he contended, when addressing the Commons in June 1936, should be non-political – to 'develop the trade of the world' and 'prevent that terrible hunger for land' which was afflicting the Dictator states.[19] In response, outspoken Labour MP Sir Stafford Cripps called for a new 'international economic organisation' to be established, which would foster and coordinate worldwide cooperation on these matters.[20] By the end of the year, other countries such as Japan were also being referred to explicitly as aggressive 'Have-Not' powers to be targeted for such measures.[21]

By the time Chamberlain came to power in May 1937, advocates of radical economic and colonial appeasement formed a substantial body in British foreign policy thinking. The new Prime Minister's long and relatively successful spell as Chancellor of the Exchequer offered hope to such figures that these issues would be tackled soon. Both the

Labour and Liberal opposition, in March and June of that year respectively, produced literature outlining their international strategies in
the economic field, with the former demanding greater equality in
wealth distribution as a central pillar of its foreign policy.[22] Their MP
David Grenfell called for 'world cooperation in the development of
raw materials and trade facilities' in particular. This, he saw, as 'the
one alternative to war'.[23] The Liberals, meanwhile, sought 'the abandonment of economic Imperialism, the relaxation of trade restrictions,
the relief of the economic terrorism in the world and the restoration
of peaceful overseas trade'.[24] This would be best achieved by termin-
ating the Ottawa system, the scheme established in 1932 which created preferential trade relations between Britain and its Empire and
closed the door to outside influence. This statement had followed
Liberal peer Lord Noel-Buxton's motion in the House of Lords during
February 1937, calling for all the existing non-mandated colonies
belonging to Britain and the other Imperial powers to be given over
to the League.

Chamberlain's accession to power would give a dynamic new impetus
to the policy of appeasement, including its economic and colonial
aspects. However, government critics maintained their pressure on the
new Prime Minister, asserting that only truly radical concessions could
avert a future war. Attlee went on a full-scale offensive in a Commons
debate during December 1937, echoing Noel-Buxton's call for a bold,
new colonial settlement: 'We do not believe in a re-dividing up. We
believe that all colonies of all powers should be held on the principle
of a mandate, first for the peoples of those territories, and, secondly, for
the whole world.'[25] Significantly, Attlee distinguished here between
a 're-dividing up' of colonies and Labour's own pro-League line. The
majority of even the most ardent pro-colonial appeasers were not keen
for these territories to be handed straight over to a regime with such
a poor track record in the treatment of minorities as Nazi Germany.
This point was echoed in the same debate by Winston Churchill, who
actually backed a degree of colonial appeasement at this juncture if it
would help avert a future war. However, the only scheme he favoured
was on the basis of a wide and general settlement, with every major
colonial power giving territories over to the League. There would be no

cession from Britain alone and no return of any former colony directly to Germany.[26]

Sinclair was more concerned with Imperial Preference during this debate, calling for Britain to 'break the shackles of Ottawa and Protection' as soon as possible.[27] The Liberal leader also placed more importance on securing closer cooperation with the world's foremost economic power, the USA.[28] A trade deal with that country was often seen as the best means to bring America into the fold, while Secretary of State Cordell Hull was one of the world's most vocal advocates of economic appeasement measures. Many pro-American elements in Britain saw the economic sphere as the best way to encourage closer Anglo-American relations. Leo Amery, for example, who presented himself as a vehement opponent of colonial appeasement – despite actually suggesting in late 1937 that Chamberlain could utilise the Cameroons as a potential 'sweetener' for Germany – advocated a reappraisal of Imperial Preference, not so much to better Anglo-German relations as to improve Anglo-American ones.[29]

*   *   *

The cause of economic appeasement received fresh impetus in early 1938 with the publication in January of the van Zeeland Report. Commissioned by the governments of Britain and France in March 1936, this plan of economic recommendations designed to avert war was produced by the Belgian Prime Minister and received widespread attention across the continent. It advocated an economic conference to be attended by all the major world powers, while supporting moves towards an internationalization of the mandate system. It also backed freer access to raw materials for all, as well as a Pact of Economic Collaboration to be agreed by as many countries as possible.[30] Van Zeeland's proposals received enthusiastic support from the main opposition parties, with Attlee echoing its recommendation for a 'calling together of the nations' and deriding Chamberlain's early performance in foreign affairs during March 1938: 'He has not been very successful with the political difficulties. Perhaps he had better turn and try to deal with the economic difficulties.'[31] Sinclair, meanwhile, outlined

Liberal policy towards Germany and Italy in more general terms:

> We will cooperate with them in setting up international com-
> missions to consider their grievances, such as the problem of
> colonies, and, on the lines of the van Zeeland Report, we would,
> in cooperation with Germany and Italy, set about curing the
> disease of economic nationalism with all its symptoms of quotas,
> tariffs and exchange restrictions.[32]

As the summer of 1938 progressed, the House of Commons witnessed calls for a more aggressive form of economic appeasement. The
majority of demands so far had been in the wider colonial sphere and
were often concerned with improving the position of the world as a
whole. In July 1938, however, several MPs called for direct loans from
Britain or the League to one specific country, China, with a view to
the military and economic ambitions of another power, Japan, being
kept in check. The latest Sino-Japanese conflict, which had broken out
a year earlier, had been progressing badly from the Chinese point of
view, with vast areas of the Yangtze valley and large tracts of coastline
already secured by Japanese troops. As a fellow League power suffering at the hands of an increasingly aggressive and Fascist-leaning
Japan, there was widespread sympathy for China's position throughout Britain. The appeasement of one country's economic troubles was,
therefore, deliberately envisaged with the express twin aim of defeating, or at least sending out a strong message, to another aggressor
power. Independent MP Eleanor Rathbone addressed the Commons
on 4 July, scornful of the government's efforts so far and calling for a
League-sponsored loan to be arranged as quickly as possible: 'Could
the Chancellor have told Japan more plainly that we were too afraid of
her to do what is our duty as a member of the League?'[33] Yet Rathbone
also appeared to stand firm behind economic appeasement in its traditional sense just minutes earlier, announcing that 'we should sacrifice
a very great deal, bits of our own empire, take risks to avoid a conflict
with Germany'. She concluded by urging Chamberlain to think carefully about 'what we are going to give away to Herr Hitler'.[34] That
she apparently favoured two opposing lines of economic policy under

the same broad banner – giving colonies to one Fascist state, while calling for loans to contain another – went unchallenged by successive speakers, and indeed gained support from several other members of the House.[35]

At first appearance, calls for loans to China do not seem like appeasement as it might be defined today, but look much more like the rallying cries for an economic war against Japan. However, these two seemingly contradictory approaches were not clearly distinguished between at the time – indeed, speakers deliberately avoided doing so for fear of provoking the Fascist powers. All this was still 'economic appeasement' when discussed in public forums like parliament or in publications such as the van Zeeland Report, the epithet being applied equally to granting concessions to Hitler as it was to tackling the financial woes of an entire continent. Thus, Sinclair could talk in late 1937 of ensuring world peace by 'restoring the prosperity of the peoples of Europe' most generally, in the very same breath as giving 'full scope to the economic interests of Germany and Italy' in specific.[36] In this context, and using the terminology of the era, a difference can be seen between appeasement in the traditional, modern sense of the word – that is, in satisfying the troubles of a belligerent, aggrieved nation – and this particular form of economic appeasement, which deliberately resisted an aggressive power as a by-product of helping another pacific one. There were few distinctions made at the time between whether the 'appeased' country was a strong bully or a weak friend, evidence, perhaps, of shifting definitions in the years after Munich and how the term 'appeasement' frequently assumed more negative connotations hereafter.[37]

The Munich Agreement in September 1938 unsurprisingly breathed new life into the calls for radical economic and colonial initiatives. Even some of the sternest critics of Chamberlain's efforts at the conference felt that wide-ranging economic measures offered a good chance of a lasting peace, if efforts were now made to build on the new mood of Anglo-German cooperation. On 3 October 1938, the first day of the Munich debate in parliament, Attlee called for an economic summit to follow on from what had been achieved. Deriding the current settlement and addressing the bigger picture, he demanded 'a real

conference, a peace conference to which people will not come merely to
rattle the sabre'. Its aim would be 'to deal with the colonial question,
to deal with the question of raw materials, to deal, above all, with the
great economic question ... to build a new world'.[38]

Lord Strabolgi, Labour's Chief Whip in the Lords, concurred with
this line, but also demanded that a comprehensive settlement of the
colonies should emerge from any such gathering.[39] The most striking
contribution to the debate, however, came on 5 October from Liberal
peer Lord Arnold. He used telling statistics to powerful effect and
his words once again underline how 'economic appeasement', in the
language of the day, could encompass concessions to both aggressive
Dictatorships in specific, as well as the wider world in general:

> It is the great inequality in the distribution of economic wealth
> and territory throughout the world which is one of the chief
> causes of international unrest. As a matter of fact six powers, if I
> may so call them, the British Empire, France, Russia, the United
> States, Brazil and China have about two-thirds of the territory of
> the world, leaving one-third to the other sixty nations, includ-
> ing Italy and Germany ... The British Empire and the United
> States have about two-thirds of the economic mineral wealth of
> the world ... Any sacrifices which the "Have" powers may have
> to make to the 'Have-Not' powers for economic appeasement
> would be infinitesimal compared with the devastation and hor-
> ror of another world war.[40]

The year ended with the most concrete proposals for economic and
colonial appeasement to date, when Labour MP Philip Noel-Baker
called for all the world's colonies to be given over to a League mandate
system for re-allocation. He asserted that 'Militarist Imperialism', at
the heart, he believed, of the recent conflicts in Abyssinia, China and
Spain, was driven by economic injustice and would only be defeated
with a comprehensive redivision of the world's territories and raw
materials.[41] In a lengthy debate during December, the notion of an
international colonial 'pool' was suggested by Lansbury as an alternative to the existing mandates. This would be administered by a global

Civil Service, with all the major powers – including Germany, Italy and Japan – taking their turn to watch over a pot of resources into which every country could dip, but which no one power could dominate.[42] While some MPs expressed a preference for the League system, and others voiced their opposition to colonial appeasement root and branch, Lansbury's pool idea emerged as an ambitious compromise between the two positions. United in opposition to government policy and convinced that Chamberlain should have been doing much more in the economic field, critics of the Prime Minister were nevertheless frequently divided over the best way to proceed.

*   *   *

A brief survey of wider opinion supporting economic and colonial appeasement at this time demonstrates similar areas of broad agreement existing alongside differences in specific emphasis. Most of the British Far-Left were also firm advocates of such strategies, and especially of wide-scale colonial re-division. Much of their support stemmed from grander Marxist anti-Imperial convictions, rather than more straightforward economic arguments, and they were often hostile to the British Empire, widely seen as the gaoler of enslaved colonial masses. However, clamouring for the liberation of natives from their Imperial bonds, they frequently supported opening trade within the colonies and a broader allocation of administrative rights as a step in the right direction. In 1936, the British Communist Party, in a widely-disseminated pamphlet, claimed that war could be ended only by eradicating Imperialist rivalries. This, in turn, could be achieved only by scrapping the present 'fallacy' of the mandate system.[43] The tiny Independent Labour Party concurred. In a 1939 pamphlet entitled *The Socialist Challenge to Poverty, Fascism, Imperialism, War*, it advocated colonial redistribution to help the natives in their struggle for freedom. Fairer access to raw materials for states like Germany and Italy was not their prime concern, however, and indeed this would have been repugnant to them.[44]

As has been suggested earlier, many pacifist groups also supported economic and colonial appeasement in the years before war. Lansbury was one of the most vocal British advocates, and bodies like the Peace Pledge Union, of which he was at one time President, enthusiastically promoted the cause. In a statement of policy issued just before the Munich Conference, the PPU asserted: 'We believe that the tension in Europe could be relieved at once if our government was willing to make considerable sacrifices of our own Imperial interests for the purpose of securing economic and political justice all round.'[45] The National Peace Council was another long-term campaigner. In a statement of policy from February 1937, it demanded 'resolute action in the economic sphere to loosen the bonds of international trading and to increase general prosperity'.[46] Similarly, the Women's International League for Peace and Freedom called for Britain to cede all its colonies to a League mandate system in January 1937, and argued that 'the Open Door must be the aim'. After all, 'the door that is open will not need to be battered down!'[47]

Unsurprisingly, the League of Nations Union also promoted the cause of economic appeasement and particularly the cession of all world colonies to a mandate system. In the month that Chamberlain became Prime Minister, the Union asserted that freer world trade would be the foremost contribution he could make to world peace through economic channels, and called for efforts to reduce quota restrictions and eradicate Imperial Preference.[48] LNU Chairman Gilbert Murray confessed that, while he was not optimistic of success in appeasing Hitler with a colonial deal, it was certainly better to explore the issue than not.[49] By the winter of 1938–1939, the General Council of the LNU had adopted a number of resolutions in the economic sphere, such as the revision of exchange tariffs within the Empire and a wholesale reconsideration of the colonies.[50]

There was also support for economic and colonial appeasement among sections of the press throughout the Chamberlain era, usually among those papers most in favour of general political measures. *The Times* was a case in point. Its editor, Geoffrey Dawson, while opposing the return of all Germany's former colonies, confessed in May 1937 that handing over a mandate to German administration would be a positive step for peace.[51] However, even some of those dailies which did not support political appeasement could also favour economic and colonial concessions, and regularly demanded greater action from Chamberlain in this field. As the Labour Party's chief supporter, the *Daily Herald* unsurprisingly backed the internationalization of all colonies in the wake of the *Anschluss*.[52] It then echoed Attlee's call for a new World Economic Conference shortly after Munich, to settle such issues as access to raw materials and natural resources.[53] The *Manchester Guardian* concurred with this proposal and, on 3 October 1938, challenged the Prime Minister over his future policy: 'Is Mr Chamberlain prepared to propose that colonies and raw materials and the other grievances of the "Have-Nots" be dealt with in the only reasonable and just way, in association with all interested States and the League?'[54]

A minority among the general public apparently supported economic appeasement measures for the duration of Chamberlain's premiership, though Gallup Poll data is ambiguous on the subject. In October 1938, only 15 per cent of those polled favoured a return of Germany's pre-war colonies, though 22 per cent did not want to risk a war over this issue.[55] Whether or not the public would have approved of freer access for Germany to the resources *in* these former colonies was not a question asked. Many letters written to newspapers supported the cause, though such evidence is largely anecdotal and issues of editorial policy must be considered. These letters came in greatest volume in the months after the *Anschluss*. H. Wilkins of Tooting Bec wrote to the *Daily Herald* on 16 March 1938 to argue that it was 'no use trying to escape the certain demand for restoration of mandates that were formerly German colonies'.[56] Horace Alexander was more thoughtful, suggesting a pooling of vital economic arteries in a letter to the *Manchester Guardian* a few days later:

> Economic appeasement is the first need, and the van Zeeland Report shows the way. The British government, without waiting for others, might declare its readiness to extend the sphere of the Open Door ... to all its dependent colonies, and it might propose a new international treaty to embody this principle. It might offer to extend the mandates system ... What about world control (or League control), in which, of course we should share, of world highways – the Suez Canal, Singapore, Gibraltar?[57]

Even the more aggressive variety of economic appeasement – if it can be labelled as such – could receive backing from the general public. In the wake of the Prague Coup, Hugh Wilson of South West London urged, in a letter to the *Daily Telegraph,* that Britain should help ease Romania's economic woes. By purchasing oil from that country, Britain would aid its economic recovery and reduce possible sources of antagonism in the region. But it would also deal a blow to German economic influence in this area and reduce the temptation for Hitler to invade Romania in the pursuit of such resources.[58]

*   *   *

The Prague Coup also shook faith throughout parliament in Hitler's promises. Indeed, from now on, Chamberlain effectively abandoned his policy of wide-scale concessions in favour of deterrence and alliances. While these events, and the subsequent reorientation of British strategy, impacted on calls for economic and colonial appeasement in the Commons – in the last six months of peace support diminished substantially – there were still a number of voices advocating such measures as the best way to avert war. Indeed, some of the immediate responses were as if little had happened in Czechoslovakia. Thus, Labour's David Grenfell was able to assert on 15 March 1939 that the 'question of land and economic security' was 'the underlying issue in Europe'.[59] A few weeks later, James Maxton of the Independent Labour Party echoed that 'the basic problem of the world today is not the problem of frontiers but the problem of poverty'.[60] Both advocated radical economic appeasement measures as the solution, while at the same time remaining fiercely critical of the broad thrust of Chamberlain's policies. Nor were such calls absent from the House of Lords. On 20 March 1939, Lord Arnold called for a reconsideration of the colonies in order to aid a Germany which had 'nothing like her fair share of the wealth and territory of the world'. He went on: 'If she cannot expand one way then she will expand in another way where she can, and that is in Central and Southeastern Europe.'[61]

By the summer of 1939, both Attlee and Sinclair had restated their general demands in the economic sphere, despite the rapid tide of events and their continuing criticism of political appeasement in general. In May, Attlee made a new call for all the world's colonies to be transferred to a League mandate system, while, in July, Sinclair backed a reduction of tariffs, quotas and fairer access to raw materials.[62] However, this would only be for those countries joining in an Anglo-Franco-Polish front.[63] Indeed, by now, for the Liberals and the majority of speakers in both Houses, economic appeasement had come to represent more aggressive measures designed to keep Germany at bay as a by-product of assisting others. As the government held its alliance talks with the Soviets, even Labour die-hards were modifying their demands to incorporate a more aggressive twin edge. Hugh Dalton's long-term commitment to economic appeasement is evident by his statement which opens this chapter. In a speech during July 1939, however, he called for new discussions with Hitler on the issues of freer trade, but also recommended supplementing the Polish Guarantee with a huge loan, designed to bolster that country's defences against the potential German threat.[64] His immediate response to the Prague Coup, meanwhile, had been to adapt his support for the economic appeasement of Germany to the resistance of that power by adopting the very same policies towards its vulnerable neighbour: 'If we are to make concessions about colonies and exits for trade or emigration to foreign countries, why not begin by making them to people like the Poles?'[65]

Again, under the official banner of 'economic appeasement' – which had been talked about for years and was never officially abandoned by the opposition – the legitimate assistance of one country or region was deliberately being conceived to have a quite different effect on the economic and military activities of another. It was emerging as a two-headed beast once again, encompassing aggressive and restrictive characteristics alongside the traditional boons and subsidies; increasingly moving towards naked economic warfare and away from appeasement as it might be defined today.[66] Inevitably, the occasional individual sailed against the tide. Former isolationist Tory MP Sir Arnold Wilson called for the internationalization of all colonies and a huge British loan to Germany during the July debate. He continued: 'We ought not to allow the bad manners of the plaintiff to blind us, as judges in our own cause, to the elements of justice and reason in his claim.'[67]

Consideration of the Alternative

Economic and colonial appeasement were perhaps the alternatives to
Chamberlain's central policy that the government experimented with
most, certainly before 1939 and the formation of the so-called 'Peace
Front' bloc of alliances. Indeed, as the introduction of this chapter
makes clear, such measures were significant facets *of* Chamberlain's
main strategy, though pursued far more sporadically and to a much
more limited extent than many of his critics called for. A detailed narrative of how far the National Government actually pursued the financial dimensions of appeasement can be found elsewhere.[68] Nevertheless,
a brief analysis of some of the key decisions and initiatives Chamberlain
undertook must now be made. A basic understanding of some of the
main things the Prime Minister did in this area is required before we
can make an informed assessment of why he did not do much more.

The idea of tackling the economic aspects to Germany's grievances had existed in Chamberlain's mind long before he became Prime
Minister. Hitler first made his colonial claims in early 1936, and
Chamberlain, as Chancellor of the Exchequer, had to respond in parliament. In what was to become the recurring official line on this topic,
he poured cold water on the idea of any transfer of a colony directly
to Germany at the present time but hinted that the issue could be
discussed again at a later date as part of a wider settlement.[69] This
strategy of ruling out a direct concession, but never closing the door
to potential colonial readjustments, was to become a regular feature of
government policy in both public and private statements over the next
few years. Chamberlain clearly hoped such questions might remain a
perpetual bargaining chip in any later dealings with Hitler on other
matters.[70] A few days after addressing the Commons, he wrote to his
sister explaining his motives:

> It was clearly impossible to declare that in no circumstances and
> at no time would we ever consider the surrender of our mandate
> over any territory that we hold now ... I don't believe myself that
> we could purchase peace and a lasting settlement by handing
> over Tanganyika to the Germans, but if I did I would not hesi-
> tate for a moment to do so.[71]

Following the Rhineland crisis in March 1936, Stanley Baldwin set up the Plymouth Committee to consider the issue of colonial concessions to Germany. The subsequent Plymouth Report, produced three months later, questioned the logic of such a move but warned against a blanket refusal to consider the matter further. This led to more discussion within the Cabinet and Foreign Policy Committee about future strategy. Crucially, while the majority of those attending such meetings were hostile to the notion of transferring mandates to Germany, it was Chamberlain and Halifax – Chancellor and Lord President respectively – who were most keen not to close the door entirely. When the Foreign Secretary, Anthony Eden, produced a draft statement of policy for consideration by the Committee on 27 July 1936, in which he proposed to rule out the transferral of any mandates, Halifax and Chamberlain spoke up, the latter claiming to be 'gravely alarmed by the wording' of the memorandum.[72] They requested that the statement be modified so as not to rule out completely any future adjustments, and a decision was subsequently taken to do so. Almost a year before he became Prime Minister, Chamberlain was prepared to consider the issue of colonial appeasement favourably, even to the point of clashing with senior colleagues on the matter.

While opposed specifically to colonial concessions at this time, Eden was a firm advocate of more general economic appeasement measures. As early as August 1936, he penned a Foreign Policy Committee memorandum recommending further consideration of raw materials and calling for close attention to be paid to van Zeeland's early work. He concluded that 'no review of the international situation which ignores the economic problems with which we have to deal, can be complete'.[73] The Foreign Office as a whole had given a good deal of consideration to economic and colonial appeasement in the wake of the Rhineland crisis. Roger Makins from the Western Department claimed that there was 'everything to be said' for the maintenance of friendly economic relations with Germany and suggested demarcating spheres of influence on the continent. He concluded: ' "A free hand" in Central and Eastern Europe should at least be equal in value to a colony.'[74] This had followed on from suggestions of Frank Ashton-Gwatkin and Gladwyn Jebb in the Economic Relations section of the

Office, who had produced a detailed memorandum on the topic during January of that year. They also earmarked Central and Eastern Europe as a sphere of influence to concede to Germany, but twinned this with a call for Britain to reconsider both its commercial policies and colonial administration as possible measures to avert war.[75]

By the time Chamberlain became Prime Minister, economic and colonial appeasement had many advocates within both the Cabinet and Foreign Office, not least Chamberlain himself. Such issues were the subject of discussion in Britain and the wider world during that spring, with conversations over possible joint initiatives to alleviate European tensions taking place between Britain and France. In the Foreign Policy Committee, Chamberlain had also pressed for talks with German Economics Minister Hjalmar Schacht in order to explore a deal based on the surrender of colonies such as Togoland and the Cameroons to Hitler in return for his assurances of good behaviour. This would be accompanied by broad trading concessions – the Anglo-German Payments Agreement was revised in Germany's favour in April 1937 – and measures to open up the British Empire in Africa to German access. Chamberlain explained his rationale in a memorandum penned on 2 April:

> We cannot afford to miss any opportunity of reducing the international tension ... [and] alleviate the economic difficulties with which these countries are faced ... Any government which turned down this invitation without at least exploring the possibilities sufficiently to make sure that there was no possible basis of agreement would incur a very heavy responsibility. Even a slight improvement in the international situation may lead gradually to a general *détente*, whereas a policy of drift may lead to a general war.[76]

By June 1937, influential figures in the Foreign Office were recommending that Britain adopt an Open Door policy throughout the Empire, as means to secure a lasting peace. Following meetings in February between Schacht and Frederick Leith-Ross, the Chief Economic Adviser to the Treasury, an Inter-Departmental Committee

on Trade Policy was established. It reported on 7 June, recommending that 'every possibility should be examined' of reducing impedi-
ments to world trade, though not abandoning Imperial Preference
altogether.[77] Gladwyn Jebb, who sat on the committee, outlined the
domestic benefits of such a policy:

> Nobody has yet explained how a country whose whole civiliza-
> tion and *raison d'être* rest on her exporters, bankers and merchants,
> can for long maintain her existing standards in any "closed sys-
> tem"; and the more intelligent of the economists agree that, if
> the international system collapses, the condition of the people
> in this country – even if war is avoided – will be solitary, poor,
> nasty, brutish and short.[78]

Accordingly, the Foreign Policy Committee met on 11 June to discuss these proposals, with Eden, in particular, keen to make progress
along the lines suggested. He argued that such measures would
improve relations with America and Japan, as well as satisfying many
of Hitler's demands. Chamberlain and Halifax also came on board in
a follow-up meeting, but only on condition that Britain should not
act alone, and that any moves should be part of a broad, international
agreement underwritten by the League.[79] The planned Anglo-German
talks were effectively killed before they could begin, however, when
the French government vetoed the scheme and refused to concede its
own mandates in Africa for use by Germany.

By the turn of the year, colonial appeasement was firmly back on
the agenda. Following Halifax's meeting with Hitler in Berlin during
November 1937, in which the colonial issue was discussed as a possible
means of improving relations, Chamberlain wrote to his sister about
his thoughts on how best to give new impetus to his pursuit of a lasting settlement:

> They want Togoland and Kameruns. I am not quite sure where
> they stand about South West Africa but they do not insist on
> Tanganyika, if they can be given some reasonably equivalent ter-
> ritory on the West Coast... Now here, it seems to me, is a fair

basis of discussion ... I don't see why we shouldn't say to Germany,
'give us satisfactory assurances that you won't use force to deal
with the Austrians and Czechoslovakians, and we'll give you
similar assurances that we won't use force to prevent the changes
you want if you can get them by peaceful means'.[80]

'I do not think it is possible', he told the Commons a month later,
'entirely to separate economic from political conditions'.[81]

In January 1938, the Prime Minister brought together his most
ambitious economic appeasement project yet when he unveiled a plan
in the Foreign Policy Committee to repartition large parts of Central
Africa for use by the Dictator powers. Voicing his conviction that 'no
satisfactory general settlement with Germany was possible which
excluded some colonial concessions', his scheme envisaged that country joining a new consortium of nations, alongside the current colonial
powers, in a mass re-division of territories.[82] A new set of rules and
regulations would be established to bind the administrative powers,
including provisos on free trade and the welfare of natives. The scheme
received a mixed reception in the Committee at first, but was eventually accepted in February, subject to refinement and conditions,
as a means of making progress towards a lasting peace.[83] Sir Nevile
Henderson, the British Ambassador in Berlin, presented these ideas to
Hitler in early March, despite being privately doubtful of the chances
of success. In the event, the *Führer* – by one account, sitting 'glowering
in his chair' – was unresponsive.[84] A few days later Germany carried
out the *Anschluss*, which suspended colonial appeasement talks indefinitely, and brought Czechoslovakia on to the agenda as the issue of
the summer.

*   *   *

Although Chamberlain carried out a degree of economic and colonial appeasement as part of his wider strategy, it was not always in
the manner envisaged by opponents advocating the cause. We need to
know, therefore, how the government's conception of policy regularly
differed from that of its critics.

Chamberlain's economic appeasement usually centred on satisfying specifically German demands, rather than grand designs to improve the world situation in general. This is in contrast to the more idealistic flavour often given to the policy by Labour, the Liberals and the extreme Left. Whereas the British Communist Party was concerned with the liberation of colonial natives, government figures tended to speak in the language of Victorian Imperialists, viewing the colonies as pawns in a huge Anglo-German chess game. Attlee and Labour, by contrast, sought to 'build a new world'. Such fundamental differences in outlook help explain how economic appeasement could assume very diverse characteristics, depending on the particular advocate and circumstances.

The Makins memorandum from April 1936 demonstrates how a substantial part of the government's economic appeasement strategy involved conceding spheres of influence to Germany in Central and Eastern Europe. For example, while the German share of Turkey's export trade more than doubled from 18 per cent to 44 per cent between 1929 and 1937, Britain's almost halved from 12 per cent to 7 per cent in the same period. The figures were similar for Bulgaria.[85] Sometimes known as a *Mitteleuropa* strategy, the idea of allowing or even encouraging Germany to expand its markets eastwards, even at the expense of other powers in the region, often underpinned wider government measures, especially in the early part of our period. It was, however, eclipsed by a tougher British policy in the region as 1939 progressed and war loomed closer.[86]

Another consideration influencing Chamberlain's appeasement strategy was a perception, in the event proved incorrect, that the German economy was on the brink of collapse. It was thought that Hitler would seize upon such initiatives from Britain to alleviate his country's dire economic situation. Public statements that the *Führer* made – such as that Germany 'must export or die' in January 1939 – served only to fuel this impression, as did his repeated complaints about global imbalances in access to raw materials.[87] Similarly, many senior figures within the Cabinet and Foreign Office wrongly believed that 'moderates' within the Nazi hierarchy would be able to convince Hitler to agree to a settlement along these lines. Gladwyn Jebb's memorandum

from June 1937 concluded that economic appeasement might appeal
to those more rational elements within the Dictator states:

> There is the further consideration that even in Germany and
> Italy action on such lines by His Majesty's government might
> encourage those (and they still exist!) who hope that the rig-
> ours of 'autarky', Nazism or Fascism may be diminished by an
> increase in international trade.[88]

Such beliefs filtered through the Foreign Office to the top of the chain
of command, with Chamberlain himself stressing that Britain should
'do all in its power to encourage the moderates'. He sanctioned discussions between Schacht and Montagu Norman, Governor of the Bank
of England, shortly afterwards.[89]

There were also domestic factors behind economic appeasement,
little appreciated by government critics. C.A. MacDonald points out
that Halifax's visit to Hitler in November 1937 directly coincided
with concern over a developing balance-of-trade crisis in Britain.
Unemployment rose by a substantial 8 per cent between December
1937 and January 1938 and the government's decision to give new
impetus to economic measures at this time was doubtless affected in
part by such factors.[90]

If domestic influences drove the government to consider economic
and colonial appeasement, so too did international ones – especially
where America was concerned. Many important figures within the
USA were favourable to such measures and indeed it was probably the
area where America sought to work most closely with Britain in solving world problems. As already indicated, Secretary of State Cordell
Hull was one of the most prominent advocates of economic appeasement during the late 1930s. While he hoped that the banding together
of nations like Britain and America in the economic sphere would
convince the Fascist powers to come on board, many people in Britain
felt that the assistance of the world's most powerful nation could only
buttress efforts for a lasting peace. Joint initiatives along the lines of an
Open Door policy in their respective territories, vast in raw materials
and capital resources, seemed an obvious way to proceed. Numerous

memoranda on such issues were produced in both the Foreign Office and State Department during Chamberlain's premiership. As the Ambassador in Washington, Sir Ronald Lindsay, told Eden in January 1936, 'if goods cannot cross international frontiers, armies will'.[91] In reply, Eden informed Lindsay of a conversation he had recently had with the American 'Ambassador-at-Large', Norman Davis. It is illustrative of the issues being considered on both sides of the Atlantic:

> Mr Davis spoke of Anglo-American relations in general ... and wondered whether it would not be possible for His Majesty's government and the United States government jointly to consider the economic situation, not only with a view to making a treaty for their mutual benefit, but also with a view to seeing what contribution, if any, could be made by them to the world economic situation ... Unless some outlet could be found for Germany economically, there was bound to be trouble sooner or later. There was much talk of a conference on Raw Materials, but this, of course, was not the root of the trouble. What Germany wanted was markets. He wondered, for instance, whether anything could be done in the way of giving Germany a special economic position in Southeast Europe.[92]

By the time Chamberlain became Prime Minister, talk was rife in both countries of an Anglo-American Trade Agreement, not only for their mutual benefit, but also to serve as a model for the wider world. Joint initiatives in the 'progressive adjustment of trade problems in the Far East' were also suggested in a letter from Hull to the new Chancellor of the Exchequer, John Simon, in June.[93] The famous Roosevelt 'Peace Initiative' of January 1938, when the President approached Britain with a secret plan for a world conference to tackle the causes of war, also contained financial dimensions, especially with regard to raw materials. The Anglo-American Trade Agreement was ratified in November of that year and the economic sphere continued to be the one where cooperation between the two powers was most widely discussed.

There was also a degree of support for economic and colonial appeasement from influential figures within the Dominions. Stanley Bruce, the Australian High Commissioner in London, was a firm advocate of such measures and produced several detailed plans circulated in the Foreign Office during Chamberlain's premiership. In March 1938, he viewed 'early action in the economic sphere as imperative' and called for 'a resumption of international lending,' as well as 'a reduction of the more extreme barriers to trade'.[94] Of the Dominions, South Africa was most enthusiastic about economic appeasement. Writing on 9 December 1937, Jan Smuts, who became Prime Minister of that country in 1939, called for closer Anglo-American relations in the economic sphere as a vital contribution to world peace: 'A real gesture is becoming necessary, and that gesture should be economic.'[95]

*   *   *

While Chamberlain's critics sometimes recognised that the financial assistance of one power could be used as a weapon against another, the government itself was compelled to explore the issue much more fully. The *Anschluss* and subsequent Czech crisis caused many within government circles to consider economic appeasement as a weapon to keep Germany at bay. Reviewing recent events, Orme Sargent suggested giving economic aid to several countries as a means to shackle German expansion. The measures he favoured are illustrative of the way in which British policy was now focussed on the Nazi menace primarily:

> The countries who might be considered for loans and credits would be Japan, Italy, Russia, Poland, and whatever Spanish government may emerge ... This list is a repellent one but necessity makes strange and unpleasant bedfellows. The candidates for direct subsidies or gifts of war materials would be the Danubian and other States, who are anxious to resist German encroachment and brow-beating.

Yet, in the same memorandum, Sargent also mooted the possibility of a very different strategy existing, one which tried to 'save the British Empire by promoting the formation of a German world empire at the expense of other countries'.[96] Again, economic appeasement and economic warfare were being considered side by side here, and largely under the same broad banner.

Turkey also emerged as a key power in Britain's strategic thinking at this time. As the gateway to the Middle East, it was one of the main obstacles to a German *Drang nach Osten*, and the decision was taken in May 1938 to grant it £16 million worth of export credits, £6 million of which was to be spent on building warships.[97] By June, the government had established an Inter-Departmental Committee on Southeast Europe to consider and, if necessary, coordinate aid for the region. The Committee produced an interim report in the winter of 1938–1939 recommending increased imports from countries in Southeast Europe, including Greece and Hungary, as well as modifying exchange tariffs and quotas in their favour.[98] For example, Britain purchased 200,000 tons of wheat from Romania in the wake of the Munich Conference.[99] The rationale for measures such as these was detailed in a Secret Intelligence Service memorandum, which recommended going head to head with Germany for influence in the region:

> Into those states ... we should inject resisting power by helping them financially and economically and making them less dependent on Germany for trade; making them realise that we and the French are strong and united; encouraging them as far as possible to look to us.

Once again, however, these sorts of aggressive moves were being considered alongside economic appeasement in a more traditional sense. In his notes on the memorandum, Alexander Cadogan spoke in positive terms about ceding colonies to Hitler and hoped that Britain would 'cut our losses' in Central and Eastern Europe. He explained: 'Let Germany find her "*Lebensraum*", and establish herself, if she can, as a powerful economic unit.'[100]

By the early months of 1939, it was clear that the *Mitteleuropa* strategy was increasingly being superseded by the much tougher variant of economic appeasement in Eastern and Southeastern Europe, designed to resist Germany and gain allies at its expense. Events such as the *Kristallnacht* pogrom in November 1938, and the war scare of January 1939 – when a series of Foreign Office and intelligence reports errone-ously pointed to an imminent German invasion of the Low Countries – seemed to suggest that the influence of the so-called 'moderates' was on the wane. Schacht's dismissal on 20 January 1939 served only to confirm this impression. The government responded by granting export credits, of £2 million and £1 million respectively, to Greece and Romania in February 1939 – countries eventually offered guaran-tees in April – and sanctioned an economic mission to Bulgaria with a view to a similar arrangement. Such moves continued to be considered until the outbreak of war, with loans and territorial concessions to Italy even being touted in July by one Foreign Office official, Clifford Heathcote-Smith.[101] Such a late approach to Germany's closest ally, in a last attempt to drive a wedge through the Axis, is indicative of the desperation to avoid war gripping the country. The lines between economic appeasement and economic warfare had, by now, virtually evaporated.

Much has been made of some of the less aggressive initiatives explored by Chamberlain during the summer of 1939, which have often been seen as a return to the policy of buying off Hitler. Statements made in parliament by Chamberlain and Halifax at this time, coming not long after the Anglo-German Coal Agreement in January, fuelled suspicions within opposition ranks that the government's new-found toughness was fast evaporating. On 19 May, for example, Chamberlain indicated that colonial appeasement was not quite dead just yet, and that it would have to form a key part of any future settlement with Germany.[102] Less than a month later, Halifax proclaimed that Britain was 'not only willing but anxious' to discuss German demands for raw materials and *Lebensraum* as soon as possible.[103]

The secret loan talks in June 1939 between Robert Hudson, Secretary for the Department of Overseas Trade, and Dr Helmuth Wohlthat, a senior German official from the Ministry of Economic Affairs, aroused most suspicion – both contemporary and retrospect-ive – that Chamberlain was once more opening the door to old-style appeasement. Though the precise details are sketchy and accounts of

the meetings differ, it is generally accepted that the Prime Minister
sanctioned several meetings between the two men at which a massive
British loan to Germany was discussed, in return for the latter's assurances of peace.[104] These meetings were leaked to the press and the
embarrassed government was forced to deny any knowledge of such
an offer. Though the exact control Chamberlain had over the agenda
of these conversations is unclear, such moves should be seen as the last
minute, tentative explorations of a government desperate to avoid war,
rather than as cast-iron evidence of a complete about-turn in policy.
The anti-Fascist Peace Front being built by Chamberlain in Central
and Eastern Europe at this time is testament to the Prime Minister's
overriding objectives in the wake of the Prague Coup.

*   *   *

Given the government's exploration of all these various measures, why
were Chamberlain's approaches in the economic and colonial field usually quite limited and ultimately without fruition? Why did Germany
never receive its colonies or a huge loan? For every economic or colonial initiative explored, there were more problems created; for every
advocate of economic appeasement within the Cabinet or Foreign
Office, there was another critic elsewhere in the government urging
restraint. While recognising that economic approaches had to form a
substantial part of his general appeasement programme, their role in
Chamberlain's mind was always subservient. As he explained to the
Commons in December 1937,

> While, undoubtedly, the economic problem must always be an
> important factor in any endeavour to bring about a better state
> of things in Europe, it is much more likely to receive favourable
> consideration if it has been preceded by some easing of political
> tension beforehand.[105]

This sort of view dominated the government long before Chamberlain became Prime Minister. As the Chancellor of a country suffering the extreme economic hardships born of the Depression,

Chamberlain was often frosty at first to any measures sacrificing British economic interests for the sake of other powers. When Eden suggested in August 1936 that Britain take the lead in attempting to improve the 'commercial, monetary and financial situation' in Germany, Chamberlain replied that he regarded the proposal as 'full of danger'. He went on: 'There is no reason to think that the German government would be willing to cooperate in the programme... the main part of the remedy is in their own hands.'[106] Coming not long after he and Halifax had argued to keep the colonial issue alive in any future dealings with Hitler, such a statement is clear evidence that Chamberlain regarded extensive pursuit of more general economic appeasement as far too risky a venture given the perilous state of Britain's finances. Vansittart expressed similar views less than a month later. As far as he was concerned, political appeasement should not be overshadowed by economic initiatives. The latter could even damage progress in the former:

I want to get on with the political arrangements... before we embark on this other sea... A political settlement would have to precede the necessary and eventual economic one. Do not let us spoil that effect by going off at half cock... else we shall fail politically.[107]

Colonial appeasement was discussed extensively during the Chamberlain period but never actually sanctioned by the government, either in a comprehensive revision of League mandates, or in the direct cession of a British territory to Germany. Indeed, there were plenty of influential figures who wanted the issue to be buried altogether. John Perowne of the Central Department of the Foreign Office claimed that it would be 'desirable to limit discussion of this question as far as possible'.[108] The Plymouth Report was highly dubious about the value of colonial concessions and spelt out some of the main problems this would raise. It argued that the vast majority of League powers, including France and most of the Dominions – not to mention the USA outside of the League – were vehemently against any reform to the current system.[109]

In April 1937, Sir Eric Phipps, then Ambassador in Berlin, also expressed his alarm at such proposals, challenging their central rationale:

> Is there any reason to assume that the restoration of the colonies would permanently satisfy Germany or even assuage German ambition for a decade? Germany possessed her colonies and her Colonial Empire was prosperous before the war, but this fact did not prevent the outbreak of war. Nor were the German people by any means satisfied with their place in the sun when their colonies were flourishing. Indeed, when one recalls the prosperity and abundance of good things in the Germany of those days, where every beer-hall was filled to overflowing ... one can only feel sceptical concerning the remedy of restoring German prosperity, whether by the cession of colonies, financial help, or any of the other remedies put forward.[110]

As already noted, Eden was hostile to any specific colonial deal, despite initially favouring economic appeasement in general. His views were clarified in September 1937, in his correspondence with Nevile Henderson regarding German military strength: 'This, like many another paper, is a very strong reinforcement for the course of keeping Germany lean.' He continued, 'I should far sooner take the risk ... of a hesitant because unready Germany taking a plunge in a weak condition than face the certainty of her bellicose hegemony a little later if fattened for the part – and fattened by us!'[111] This issue of economic and colonial appeasement making Germany so strong as to pose an immediate danger to Britain and its Empire was a recurring dilemma. Military and strategic planners such as Admiral Drax constantly warned that any colonial territory ceded to Germany would be likely to be equipped with naval or air bases within a short space of time and thereby provide the perfect launch-pad for the invasion of other territories.[112] One of the reasons Chamberlain's Central Africa repartition scheme was allowed to fade from view was because most of the Foreign Policy Committee were concerned that Tanganyika and Kenya, both within the proposed zone for revision, could easily fall directly into German hands.[113] Imperial Preference was not abandoned and an Open Door policy was never sanctioned because of the fears that Japan would only seize the opportunity to expand its own military influence in the void left by British trade.[114] The harsh strategic realities of the day meant that ambitious proposals for economic and colonial appeasement had to be reined in dramatically.

Many people within the government, not least Chamberlain himself, felt that a great number of Germany's economic problems were of its own making, and that Hitler's claims of raw material starvation were vastly overblown, amounting to little more than Nazi propaganda. An Inter-Departmental Committee on the Question of Raw Materials, which reported to the Foreign Office in January 1936, asserted that Germany was not actually lacking in such mineral resources, or access to them, and that the return of colonies would be unlikely to solve its problems anyway.[115] Subsequent historical research tends to confirm these suspicions. David Meredith has pointed out that Germany actually increased the amount of cocoa it bought from West Africa by more than one-fifth, trebled its purchases of sisal from Tanganyika and raised imports of rubber from Malaya and Ceylon by 40 per cent between 1932 and 1938. Three-quarters of all the copper bought from Cyprus during this time went to Germany.[116] As early as February 1936, Phipps suggested that claims of a German economic crisis were exaggerated and that most of its problems were easily remedied. Hitler, he wrote irritably, was 'providing marriage bonuses for servant girls to induce them to marry and propagate the species [and] giving large tax reductions to large families. At the same time he is bitterly complaining that Germany is overcrowded and is in dire need of territorial expansion'.[117]

* * *

The issue of native rights and welfare also undermined the viability of colonial appeasement. Germany's chequered history with regard to minorities and issues such as the treatment of black athletes at the 1936 Berlin Olympics constantly resurfaced in the minds of government figures. William Ormsby-Gore, Colonial Secretary until May

1938, regularly asserted that Britain's first duty was to the inhabitants of these territories and the Plymouth Report had also expressed strong reservations on this issue.[118] The views of the indigenous populations themselves also played an important role, with Ormsby-Gore and John Simon both pointing out that the vast majority of Africans would be opposed to Chamberlain's repartition scheme when it was first discussed in January 1938. Home Secretary, Samuel Hoare, and Minister for the Coordination of Defence, Sir Thomas Inskip, were other Cabinet members initially opposed to the plan. It was well known that the majority of Tanganyikans, in particular, would be against a return to German rule, regardless of any grand schemes for the rest of the continent.[119]

Opposition to economic appeasement within the government was not confined to the colonial sphere. The practicability of the more aggressive schemes, designed to strangle Germany as a by-product of assisting others, was also routinely questioned. As already noted, it was decided not to adopt an Open Door policy in the Far East during June 1937 for fear of provoking further Japanese aggression in the region.[120] One year later, the Foreign Policy Committee decided against offering a loan to China in order to resist Japanese belligerence, with Chamberlain outlining his fear of antagonising the latter power. Simon, who had now succeeded Chamberlain as Chancellor, was also dubious about the practical effects of such a loan: 'We would run very substantial risks of doing China little, if any, good while creating the maximum amount of trouble and danger with Japan.'[121]

Economically assisting states in East and Southeast Europe, as a means to resist German influence there, was also discussed at this meeting, with similar results. Chamberlain indicated that the rationale for such aggressive moves was unsound when he suggested that a *Mitteleuropa* strategy might still be the best way forward, allowing Germany to grow fat and weary. Simon, meanwhile, held on tightly to the purse-strings. Surely, he argued, Britain could not afford the colossal expenditure required to cause Germany even to think about changing its policy in the region.[122]

The interim report of the Inter-Departmental Committee on Eastern and Southeastern Europe, produced in October 1938, also urged caution

in this area. Large amounts of capital investment into powers such as
Hungary was not deemed viable due to the risk of over-loading the
small economies of such agriculturally-based powers, whilst antagonising Germany into possible counter-measures.[123] The Committee
recognised that business of this kind, as with all aggressive economic
appeasement moves in the region, left Britain open to a degree of
blackmail at the hands of the 'appeased' powers. As Halifax pointed
out, these states all knew that Germany would be just as anxious to
increase trade with them as Britain was.[124]

Nor can domestic financial issues be ignored in understanding why
economic appeasement never really got off the ground. Behind much of
Chamberlain's foreign policy strategy lay a belief that a sturdy economy
would emerge as a 'fourth arm of defence' and that Britain would be
stronger in the long run, should war come, if it maintained balanced
budgets at the expense of an immediate vast rearmament programme.[125]
The very *raison d'être* of the National Government was to achieve financial stability in the wake of the Depression. Economic appeasement,
unsurprisingly, fell victim to such a protectionist outlook. Simon, as
Chancellor, routinely opposed the majority of the more radical measures.
Chamberlain, the ex-Chancellor, urged similar caution with any move
that might weaken Britain's financial hand extensively, or strengthen
Germany's. Leading businessmen also tended to oppose economic and
colonial appeasement and frequently lobbied the government in this
sense.[126] As Antony Best points out, the economic appeasement of Japan
during Chamberlain's premiership was so limited in part as a result of
these domestic pressures. Textile industrialists from Lancashire, direct
rivals of Japanese competitors for markets in India, did not respond
kindly to talk of an Open Door policy in the Orient.[127]

Moreover, internal political factors also undermined economic and
colonial appeasement measures. Gustav Schmidt argues that, in addition to lack of support from the opposition, much of industry and the
trade unions, infighting within the government itself meant that such
initiatives were often doomed from the outset:

> A coalition of officials, advisers and Cabinet Ministers prevailed
> time and again, which maintained that economic and financial

measures were admissible as supplementary measures but could never properly prepare the ground for a lasting arrangement between political powers.[128]

Pro- and anti-economic appeasement factions within the government grew to resent one another and competed for the attention and financial resources which only senior Cabinet figures could give. Even setting up the bodies to consider such initiatives, such as the Inter-Departmental Committee on Southeast Europe, could provoke fierce arguments. In this case, President of the Board of Trade, Oliver Stanley, opposed the high costs involved to get the Committee up and running and his concerns were echoed by Simon at this time.[129]

Wider international factors fuelled the impression that economic appeasement would be unworkable in anything more than a piece-meal manner. The vast majority of schemes contemplated by the government relied on international approval – and often direct contribution from other countries – and this was rarely forthcoming in a period of such global instability. A revision of the mandates would require the backing of the rest of the League and consent from the colonies themselves. Scrapping Imperial Preference needed blanket Dominion support, as well as extensive consultation with the USA. Plans to repartition Central Africa had to have the go-ahead of the current administrative powers, as well as the natives in the countries involved. Save for Britain giving one of its own colonies directly to Germany, all of these initiatives were large, complex and would require many nations taking part over long periods of time if they were to be successful. The government knew this only too well, even if its critics could speak rather casually of building 'a new world'. The Plymouth Report pointed out that the majority of the colonies, as well as the USA, France and Belgium, had serious objections to any wide-scale territorial adjustments.[130] Dominions Secretary Malcolm MacDonald was constantly at pains to stress that the majority of the Dominions were against colonial appeasement or an Open Door policy, despite positive indications from some figures within countries like South Africa.[131] At the Imperial Conference in May 1937, when Chamberlain asked the New Zealand Prime Minister, Michael

Savage, what he thought of British proposals for economic appeasement, he was greeted with the sharp reply: 'bunkum from end to
end!'[132]

Despite the economic sphere being the one where the USA was most
keen to work with Britain, that power was still gripped by powerful
isolationist sentiment and remained wedded to its neutrality legislation.[133] This permeated financial matters, fostered mutual suspicion,
and served to paralyse joint efforts to get real work done, especially
in the Far East. When, in the summer of 1938, Halifax asked Ronald
Lindsay whether the USA could sanction a loan to help ease China's
economic troubles, the Ambassador replied that 'he doubted whether
American opinion would favour any action so direct ... Opinion would
very much prefer to continue on some such line as that on which they
were already acting'.[134] Britain, therefore, turned away from most of
the schemes touted by figures such as Cordell Hull. Moreover, many
within the government, including Chamberlain, distrusted American
intentions in the economic arena. It was felt that despite the fine words
of men such as Hull, the USA was dragging its feet in the financial
realm as much as the diplomatic, and only made moves of significance when the end result would benefit America itself. The Anglo-
American Trade Agreement was a case in point, being designed, many
Britons felt, to placate Congress rather than to make a genuine contribution to the world economy.[135]

*   *   *

A brief survey of wider opinion indicates as much opposition to
radical economic and colonial appeasement measures in Britain as
there was support for them, and suggests that Chamberlain was right
to regard both options as unrealistic policies for extensive pursuit. For
every advocate in the House of Commons, there was a critic who spoke
out in opposition. The majority of Conservative MPs regarded colonial
re-division as tantamount to treason. Leo Amery was fiercely opposed
to the return of all of Germany's pre-war colonies, suggesting as early
as February 1936 that such a move would have little effect on the balance of power:

Is Germany going to be less afraid of Russia if she has Togoland given to her? What colony could we offer to Japan to make her less afraid of Russia? ... What Germany wants today, and what she claims, is space for settlers, room for enlarging effectively her economic entity. She is not going to get that if you give her Togoland or even Tanganyika. Does anyone suggest that we should give her half of Australia, or half of Canada?[136]

Even a number of Labour figures were opposed to colonial appeasement. In the wake of the Rhineland crisis, Morgan Price voiced his concern about the suitability of Germany as an administrator of such territories: 'I should certainly not agree to handing any territory, in which we are now responsible for the state of the natives, to those who treat Jews in the way they are doing, and who are developing a crazy, unscientific racial theory.'[137] Some left-wing parliamentarians felt more comfortable expressing their views on such matters in private during these years, sailing as they were against their official party line. On 6 June 1938, National Labour MP Harold Nicolson, who had long been sceptical of colonial appeasement, used his diary to bring the central dilemma of the question into focus: 'If we assuage the German alligator with fish from other ponds, she will wax so fat that she will demand fish from our own ponds. And we shall not by then be powerful enough to resist.'[138] By the time of the Munich debate in October, Labour's Frederick Bellenger seemed to concur wholeheartedly: 'No loans for Germany or Italy will buy peace ... No colonial settlement will bring disarmament.'[139]

The lengthy colonial debate in the Commons during December 1938 allowed sceptics a wider platform to elaborate their views. Even those broadly favouring economic appeasement measures, such as Labour's Philip Noel-Baker, could stress that direct cession of a colony to Germany was undesirable. He first questioned Hitler's claim of a 'moral right' to own a colony, given his regime's treatment of minorities, before pointing out that the vast majority of raw materials the *Führer* demanded – such as oil, iron and coal – could not be found in great quantities in these territories. Similarly, he argued that neither Togoland nor Tanganyika would be big enough to provide adequate

Lebensraum for Germany, if Hitler's claims on his population expansion rates were to be believed.[140] Tory MP Ian Orr-Ewing, meanwhile, took a more domestic angle, pointing out that the government had a responsibility to its taxpayers in keeping the Empire for British exploitation. Hardworking Britons who paid for the upkeep of the colonies should get 'some reasonable return', he asserted, and attacked the huge administrative costs of any territorial concessions.[141] His colleague Sir Walter Smiles boomed, 'No surrender, not an inch to anyone', before reminding the House that many British ex-patriots now lived in these regions. Their homes and businesses would be at risk in any vast redivision of territories.[142]

Political pressure groups such as the Colonial Defence League favoured a general reconsideration of the colonial issue, while remaining fiercely opposed to a return of Germany's former territories in specific. In a pamphlet produced in 1938, the League, which counted Amery and Nicolson among its members, spelt out the wider strategic implications of such a move:

Tanganyika is crucial for air, rail and road communications in Africa. Kenya and Uganda would be surrounded by Germany and Italy if Tanganyika fell. South Africa would be in range of German bombers. Ports in these areas would be open for German ships and submarines. West African domination leads to British weakness in the Mediterranean.[143]

It is unsurprising that the anti-appeasement press could also be critical of economic and colonial initiatives. To give just one example immediately after the Prague Coup, the *News Chronicle* asserted bluntly that 'this country should do nothing which will enable Germany to overcome its economic difficulties or increase its war resources'. It went on: 'It should rather be our aim to increase those difficulties and diminish Germany's power to wage war.'[144] Insofar as we are able to gauge public opinion on these matters, the majority seemed very sceptical of wide-scale economic and colonial appeasement, and especially breaking up the Empire to assuage Germany. Of those polled just after Munich, 85 per cent thought that Germany should not have its former colonies returned, with 78 per cent willing to fight rather than hand them back.[145] Views hardened even more as time moved on. In July 1939, while more people thought that Britain should give a loan to China than do nothing about Japanese aggression in the Far East – 17 per cent compared to 15 per cent – a larger portion of 22 per cent called for straightforward military action against Japan as the better policy.[146] The position of the people on this issue was clear.

Conclusion

Economic and colonial appeasement, carried out in a radical manner by giving away colonies or adopting an Open Door policy in the Empire, were clearly stated alternatives to the strategy Chamberlain pursued. While the Prime Minister explored these policies himself, it was only ever in a tentative manner and to a much more limited extent than many critics demanded. Support for such moves among the political class was considerable. Most members of both opposition parties claimed that the economic sphere was one where the government was failing and could do much more. Economic appeasement could work on differing levels and with differing aims. It encompassed both macro- and micro-scopic initiatives – aiding one country or tackling the problems of an entire continent – and could have an aggressive bent to it if it was pursued with the intent of restraining the actions of one power as a by-product of assisting another.

Economic and colonial appeasement formed a sizeable part of Chamberlain's wider policy. When discussion of the latter was going to be dropped by the government in 1936, it was Chamberlain and Halifax who kept the option open for further consideration. It is fair to say that the Prime Minister favoured the specific colonial elements of the policy more than the wider economic generalities. At the same time, it was also Chamberlain and Simon who often had the final say in urging caution with grand economic appeasement measures later on. There was as much Foreign Office and Cabinet opposition to the policy as there was support for it.

Was Chamberlain right to restrain economic and colonial appeasement in the way that he did, never allowing them to become more

than a limited part of his wider strategy? It is understandable why
such initiatives were deemed unrealistic for excessive pursuit. Had the
Prime Minister followed these policies in a more radical manner, he
would have gained the limited support of many former enemies but
lost that of his own party and large sections of the public, especially
if he had given away a colony to Germany. For every colonial or economic appeasement measure explored, practical difficulties and strategic realities blocked implementation. The power of the purse played
an important role here. The National Government simply did not have
enough money to make economic solutions to the world's problems a
central priority. Economic and colonial appeasement needed to be supported internationally if they were to have any hope of success. The
task of building Attlee's 'new world' was so big and the time scale
would have been so vast that it would have taken a whole generation
of concerted multilateral effort to begin to bring it about. Simply put,
wide-scale economic appeasement measures would have been much
too slow and cumbersome to solve the very immediate problems of
the late 1930s. The fact that very few other countries were willing to
cooperate meant that most British initiatives were hamstrung from
the outset. In this era of paranoia, caution and extreme protectionism,
Britain could ill afford to be the only country seeking to solve these
issues. Could Britain give its colonies to the League if France would
not do the same? Could Chamberlain do anything in the way of an
Open Door without real assistance from an America so distrusted and
committed to isolation? The views of the indigenous populations and
of the Dominions also had to be considered.

Three fundamental concerns existed within the government about
economic appeasement: would giving money or territory to Germany
sate the Imperial Eagle or merely whet its appetite for more?; if
Germany was not given a colony or region to exploit, would it then
go to war in order to have its place in the sun?; finally, was it morally
'right' and would the British people stomach it? Even committed pro-
appeasers such as Gladwyn Jebb recognised that there was an element
of 'Danegeld' about it all.[147]

With all this in mind, we are tempted to ask these questions: Could
Hitler ever have been appeased with a colony? Would Tanganyika have

had any affect on the *Anschluss* or the subsequent Czech crisis? The
extent to which Hitler was even interested in the colonial sphere is
highly questionable. Even at the time it was open to doubt. As Nevile
Henderson asserted in early 1939, 'I should keep away from the colonial question. I think that Hitler...fully realises that the question
must wait a long time yet'.[148] Furthermore, it was rare that Hitler did
not hold the diplomatic initiative. Britain and the world responded to
his every sudden and dramatic move and, if the *Führer* was not concerned with colonial or economic appeasement, it was rarely discussed
in Anglo-German diplomacy – certainly less than it was considered
within the Foreign Policy Committee at home. As Newton points out,
'he had no particular interest in extra-European expansion...Hitler's
purpose in raising the issue had been merely tactical'.[149]

Historical literature on economic appeasement has been limited
in its exploration of viability, but several important recent texts suggest that Chamberlain was right to keep such measures as background
considerations. The fact that it is sometimes noted that allied soldiers
were shot at with shells containing copper bought from British Empire
sources suggests that hindsight judges economic appeasement to be a
tragic mistake from the British point of view.[150] Moreover, extreme
economic and colonial appeasement might only have made the situation worse. Would colonies or a loan have stopped Hitler pursuing
an expansionist policy in Europe and averted the Second World War?
And would Germany's chances of winning that war have been hindered in any way, or rather improved, by extra material resources of
this kind?

If it is generally accepted that appeasement was a failed policy
because it did not allow for Hitler's insatiable appetite for war, it is
highly doubtful that the economic dimension, pursued more vigorously
than it was, would have enjoyed greater success. The racial and eugenic
elements of Nazi ideology would not have been destroyed by bursting
German banks. Instead, economic regions to exploit would probably
have whet the Fascist appetite for more in the way that Manchuria,
Abyssinia, the Rhineland, Austria and the Sudetenland obviously
did. When the German tiger had conquered most of Europe by 1942
and had acquired the economic and *Lebensraum* resources of almost an

entire continent, it did not stop and settle down to sleep. Rather, a snowballing process occurred where the attainment of resources only fuelled the inclination and capacity to gather yet more and perhaps even necessitated further expansion. Moreover, there were Imperial factors to be considered with the colonial issue, and it would only have increased the danger to the British Empire had they been ceded to one Dictator state or another. It is difficult to believe that an opportunist as skilled as Hitler would not have utilised, say, Tanganyika as a springboard for assaults in surrounding areas during the war itself.

Many of the underlying causes of unrest in the 1930s were driven by economic factors and this made it tempting, especially to minds of the political Left, to postulate grand economic solutions. However, the most important causes of the war were not financial in character, and so economic gestures like these could not ultimately prevent that war, nor is it likely that they would have hindered the Nazi military effort in any way.

3

LEAGUE OF NATIONS

We must not surrender faith in the League and in a collective peace effort ... The worst enemies of peace today are those who discredit the League. Faith is the first essential in peaceful and democratic communities. The only alternative is fear and force.[1]

(Fred Simpson, House of Commons, March 1937)

Introduction

A large number of Chamberlain's contemporary critics contended that the National Government should have pursued a policy of vigorous support for the League of Nations as an alternative to appeasement in the late 1930s. Standing by the League and its central pillar of collective security would, they claimed, have deterred the Fascist powers from their foreign adventures and offered the surest way to a lasting peace.

This chapter will examine the origins and viability of the policy of committed support for the League of Nations as an alternative to Chamberlain's strategy. Whereas the majority of the other rival options considered in this study envisaged the Prime Minister steering Britain towards a new path – at least one not trodden during his own period in high office – the League of Nations already existed as an alternative to appeasement which the Prime Minister turned away from. Broadly speaking, for much of the 1930s, the League represented the *status quo*, and Chamberlain's decision to abandon it in his attempts to revise the post-war settlement provoked anger amongst many contemporaries across all parties and shades of political opinion. With its grand ideals of a new and better world following the horrors of the Great War, the League had enjoyed enormous popular support since Versailles and the launch of Woodrow Wilson's radical vision. Its effective abandonment by the British government in the final years before the Second World War was not easily forgiven and led to bitter recriminations from many opponents when war eventually broke out, and in its emotional aftermath, as blame was apportioned and the United Nations took its first tentative steps. The National Government had, after all, won the 1935 General Election on a platform of firm League support.

Of all the alternatives considered in this study, the League is probably the one about which most is already known. This is testament to its centrality to world affairs during the 1920s and 1930s and its popularity among those discussing foreign policy, both at the time and ever since. It must, therefore, occupy a key position in any discussion of alternatives to appeasement. Unsurprisingly, given the popularity of the League for much of the interwar period, many among the orthodox school of appeasement historians had much to say on this important institution. Just about every memoir written by Chamberlain's political contemporaries contains at least one passing reference to the League itself or a brief assessment of the strengths and weaknesses of collective security. The fact that most of these figures wrote in the 1950s, when the United Nations was emerging from the wreckage of the failed League, and the Cold War was at its peak, no doubt influenced this trend.

Many government critics later condemned the records of Baldwin and Chamberlain *vis-à-vis* Geneva. Churchill viewed the League as a shamefully deserted mechanism, which might have changed the course of history had it been used with greater conviction in the mid-1930s. In his introduction to *The Gathering Storm*, he asserted that 'it was a simple policy to keep Germany disarmed ... to build ever more strongly a true League of Nations capable of making sure treaties were kept, or changed only by discussion and agreement'.[2] Writing of the government's response to the 1935 Abyssinian crisis, Churchill lamented how it 'had led the League of Nations into an utter fiasco, most damaging, if not fatally injurious to its effective life as an institution'.[3] The Rhineland affair in 1936 was another important turning point:

> There was, perhaps, still time for an assertion of collective security, based upon the avowed readiness of all members concerned to enforce the decisions of the League of Nations by the sword ... There is no doubt that had His Majesty's government chosen to act with firmness and resolve through the League of Nations they could have led a united Britain forward on a final quest to avert war.[4]

Harold Macmillan was equally firm in his criticism. Echoing Churchill's contention that Britain had spurned the opportunity to use much tougher League sanctions against Italy during the Abyssinian conflict, Macmillan's views were clear: 'It was to the League, fortified, strengthened, and encouraged by British and, it was to be hoped, French leadership, that we must look in order to rally resistance to the growing German menace.'[5] Like Churchill, Macmillan presented the League as a viable alternative to appeasement in the final years of peace, a workable rival strategy which should have been pursued much further and which might have averted war:

> Such a lead by Britain might have brought fresh energy and unity into France; it would have steadied Central and Eastern Europe and probably, in due course, brought Russia into a genuine partnership with the West. It would certainly have thrilled public opinion in the Dominions and perhaps galvanised their governments into activity. It might, who knows, have succeeded in leading the American people at least some steps along the road of international responsibility which they were destined within a few years to tread.[6]

As a former League of Nations Union Chairman, Gilbert Murray unsurprisingly concurred with this view. In 1948, he confidently asserted that 'the whole course of history would have been different' if only Chamberlain had stood by the League.[7] Similarly, Clement Attlee resolutely defended at least the ideal of collective security, if not quite the League itself: 'One must have collective defence. It was sneered at at the time by people like Neville Chamberlain, who called it midsummer madness, but now, of course, it is orthodox doctrine.'[8]

If Chamberlain's critics were quick to attack the government for spurning the League option in trying to save peace, many of the Prime Minister's allies were as eager to defend their leader's record. Both Halifax and Simon stood full-square behind the government's strategy. In his 1957 memoir, *Fullness of Days*, the former asserted that 'it was obviously idle to pretend that there was such a thing as collective security on which nations could confidently rely for their own protection'.[9] Similarly, Simon criticised a body which essentially sought to defend an unjust *status quo* in Europe and left only 'a legacy of unappeasable quarrels, which would make the state of the world more dangerous than ever'.[10]

Other colleagues of the Prime Minister agreed that the League had a limited value in the face of the Fascist threat. Two major figures at the Foreign Office during Chamberlain's premiership, Lords Vansittart and Strang, both gave damning assessments of Geneva's chances of averting war. The former, by no means a defender of Chamberlain's reputation in general, stressed that while the principles of the Covenant were sound, the conditions of the day were wrong for their application. With America, Germany and Japan all non-members, and Italy withdrawing in 1937, Geneva's machinery was incomplete and unworkable.[11] Strang, head of the Central Department between 1937 and 1939, blamed a crisis of will. How could the League hope to save the world with only 'paper commitments that passed for a system of collective security'?[12] Samuel Hoare defended his own period in office by condemning other nations' attitudes to Geneva. Britain, he asserted, could not have afforded to be the only power propping up the whole collective system.[13]

Even fierce critics of appeasement admitted in retrospect that the League was an unworkable solution to the Fascist problem. Leo Amery concluded that League economic sanctions were futile in a world where non-member states such as the USA were free to trade with whomsoever they liked.[14] Alfred Duff Cooper, Chamberlain's First Lord of the Admiralty, claimed that, after the Rhineland affair, the League amounted to no more than 'dead, empty words' and wrote an allegorical pamphlet in 1940 entitled *The Funeral of the League of Nations*.[15] In this, he attributed the death of collective security to a lack of universal membership and coordination of intent.[16]

Both Eden and Attlee, two of the most committed League advocates in the 1930s, revised their opinions with the passage of time. The former admitted that, by 1938, it 'was a very different proposition from the League which had voted so solidly in favour of sanctions'. He went on, 'I could not believe that Geneva would be, at least for some time to come, an adequate guardian of peace'.[17] Attlee, despite standing by collective security in general, made a bold admission that his Party's official line had been somewhat naive:

(Williams): How far do you think it was still possible to depend on the League of Nations as an effective organ after the march into the Rhineland and after Abyssinia?
(Attlee): Well, Germany was out. And Russia had more or less gone when Litvinov [Soviet Foreign Minister until 1939] dropped out of favour. After that I don't think there was much chance.[18]

Those among the orthodox camp on Chamberlain and appeasement, therefore, produced as many damning verdicts on the League as they did positive, with even government critics later admitting to the numerous frailties of the Geneva system.

The vast majority of historians from the revisionist period of appeasement historiography concurred with such brutal assessments. E.H. Carr viewed the League as doomed to failure because the lofty ideals of its creators were ill-suited to the harsh realities of the era:

The metaphysicians of Geneva found it difficult to believe that an accumulation of ingenious texts prohibiting war was not a barrier against war itself... Once it came to be believed in League circles that salvation could be found in a perfect card-index, and that the unruly flow of international politics could be canalised into a set of logically impregnable abstract formulae inspired by the doctrines of nineteenth century liberal democracy, the end of the League as an effective political instrument was in sight.[19]

A plethora of historians succeeding Carr reinforced this view. F.S. Northedge followed up his damning 1966 assessment of the League as merely a guardian of the *status quo* with a comprehensive analysis of the weakness of collective security some 20 years later.[20] His main argument was that collective security was too radical a notion for those used to the 'old' diplomacy of the pre-Great War era. They tried to practise both at the same time and succeeded with neither.[21] While the absence of several great powers dealt an early blow to the League's chances of success, it was the novelty of the system that was its undoing:

> Nothing like the League or the Covenant had ever been seen or tried before... When member states realised that it was they themselves who had to act, that the League was in effect nothing more than the sum of its members, the old allurements of safety, the old methods and the old game tended to return to the forefront.[22]

Other historians have developed the Northedge thesis into what has become the standard view of the League as a tragic failure as a peacekeeping organ, save for minor successes in the humanitarian field. Paul Kennedy asserts that 'it is difficult to conclude in retrospect that the existence of the League proved an advantage to Britain'.[23] Donald Birn admits that members of the League of Nations Union failed to educate the government sufficiently about what collective security would really entail, preferring to retreat behind their own rhetoric in a flawed attempt to win mass support.[24] More recently, Peter Beck re-emphasises many of these points, whilst also challenging Murray's assertion that Geneva could have averted war. For example, he reminds us that even the Russo-Finnish conflict of 1939, a campaign involving two non-Fascist powers, went unchecked by the League.[25] Though Russia was eventually expelled because of this invasion, no military action was taken by the other members.

Notwithstanding Susan Pederson's recent attempt to call scholars 'back to the League of Nations', particularly with regard to the analysis of the personnel, mechanisms and culture of Geneva, the anticipated flood of new research has so far amounted to little more than a trickle.[26] Indeed, a truly comprehensive post-revisionist exploration of the League option has yet to be undertaken. While the continued existence of the United Nations and ongoing debates about multilateral solutions to international crises keep this topic alive, the damning verdict of history with regard to the League alternative to appeasement seems to have been settled some time ago.

Support for the League was much more complex and ambiguous in nature than is often recognised. Praise for the Covenant, from both government and non-government figures alike, varied widely in character and extent. Indeed, some people merely used the terminology and language of the League to cloak other, more cynical policies, far removed from, and sometimes even antithetical to, the original ideals of the League's founding fathers. League support was advocated by many who actually backed the far more *Realpolitik* option of alliances, and these two alternatives – the 'old' and 'new' diplomacies – actually merged and interacted on numerous occasions throughout the late 1930s.[27] Defining a term like 'collective security', therefore, becomes a problematical issue. This phrase was used by many at the time in its original sense to describe the idealists' favoured strategy of all 50-plus member nations acting together against an identified aggressor in the pursuit of economic or military sanctions. And yet the term was also used to describe naked balance of power diplomacy, limited agreements and pacts, often by those seeking legitimacy or vindication for the policies they supported. Collective security has also evolved as a strategy over time, of course, particularly considering the development of the modern United Nations. Such nuances will be explored in more detail below.

Origins and Nature of the Alternative

Having existed since 1920, the creation of the victors of the Great War, the League still had many staunch advocates in Britain in the mid-1930s. But events such as the Manchurian, Abyssinian and Rhineland crises had dramatically shaken faith in the League as an effective instrument in solving global disputes. One critic described it in the wake of the Rhineland affair as 'a lamentable failure'.[28] However, supporters of the Covenant maintained that adherence to its broad values – and specifically the bedrock policy of collective security – remained the best guarantee of future peace. Though League approval existed long before Chamberlain's premiership, it was during this period that calls for it to be revived grew louder as war loomed nearer.

Labour and the Liberals had long placed high value on multilateral efforts to maintain law and order. The League, therefore, emerged as the opposition's most consistently backed option to deal with the Fascist threat. It became the official foreign policy of these parties and government rearmament programmes were supported by them only if they were believed to be for collective security purposes. Indeed, of all the alternatives to appeasement considered in this study, the League enjoyed the widest support, certainly in the earlier part of our period. As time passed and events in the last year of peace began to turn even the most ardent enthusiasts away from the belief that the League could stop Hitler in his tracks, support for what it represented – its language and ideals – remained unbowed. The League also had a number of vocal supporters amongst the Conservative Party, at least before 1939, although scepticism about its value was also highest in Tory circles and remained so.

The issue of sanctions had been discussed in early 1936, in the wake of the trade restrictions imposed upon Italy by the League Council following the invasion of Abyssinia in October 1935. Major figures from all parties now called for their intensification, with oil and coal embargos advocated as a means to slow down the Italian war effort. While Sinclair claimed that League sanctions were 'the only means' of ending the conflict, Attlee assaulted the government's policy more broadly:[29]

> We on this side believe that this war need never have arisen if the government had stood firmly by the League from the start ... If our government had taken a firm line the other countries of the League would have fallen in. I believe there would have been support from the United States of America and I believe it might immeasurably have strengthened the whole collective security system.[30]

Possible sanctions against Germany, a non-League member from 1933, were rarely advocated after the remilitarization of the Rhineland, as Hitler was widely perceived only to have rectified an old injustice left over from 1919. However, discussion of sanctions for Italy's ongoing African adventure continued and the general role of the League was brought into sharper focus by developments in Central Europe. Labour spokesman Hugh Dalton ruled out supporting sanctions against Germany, but reiterated his party's backing for a League of Nations international police force and 'particularly an international air force' to supersede their national equivalents.[31] In the same debate, Conservative MPs Robert Boothby and Winston Churchill both stressed that any concrete Anglo-French military pact resulting from the Rhineland crisis should not supersede collective security, but merely form one part of it.[32] Across two debates in March and April, Churchill stressed that 'pacts of mutual aid and assistance' should be agreed under the auspices of the League as a starting point in real collective security.[33] He concluded: 'There is safety in numbers and I believe also that there may be peace in numbers.'[34] Many Liberals agreed. Geoffrey Mander called for the stiffening of sanctions against Italy:

> Members will probably say 'sanctions means war' ... I venture to say that the precise opposite really represents the position. It is the belief that sanctions will not be applied or that they will be applied ineffectually or half-heartedly that means war.[35]

In the House of Lords, Viscount Cecil, the LNU President, called for intensified sanctions against Italy and maintained that the 'big, broad, general systems' which the League represented provided the best route to British safety.[36] Labour's Lord Strabolgi concluded the debate from the opposition benches, claiming that he saw 'no alternative at all' to the League and calling for efforts to reinvigorate the drive for collective security.[37]

Abandonment of League sanctions on Italy in the summer of 1936 provoked fury among the ranks of Geneva supporters. The National Government bore much of the brunt here, exacerbated in June by Chamberlain's famous reference to the maintenance of sanctions as 'the very midsummer of madness', given Italy's obvious victory.[38] Labour's deputy leader Arthur Greenwood claimed that 'Abyssinia stands as a ghastly monument to the treachery of nations who were sworn to stand by her'.[39] Attlee agreed that Baldwin, by his part in the decision, had 'killed the League and collective security'. Moreover, he had 'never honestly tried to make an effort'.[40]

By the end of the year, Winston Churchill began advocating a policy that became known as 'Arms and the Covenant', a somewhat inconsistent position given that the League was often associated with disarmament for much of the interwar period. Along with fellow Tory enthusiasts like Macmillan, and leading figures from other parties and trade unions, he organised a huge rally at the Albert Hall in December 1936 in support of this line. This 'tremendous gathering' would be presented as a missed opportunity to save peace by rallying the country around a League banner. At the time, however, the abdication crisis stole much of its thunder and its impact was less than hoped.[41] Following Churchill's vigorous lead though, many other prominent League supporters attempted to reinvigorate the cause by signing a cross-party pledge in *Headway*, the League of Nations Union magazine. Under the banner 'Save the League: Save Peace', the signatories declared their firm belief 'that war can be averted and a stable peace permanently maintained if the nations which are Members of the League will now make plain their determination to fulfil their obligations under the Covenant'. It went on: 'Only so will the peaceful settlement of international disputes become possible'.[42] The statement was signed by, among others, Attlee and Dalton from Labour, Sinclair and Lloyd George from the Liberals, Churchill from the Conservatives, Cecil and Gilbert Murray as representatives of the LNU, and Cosmo Lang, Archbishop of Canterbury.

*   *   *

The position at Chamberlain's assumption of power was clear. Although rocked by the Abyssinian and Rhineland debacles, many League supporters from across all parties maintained that it should be strengthened and revived. Collective security, Geoffrey Mander asserted in March 1937, if pursued with 'more vigour and determination' by the government, still represented the best hope for peace, rather than acquiescing in the foreign adventures of the Fascist powers.[43] Attlee's Commons statement on the Spanish Civil War in June is further evidence of the strength of such views. Here the Labour leader called for an end to non-intervention and for the League to be utilised in resolving this conflict. Furthermore, he asserted, a Geneva policy was 'the only way in which you will maintain the British Commonwealth of Nations'.[44] By the close of the year, other Labour MPs, such as Albert Alexander, were calling for League sanctions to be utilised against Japan, over its ongoing conflict with China.[45]

Around this time, Churchill launched a new drive for his policy of 'Arms and the Covenant', claiming in the Commons during December 1937 that 'armaments alone will never protect us'.[46] However, Churchill's enthusiasm for the League was not all it might seem to be, increasingly representing little more than a cloak for his developing strategy of alliances. By adherence to the League, he asserted, 'we consecrate and legitimise every alliance and regional pact which may be formed for mutual protection, and ... win for us a very great measure of sympathy in the United States'.[47] This statement, taken with his earlier calls for 'pacts of mutual aid and assistance', is illustrative of how Churchill saw the League now as the means to rubber stamp other agreements far more limited in scope than collective security originally envisaged. This was meant to be an idealistic, multilateral arrangement designed to replace those narrow blocs and alliances of the old diplomacy, which were widely held to have contributed to the coming of the Great War. For Churchill, the Covenant would also be a moral banner under which Britain could win support and cooperation from the USA, the strongest world power, but not yet a League member.

Whereas the League was the end in itself for many within the Labour and Liberal ranks, it was becoming more of a means to an end for opportunists like Churchill. This is not to suggest that such figures had always held these views or that they did not once support collective security in its original, more altruistic sense. Harold Macmillan, a leading figure from the 'Arms and the Covenant' camp, was originally disturbed by the links between the League, collective security and old style alliances.[48] In a private letter to *The Times* editor Geoffrey Dawson in the wake of the Rhineland crisis, he spelt out the implications for the League of a possible imminent Anglo-French agreement:

> The danger is not in an alliance – the League itself is an alliance – but in allowing an alliance, designed to be the nucleus of a true European society upholding a principle of security which can be applied to all alike, becoming an alliance which is in fact a challenge to that principle.[49]

Churchill's attitude at the time of the March 1938 *Anschluss* confirms that his views were shifting. He used this event to call for a Grand Alliance against the Fascist powers, with the League now mentioned only briefly as the vehicle through which any future discussions with Germany might take place and as the 'moral basis' for rearmament.[50] The Covenant part of 'Arms and the Covenant' was now retreating in the face of a naked *Realpolitik* pact, though admittedly one he described as 'agreeable with all the purposes and ideals of the League'.[51] In the same debate, however, other speakers, mostly to Churchill's Left, argued that events merely demonstrated that the League itself needed to be revived by Chamberlain. Geoffrey Mander was clear: 'It is said that the League is dead, but the League at present is like a motor car without petrol and without a driver. It is there and you need only fill the tank and put your chauffeur there and he can at once drive straight ahead.'[52]

Attlee used the *Anschluss* to reaffirm that the government needed 'a return to League principles and League policy ... as the only way to maintain peace' and he called for a meeting of the Assembly to discuss what should be done in response to the crisis.[53] Sinclair claimed that, 'above all', Britain should now base its foreign policy on the principles of the Covenant and work with its neighbours to 'combine our resources in a system of collective security against aggression'.[54] A few days later, however, on 24 March, Sinclair demonstrated that his thinking was moving away from the idealistic position of many League zealots and towards Churchill's more limited and pragmatic view. His call for the government to 'rally the peace-loving powers in a system of mutual assistance against aggression' suggested that he was now thinking along the lines of limited, regional pacts as a basis upon which to build all-inclusive collective security later on.[55] Philip Noel-Baker rejected even contemplating this sort of line when he concluded the debate from the Labour benches: 'We stand for no alliance but the great alliance of the League against armaments and war. What we want to do, and what we believe can be done, is to revitalise the Covenant of the League of Nations.'[56]

The view in the House of Lords mirrored and sometimes even magnified that within the Commons, the political experience of many of the figures here meaning they were more likely to have been active at the time of the League's inception. Labour peers Lords Snell and Strabolgi echoed their colleague's comments in the lower house, both demanding that the League be rebuilt and supported by the government as the surest way to a lasting peace.[57] The latter stressed that it could be an instrument for ending grievances in Europe, if only the 'the Chamberlain policy' were reversed.[58]

The Munich Agreement prompted further debate on the League and collective security. Neither, however, dominated the discussion in parliament in the way they might once have done, evidence that other solutions to the Nazi problem were increasingly being considered. Chamberlain was scolded as much for not standing by the League in the past as he was for not supporting it now. Attlee opened the debate on 3 October by explaining that Britain was currently in such a humiliating position because of the government's failure to support the League in Manchuria, Abyssinia, Spain and Austria.[59] Indeed, almost every reference to the League in his speech was retrospective and full of sombre regret, rather than hope for its successful use again in the future. Herbert Morrison's opening attack on 4 October was in the same vein.[60] Churchill's bitter salvo a day later barely mentioned the League at all – in fact, half of 'Arms and the Covenant' seemed to have been jettisoned altogether.[61]

If Munich had done little to enhance support for the League, the opposition had not yet abandoned it completely. Dalton and Greenwood both submitted that there was no other way to secure

peace than by collective security methods.[62] The latter's speech indicated that the League itself was less important than the grand ideals it
embodied.[63] More junior figures, such as Josiah Wedgwood and James
Griffiths, called for the League to be revived and strengthened,[64] the
latter asserting that 'we have, first of all, to get back to 1918, to the
one decent thing that came out of it'.[65] Many Liberals also called for
the League to be remade as an alternative to the sort of agreement
embodied at Munich. Lord Davies scolded Chamberlain on 4 October
for abandoning collective security during the height of the crisis,
before concluding: 'You can make it workable if you create the proper
machinery'.[66]

Even a few Tories still advocated strengthening ties with Geneva,
though these were now the rare exception in a party which stood
firmly behind appeasement with its back to Geneva. Edward Grigg
and Derrick Gunston spoke in succession on 6 October about the need
to create a truly universal League, the implication being that they
wanted America included in any revived system.[67] In the Lords, meanwhile, Londonderry and Lytton reaffirmed their support, the former
placing blame squarely at the door of his own government, among
one or two others: 'It is not the League of Nations that has failed, it
is the members of the League of Nations who have failed.'[68] Lytton
concluded that peace could 'only flourish in the soil of justice. There is
no other soil in which it can permanently grow'.[69]

*   *   *

Extra-parliamentary opinion displayed similarly strident viewpoints
on this issue. The League of Nations Union was as old as the League
itself and reflected the opinions of its founder and Honorary President
Viscount Cecil, who had played a leading role in the creation of the
League during the 1919 peace settlement. Liberal academic Gilbert
Murray, LNU Chairman in the late 1930s, also drove much of its policy. A 'pacificist' body, with strong links to many pacifist groups, the
Union's highpoint came in the late 1920s and early 1930s. However, it
still numbered just under 200,000 members by 1939, drawn mostly
from the political Left, though not usually the extreme Left.[70]

Unsurprisingly, the group consistently advocated closer ties with the League as an alternative to any policy relying on peace through wide-scale concessions. In June 1936, Cecil wrote to the Foreign Secretary Anthony Eden claiming that collective security was the 'only solid hope' of deterring aggression and advising that League sanctions against Italy be intensified.[71] Only a few months earlier, Murray had outlined his belief that alliances and other limited agreements were no substitute for the grand ideals of the Covenant: 'I think the difference between collective action unanimously undertaken by a complete all-inclusive League and an attempt at collective action by certain nations in a very incomplete League is the difference between peace and war.'[72] The Union intensified its efforts once Chamberlain assumed the premiership. As international tensions increased and the government moved further away from a Geneva-based strategy, Murray launched a scathing attack on Chamberlain in a letter to a colleague in April 1938:

He first destroyed collective security by announcing that we would not defend anybody, and then justified his isolationism by saying that collective security was dead ... If Britain and France give a lead and genuinely support the League, the small states will be overjoyed.[73]

The Munich Agreement was, for Cecil, a missed opportunity to stand firm behind the League and call Hitler's bluff. In the Lords on 3 October, he asserted that Anglo-French mobilisation just prior to the conference – together with the threat of France and Russia fulfilling their joint obligations to Czechoslovakia – had demonstrated that the principles of collective security were sound: 'No one can doubt that if we had chosen to use it ... it was utterly unthinkable that Germany would have resisted.'[74] Whether a simple tripartite pact such as this would have constituted true 'collective security' is another matter. As late as 2 January 1939, the Union reiterated its belief that there were 'no other effective measures of preventing disturbances of the peace than insistence upon the principles which underline the Covenant of the League'.[75] It is, however, important to note the precise wording of this statement. A phrase like 'principles which underline the Covenant of the League' allows a degree of flexibility in interpretation which a simpler 'the League', alone, does not. Even Union members' convictions had weakened from the lofty, idealistic heights Murray scaled in the spring of 1936. The fact that the LNU supported Chamberlain's efforts to construct his Peace Front in the summer of 1939 shows that even the most ardent League supporters now accepted that limited alliances would be the best substitute for the grander ideal as the descent to war quickened.

Other smaller groups, often formed by leading LNU members or linked to various pacifist bodies, also promoted the cause. The New Commonwealth Society, of which Churchill and Macmillan were sometime activists, frequently lobbied the government on the benefits of a League policy and had begun to make 'real progress' in its calls for an international police force by the beginning of 1938.[76] The Council of Action and the Next Five Years Group were both established in the mid-1930s, by Lloyd George and Macmillan respectively, and heartily endorsed both collective security and measures of colonial and economic appeasement. Larger pacifist groups such as the Peace Pledge Union and the National Peace Council also regularly called for the League to be revived. The latter sent a letter to the Foreign Office in February 1937, strongly condemning the government's programme and asserting its belief that 'the best safeguard of national security and peace and the best defence of democracy lie in the pursuit of a courageous and practical policy of international cooperation'.[77]

Far-Left politicians rarely joined the LNU and most were openly hostile to an organisation traditionally perceived to be no more than a clique of Capitalist powers, promoting the enslavement of colonial masses through the mandate system. However, the left-wing ideal of a world run by multilateral consensus, as opposed to major states and old Empires, still appealed to many members of such groups. Calls for a radically reformed League were, therefore, sometimes voiced by Far-Left spokesmen. James Maxton of the Independent Labour Party called for a much stronger League, prepared to use 'armed force methods', in the wake of the Rhineland crisis.[78] Similarly, a Communist Party pamphlet from January 1937 bemoaned 'the National Government's deliberate abandonment of collective security that plunged the world into a new armaments race', before advocating a prompt return to a Geneva strategy.[79]

The national press, as usual, reflected the concerns of many anti-appeasement groups and figures. Unsurprisingly, the pro-Labour *Daily Herald* supported the League cause wholeheartedly for much of the decade. In the wake of the *Anschluss*, it asked of the government: 'Will they see now that the only chance for the future is to rebuild the system they have shattered?' It continued: 'There is no escape from danger save by working with redoubled power, taking every difficulty as a spur, for the reconstruction of the collective system.'[80] In response to the Munich Agreement, the *Herald* took a line not unlike Cecil's:

> We have refused to take collective security seriously. We were saved from war because at the last moment it was called into being through the collective preparedness of Britain, France and Russia... Two things are necessary to secure peace. One is that there shall be a firm collective resistance to aggression... The second is a removal of the causes of war.[81]

It is noticeable that the *Herald* closed here, in common with other League advocates, with a claim that the League could be used alongside appeasement, and not just as a direct alternative to it. However, it was the loftier characteristics of Chamberlain's policy to which these critics referred – peace through international negotiation – and not the aspects of coercion so roundly condemned at the time of Munich.

Other papers also backed the League option, though rarely with the passion of the *Herald*. Following the *Anschluss*, the *News Chronicle* produced a detailed article entitled 'The Only Real Way to Peace'. In this it called for Chamberlain to 'recognise that the badly shaken system of collective security needs to be rebuilt... It is only when the principles of collective security have been thus transformed into a living reality that we can begin to "bargain" with Germany'.[82] The links between collective security and alliances were not so much an issue for the *Chronicle*, indeed it attempted to persuade its readership of the benefits of a League-based policy by linking it *with* these older strategies: 'Collective security is simply an up-to-date way of giving sense to an old saying: "United we stand, divided we fall." Or, if you prefer: "Hang together or hang separately." '[83] Of the smaller newspapers, the *Economist* and *Spectator* were among the most committed League supporters during this era.

The general public backed the League with more commitment than they did any other rival policy, at least before the Munich Agreement. The National Government had, after all, won a landslide victory in 1935 largely because of its avowed support for Geneva. Politicians regularly called for the government to stand by the League by claiming that this strategy enjoyed the majority support of the British people. Wedgwood's bold assertion in February 1937 that 'the public opinion of this country, Conservative and Labour alike, is overwhelmingly strong in favour of the League of Nations and collective security' is just one illustration.[84] Similarly, letters from the general public to newspapers supporting the League rather than appeasement abound at this time. G.M. Bearne of Kingsley Way, North London, felt compelled to write to the *News Chronicle* shortly after the Munich settlement demanding 'something better' than appeasement and concessions: 'We want to find the way out which will change the circle into an ascending spiral. In a word we want Federation – a strong and enduring League of Nations.'[85]

It is Gallup Poll data, however, that gives the clearest indication of public support for the League option during Chamberlain's premiership. A huge 71 per cent backed continued adherence to the Covenant in June 1937, just a month after he had become Prime Minister.[86] Asked in December if Britain should remain a member of the League, 72 per cent answered in the affirmative, this despite the effects of the Abyssinian and Rhineland crises.[87] The highest levels of peace-time approval for Chamberlain – and by inference for his policy of appeasement – was 59 per cent in early 1939, far inferior to levels of support for the League.[88] Was this, then, the 'people's alternative'? Unfortunately, Gallup asked no more questions about the League before the outbreak of war, though no other policy gained as much popular support in their polls before events in Munich.

* * *

The Prague Coup all but ended even the most ardent League support-ers' hopes that a solution to the Nazi menace could be found within the Covenant. While support for the League and collective security contin-ued to be voiced by the opposition until the outbreak of war itself, few genuinely believed that the grand ideals of the League's founding fathers could now stop Hitler in his tracks. Indeed, backing for the League was often only lip-service, rather than true conviction, or else a retrospective attack on the government for placing Britain in the position it was in by abandoning Geneva in the past. Collective security was increasingly used merely as a cloak to disguise rapidly growing support for Chamberlain's new Peace Front policy of alliances. Thus, on 3 April 1939, Churchill was quick to praise the way in which the 'letter and spirit of the Covenant' were being maintained when he welcomed the Polish Guarantee, issued three days earlier.[89] This was a dubious statement to say the least.

A handful of leading opposition figures even tried to pass off the government's pursuit of alliances as their own League programme and derided Chamberlain for only now adopting the collective security strat-egy they had called for all along. On the same day that Churchill spoke, Sinclair welcomed the Polish Guarantee as a sign that 'now, once again, it is common ground that the rule of law, buttressed by collective secur-ity... is the indispensable foundation of peace and order in Europe'.[90] Labour peer Lord Snell felt able to taunt the government later that month for its 'new conversion to a policy that we have long preached'.[91] In the months after Prague, many senior pro-League figures advocated closer ties with Russia in particular and called for the Soviets to be welcomed into the collective system.[92] Alliance talks officially began in May.

Many old League advocates thus became almost self-delusional, as if trying to convince themselves that the naked pacts they were now advocating were acceptable because they were, in fact, collective secur-ity in action. The *Daily Herald* claimed on 21 March: 'The new Grand Alliance which must be formed will derive in spirit not from preda-tory or self-seeking alliances of the old world, but from the principles of the League.'[93] A day later, it stated that 'there must be no turning back from collective security now'.[94] The writers at the *Herald* knew only too well, of course, that any Grand Alliance currently being con-sidered would consist merely of a handful of nations, rather than an

all-inclusive collection, and might indeed include Russia, at best a quali-
fied supporter of Geneva principals. Indeed, the Soviets were eventually expelled from the League following their invasion of Finland later
that year. Lord Strabolgi complained during April 1939 that the policy
of guaranteeing Poland – and the concurrent alliance talks beginning
with countries such as Greece, Turkey and Romania – gave 'the disad-
vantages of a system of collective security and none of the advantages of
the Covenant'.[95] Others hoped that limited alliances now might be the
foundation around which a true collective security would be built later
on. Thus, before the Polish Guarantee was even given, Viscount Cecil
expressed his desire that the 'nucleus of a new Confederation of Nations,
or League of Nations' would be found in the security arrangements currently being discussed. He also hoped that Russia and the USA might
one day be added to this system.[96] Tory peer Lord Mottistone called
for a new 'League for Fair Play' or 'League of Humanity' to be built
around the current Peace Front, in order to secure the long-term future
of Europe once the current troubles had died down.[97]

Many advocates of European Union had also seen in a revived
League their best hopes of achieving this ultimate goal. Hugh Dalton
wrote in his diary on 11 and 12 March 1936, during the Rhineland
crisis, *not* of his hopes for collective security in general, but his wish
for an 'all European Pact of Mutual Assistance against aggression' in
specific.[98] This suggests that even the most ardent Geneva supporters
had a Europe-first regional mentality. Viscount Cecil, among others,
was a committed advocate of closer European integration as a means to
secure peace and viewed the League as the best instrument to achieve
this end. Talking in the Lords of reforming and rebuilding the League
shortly after the *Anschluss*, he stated: 'Let us have in our minds by
all means, as I think we ought to have, the ultimate possibility of a
United States of Europe.'[99]

Other academics and thinkers of note went even further than this.
Shortly after Munich, writer Arthur Moore penned a pamphlet entitled *The Necessity for a British League of Nations*:

We have before us for purposes of study a remarkable example of
a united effort to secure permanent peace and common protection

against aggressors: The League of Nations ... We might do all we can to popularise here and in other Empire countries the idea of a still larger federation, a Federal British Commonwealth or League of Nations, which will have an authority and centre of its own ... based upon our collective security and a pooling of defence forces.[100]

Seeds for the future United Nations were also being sewn. Henry Gillett, Mayor of Oxford, wrote several times to Lord Halifax in the final year of peace with his thoughts on the subject. Lamenting that neither Geneva nor alliances 'really function satisfactorily', he was convinced that the League should incorporate America within it and evolve into 'the beginning of a World State':

If it was possible now for England and America to move together towards the formation of this union of democratic nations, the advantages would be very great – first, in a united foreign policy; second, they would be strong enough now without further rearmament to withstand aggression.[101]

Consideration of the Alternative

Is the broad verdict of history correct and was Chamberlain right to abandon the League in favour of other methods of securing peace? Before this question can be answered, we must first outline briefly the extent to which the National Government actually worked within the Geneva system. After all, it has become something of a truism that Chamberlain washed his hands of the League from the first day of his premiership. It was not until early 1938, however, that the break became final.

In the wake of the Rhineland crisis in March 1936, Chamberlain announced in the Commons that the Covenant represented 'the keystone' of British foreign policy.[102] In a letter to his sister in April, he suggested that the League would be discredited if Britain withdrew support for sanctions on Italy: 'If that happens our whole European policy is threatened.'[103] Just a few days later, in the Western Department of the Foreign Office, Roger Makins claimed that the League was valuable to Britain not only for the security it gave, but also for the aid it afforded London in maintaining smooth relations within the Empire.[104]

During the summer of 1936, however, there was a widespread evaporation of this confidence in Geneva, as the repercussions of the Abyssinian and Rhineland debacles became clear. These few months saw the early stages of a creeping disillusionment on the part of Chamberlain and other senior government figures, as evidenced by his famous 'midsummer of madness' description of sanctions in June. They were eventually withdrawn in July. Instead, Chamberlain's support for the League came increasingly to rest upon wide-scale reforms. At first appearance, these seemed aimed at strengthening the collective system through the consideration of such things as an international police force to supersede national armies. It was hoped that Germany would also be welcomed on board. However, Chamberlain was also keen on more limited regional pacts, which would actually amount to the gradual dismantling of true collective security. Indeed, these represented a sort of halfway house between the League's multilateral ideal and the old diplomacy of blocs and alliances. A diary entry from April 1936 is illustrative of his thoughts: 'The League of Nations ... should be kept in being as a moral force and focus, but for peace we should depend on a system of regional pacts, to be registered and approved by the League.'[105]

A Foreign Office paper from July of that year, circulated in the Cabinet and Foreign Policy Committee, gives more detail on government recommendations in this area. It talked not only of a possible 'Mediterranean Pact' that Britain would adhere to, but also of an 'All-European Pact of Mutual Assistance', evidence that figures such as Dalton were not the only ones thinking in a continental mindset.[106] Indeed, throughout the Foreign Office, important officials such as Under-Secretaries Viscount Cranborne and Lord Stanhope were particularly keen on this idea.[107] Along with Chamberlain, Malcolm MacDonald was most impressed by these proposals within Cabinet, anxious as he was to carry Dominions opinion with him in any wide-scale revision of the collective system.[108]

By August 1936, while Chamberlain talked in the Foreign Policy Committee of 'every effort' being needed 'to strengthen and re-establish' the League system, he undermined this by suggesting that these regional pacts might operate outside League jurisdiction: 'He did not think that the failure of the Council or the Assembly to approve a pact should render that pact invalid ... The validity of a pact should not depend upon the prior approval of the League.'[109] In public pronouncements, however, Chamberlain paid the customary lip-service to Geneva. Outlining policy in November 1936, he asserted that 'all regional pacts must be subject to our general obligations under the Covenant. They are not intended to be a substitute for them but an addition to them'.[110]

It is clear, then, that while maintaining an official line of support for the League, many senior figures within the government, not least Chamberlain himself, were actually planning in the latter part of 1936 to rebuild the system in a way far removed from, and even antithetical to, the original ideals of its founding fathers. Though these planned reforms never came to pass, the following year carried on in much the same vein, with increased private expressions of concern about League viability accompanied by public pronouncements of continued good faith. By the time Chamberlain had assumed the premiership, a strange dichotomy had set in, as the government sought to reconcile its growing doubts with the official, popular line of support. In November 1937, for example, Eden stated that, in the mission for a lasting peace, while 'the League of Nations is at present seriously handicapped ... we believe it still proves the best means for obtaining that result'.[111]

Despite Chamberlain's dogged pursuit of appeasement in the final years of peace, he could still use the language of the League for his own purposes. The government never officially abandoned the League – rather it was put into a state of 'suspended animation' – and Britain remained a member through to the outbreak of war and beyond.[112] As an instrument to halt the Fascist march, however, its use became more valuable as a shroud to cover other, more practical policies such as pacts and alliances. Thus, the comments Chamberlain made in his diary in April 1936 about the moral weight of the League were relevant again two years later when his government considered a

possible tripartite pact with France and Czechoslovakia following the
Anschluss. In the Foreign Policy Committee, Lord Halifax observed
that 'this could be best pursued if it were sustained by the moral
sense of the world, and for this the League of Nations offers a convenient framework'.[113]

A year later, when the government actually started to make alliances after the Prague Coup, Alec Randall of the League section of
the Foreign Office suggested calling upon Geneva in the event of
hostilities. This was not because he expected any practical assistance for Britain from the other member nations, but because of the
moral authority the League would give 'in our position in regard to
measures affecting the neutrals'.[114] Clearly, the government considered
that the value of the League as a lever on countries like the USA,
Netherlands and Belgium was greater than it was on Nazi Germany.
Even an unsuccessful League approach would win favour with these
powers, and this might one day turn into material support, or at least
make it extremely difficult for such countries – and world opinion – to
side with the aggressor.[115] When Chamberlain was actually discussing
an alliance with the Soviets during the summer of 1939, Alexander
Cadogan noted that he and the Prime Minister had considered trying
to get 'a League umbrella for our Russian arrangement'.[116]

*   *   *

Why, then, did the government abandon the League in favour of
appeasement? The issue of incomplete membership haunted Geneva
all through the Chamberlain period and limited its effectiveness as a
realistic option. In the wake of the Rhineland crisis, Halifax rebuffed
calls for sanctions on Germany by claiming that 'a League that is
50 per cent or 60 per cent representative cannot be expected to be
100 per cent effective'.[117] A fortnight later, Viscount Cranborne argued
that Britain could not be expected to carry the League on its back by
imposing sanctions alone: 'That policy is heroic, but not collective,' he
asserted.[118]

The Rhineland affair dramatically impacted upon government
opinion on the League, as has been shown. While Chamberlain

claimed in public that it still represented 'the keystone' of British policy, his doubts were growing in private. Had not the League's failure over Abyssinia just bequeathed this current crisis? Austen Chamberlain, the former Foreign Secretary who had helped bring Germany into the League, announced on 26 March 1936 that the time was ripe for some 'hard thinking' about Geneva, 'and whether collective security is any more than a pretty phrase to adorn a meaningless speech'.[119] His half-brother echoed these concerns later that day. The League, he asserted, 'must have far clearer ideas, far more definite arrangements among its members as to what part each is going to take in the arbitrament of force'.[120] He was worried that failure to achieve this would result in a League only likely to provoke more trouble from Hitler in the future. Indeed, little more than a week later, Chamberlain complained to his sister that Geneva had 'once more conspicuously failed to do more than exacerbate feelings all round'.[121]

Less than a fortnight after Chamberlain's 10 June 'midsummer of madness' reference to sanctions, Baldwin stated that Britain could not carry the League on its own and put the recent crisis down to a lack of will from other members states – a 'reluctance of nearly all the nations in Europe to proceed'.[122] Lessons were also being learnt in the Foreign Office. Roger Makins felt that the Rhineland affair demonstrated the difference in priorities between the League's two foremost powers: 'My conclusion', he asserted, 'is that we ought to withdraw from the League and refuse to cooperate with France in working out a security system for Europe'.[123] This issue had been widely foreseen earlier that year, when Cabinet minutes from January record that 'no one thought that France was likely to move in the matter of collective security, except where her own frontier was in danger'.[124] Eden later echoed this point about Anglo-French discord undermining the League, while Northedge asserted that it was a fundamental difference in outlook, rather than strategic priorities, which so hampered its efficiency.[125] It could be argued that successive French governments of the 1930s saw the League as a tool to keep Germany at bay and maintain the Versailles system, while Britain, especially in the Chamberlain era, needed it to be a catalyst for change in Europe and an engine for Franco-German *rapprochement*.[126]

Makins was not the only senior Foreign Office official to question Britain's membership of the League during the summer of 1936. Others advocated effective withdrawal in late June of that year by notifying the Assembly that Britain would no longer adhere to the coercive clauses of the Covenant. Gladwyn Jebb declared that 'personally, I have held for a long time that collective security was dead ... I cannot help feeling that it would be better to have no obligations at all'.[127] This line was supported by influential military and naval figures. Admiral Drax slammed the League's 'pathetic weakness' in an Admiralty paper written in July.[128] While a definite decision along these lines was never taken, the fact that so many important figures contemplated effective withdrawal is indicative of how low the League had sunk in their eyes following the Abyssinian and Rhineland debacles. In August 1936, Chamberlain described collective security as a 'palpable sham' and once again underlined how lack of unity was crippling the system: 'No one would have any confidence that if he ventured into the lion's den he would be followed by anyone else.'[129] This view dominated government opinion for the rest of that year and well into early 1937. The relative low regard in which Churchill was still held by many within the Conservative Party meant that 'Arms and the Covenant' made little headway in high political circles. The kindest public pronouncement that Eden, generally regarded as a Geneva enthusiast, could bring himself to make, was that the League was currently 'in state of convalescence'.[130]

While the government's low opinion of collective security had essentially been formed before Chamberlain assumed the premiership, events thereafter served only to reinforce this view and convince the new Prime Minister that an alternative was needed. His early efforts to court Italy and reinvigorate the Stresa Front in the summer of 1937 demonstrate that he viewed a flagrant abuser of the League such as Mussolini as a more realistic partner with whom to secure a lasting peace than the League itself. The much vaunted international conference in September to deal with Italian piracy in the Mediterranean was held in Nyon, rather than Geneva, and invitations to this were extended to non-League powers. In October, Chamberlain's frustration with the opposition's continued insistence upon the League option boiled over into an angry outburst in the Commons:

> Honourable members forget that the League is not an end to itself, it is a means towards an end, and if the League is temporarily unable to fulfil its function to achieve that end, what is the use of repeating parrot-like that we believe in the League? ... We have to find practical means of restoring peace to the world.[131]

It is clear that Chamberlain was planning something drastic by the turn of the year. To Leo Amery, a long-term Geneva critic, he wrote, 'I do not dissent from your views about the League' and indicated that only diplomatic protocol and the need to keep in step with France were holding up a radical step or pronouncement.[132] Even Eden seemed to suggest that the methods of appeasement, which he soon claimed to despise so much, would be preferable to a League policy at this time. He questioned what was meant when people talked of a general settlement: 'Do we mean to try for some multilateral settlement on a grand scale, in which all governments concerned would participate on an equal footing?' This, he felt, would 'stand very little chance of success'. He concluded: 'One alternative would be to envisage in the first place – as the Germans presumably wish – a purely Anglo-German settlement.'[133]

The effective final break with the League came in early 1938 when Chamberlain announced the death of collective security. Coming just days after Eden's resignation speech – in which the latter made no mention of the League at all – Chamberlain spelt out his views to the House of Commons:

> Does anybody here believe that the League, as it is constituted today, can afford collective security? ... I do not believe it now ... We must not try to delude ourselves, and still, more, we must not try to delude small, weak nations into thinking that they will be protected by the League against aggression ... I believe that the policy of the party opposite, if persisted in, this policy of holding

their hands and turning their backs, of making speeches and doing nothing, is a policy which must presently lead to war.[134]

Of all possible alternatives, Chamberlain backed appeasement as his strategy of choice. In response to the *Anschluss*, the new Foreign Secretary Lord Halifax asserted that he could not see 'any useful purpose' in invoking the League, a point Chamberlain concurred with in a letter to his sister.[135] In this, he claimed that collective security could not offer any hope of preventing such events, 'until it can show a visible force of overwhelming strength, backed by determination to use it'.[136] The Committee of Imperial Defence supported this line, stating that 'recent experience' showed collective security to be of 'illusory value'.[137] It is popularly believed that the League Secretary General, Joseph Avenol, was tending to the Geneva gardens at the time the *Anschluss* occurred.

At the Munich Conference, the League was sidelined completely. The only reference to Czechoslovakia in the League Council session index at this time was in relation to drug trafficking and not the Sudetenland.[138] Appeasement rather than the Covenant was the order of the day and, indeed, it had seemed to be successful in averting war. Chamberlain used the Munich Commons debate in October to round on those opposition critics who claimed that collective security was the policy needed, while they were really envisaging an old style alliance with the Soviets under a League of Nations banner:

> That is what some Gentlemen call collective security ... but that is not the collective security we are thinking of, or did think of, when talking about the system of the League of Nations. That was a sort of universal collective security in which all nations were to take their part. This plan may give you security; it certainly is not collective in any sense.[139]

The Prague Coup in March 1939 gave rise to virtually no consideration of the League within the government. Indeed, there was a widespread concern that association with Geneva might just undermine Chamberlain's new initiatives or suggest a weakness on Britain's part. During the Foreign Office discussions in April, which considered tying possible new alliances to the League as a means of influencing neutral powers, fears were expressed that such a move would suggest Britain was attempting to leave itself an escape route, on some Geneva technicality, should hostilities break out.[140] By 1939, it was clear that the League was strongly associated with cowardice and shirking responsibilities, or at least that Chamberlain and his senior colleagues believed this to be the case.

The Dominions complicated matters further and Britain had to carry the Empire with it in any reconsideration of League policy. In South Africa, Jan Smuts was a League enthusiast and founding father, but Australia and New Zealand were much less keen on the Geneva system as a whole. In these countries, it was popularly held that collective security had done little to check Japanese belligerence in the Far East and served only to distract Britain into dangerous European entanglements, far removed from their own spheres of interest. Canada was often openly hostile to the League, and many of its leading politicians and businessmen had echoed Foreign Office calls for British withdrawal in the summer of 1936.[141]

*   *   *

Wider parliamentary opinion suggests that Chamberlain was by no means alone in rejecting the Geneva option to deal with the Fascist threat. Criticism within the House of Commons was widespread, with the vast majority of Tories sceptical about the League from an early date, and almost universally hostile once Chamberlain had himself abandoned Geneva in favour of appeasement. Indeed, in the last 18 months or so before war, the future of the League became a party issue, with Labour and the Liberals still claiming support and the Conservatives firmly against.[142] For example, it was deemed 'the worst will o' the wisp that has ever been followed' by Tory MP Alfred Wise on the day after Eden's resignation.[143] Chamberlain's announcement that he was abandoning the League in favour of appeasement at this time led many others to follow suit. Former pro-Leaguer, turned ardent pro-appeaser, Lord Lothian, illustrates this trend in a letter to

Gilbert Murray from February 1938: 'It was the painful experience over Abyssinia which finally convinced me that League collective security could not, and indeed ought not, to be made to work unless the League could also do collective justice.' In a variation on the *status quo* argument, he then suggested that the League's 'total inability to do justice to Germany in the years after the war', as well as its 'moral failure ... to recognise that justice comes before peace' were the main reasons for its downfall.[144]

Leo Amery was one of the most committed opponents of the Geneva system. As early as March 1935, he asserted that 'we might as well call on the man in the moon for help as make a direct approach to the League'.[145] Amery made some of his most eloquent attacks on collective security in a speech during September 1936, arguing that it was little more than a 'dangerous and mischievous dream'. He also thought the coercive clauses of the Covenant should be abandoned: 'Whenever the question of coercion has been raised, whether in connection with Manchuria, Abyssinia, and so on, the League has failed'.[146] In November 1937, he wrote to Chamberlain demanding an end to 'the lip-service paid to collective security and the League's ideals'. He went on: 'There is nothing so fatal as sticking to the carcasses of dead policies.'[147]

Other political parties and pressure groups mirrored the majority of Conservative MPs in opposing the League alternative. It is unsurprising that the British Union of Fascists echoed the critical views of Geneva regularly expressed by Hitler and Mussolini. A BUF pamphlet from 1936 asserted that it was 'merely an instrument to maintain the Versailles Treaty' and claimed, 'the sooner the League is destroyed the better for mankind'.[148] The Far-Left could also be fiercely critical. Sir Stafford Cripps, the outspoken Labour MP who was expelled from the party in May 1939, denounced the League as a club of 'Capitalist Imperialists'.[149] While Independent Labour's James Maxton thought the League should have been strengthened in the wake of the Rhineland affair, he had fallen into line by the time of Eden's resignation two years later: 'We never believed that the League of Nations was anything more than a utopian dream in a Capitalist Society.'[150]

Not even all pacifists saw the League as the surest route to peace. Numerous members of the Peace Pledge Union came to view collective security as just another by-word for war – military sanctions, of course, were effectively this – and believed economic sanctions would only hurt the innocent masses in countries like Italy, while the real trouble-makers such as Mussolini went unpunished.[151] Even the League of Nations Union eventually had to admit to the obvious frailties within the Geneva system. Gilbert Murray's private papers demonstrate a clear decline in his view of the League's effectiveness as time moved on. By May 1938, he too was advocating more limited regional pacts, the League 'having failed as an instrument of coercion'.[152] National Labour's Harold Nicolson, a staunch member of the LNU, noted during November that the group, as well as the object of its affections, was fading fast:

LNU meeting. Liddell Hart [government military advisor] puts forward an admirable memorandum in which he suggests that as the League is practically dead, the Union should turn itself into some sort of Union for the protection of democracy and liberty … These ancient League enthusiasts have ceased merely to have bees in their bonnets and have actually become huge bumblebees themselves.[153]

Opposition to the League also grew in more public spheres. Hans Morgenthau, Professor of Law and Political Science at Kansas University, published a book in Britain during the summer of 1938, fiercely critical of the League as a body of grand ideals but little action. Furthermore, the priorities of the nation-state would always override any multilateral impulses.[154] Francesco Coppola, Professor of International Law at the University of Rome, publicly challenged Gilbert Murray on the merits of the League at the International Studies Conference during June 1935. Here, Coppola condemned the system as 'absurd' and 'anti-historical', maintaining that arms and allies were the surest way to protect a nation.[155]

The hostility of the national press to the League option also increased as time moved on. The pro-isolation *Daily Express* was a long-term critic, describing sanctions as a 'flop' in March 1936.[156] By 1 October 1938, the *Express* boomed triumphantly that Chamberlain's appeasement 'destroys the ghost of collective security, that apparition growing dimmer each day yet still troubling our peace of mind'.[157] The *Manchester Guardian*, on 5 October, decided that the League and collective security had now gone, 'even as watchwords'.[158] After events in Prague during March 1939, even the *Daily Herald* had to admit that the League was now irreparably 'broken'.[159]

While Gallup failed to ask any more questions about the League in Britain after December 1937 – significant in itself, perhaps – it is evident that public approval decreased considerably as events reinforced Geneva's redundancy. Popular support for antithetical policies such as alliances rose markedly throughout late 1938 and early 1939.[160] There was also a sharp increase in letters to newspapers criticising the League, particularly after the Munich Conference. C.J. Robins of Croydon wrote to the *Daily Telegraph* on 1 October 1938 to ask whether multilateral efforts over the previous twenty years had even been worth it: 'Might it not have been better for the world if President Wilson's 'ideal' League had been left as a skeleton framework for a later generation to fill in?'[161]

Conclusion

The League of Nations and collective security enjoyed widespread support as alternatives to appeasement in the late 1930s – from the Labour and Liberal opposition, a committed but small band of Tories, from large pressure groups such as the League of Nations Union and from significant sections of the press and general public. As time passed, support from all areas of politics and society diminished substantially and had all but evaporated by early 1939, though its lofty ideals survived and received new life after the war in the form of the United Nations.

The National Government considered pursuing a wholehearted League strategy in only the early 1930s, before the Abyssinian and Rhineland debacles graphically illustrated the frailties of the Geneva system. By the middle of 1936, it even contemplated withdrawal altogether. Indeed, it could be argued that Chamberlain had made his mind up about the viability of this alternative long before he assumed the premiership and then struggled to extricate himself from its shackles once he took power. What support he did give to collective security was largely on the basis of regional pacts – a limited, distorted version of the system, which actually had more in common with those old alliances that the League was meant to replace. In the last year of peace, the moral authority of the League was greater than its deterrent value for Chamberlain, his senior colleagues and many political opponents.

Given all this, then, it is clear that most criticism of the government with regard to the League was muddled. Irrespective of its viability in averting war, a significant portion of League support rested upon ideas alien to the original ideals of the founding fathers. Churchill's 'Arms and the Covenant' is an example of this, the 'Covenant' part increasingly being used more to disguise a policy of alliances and rearmament than to signal a true commitment to the ways and means of Geneva. Many League supporters' attacks on the government lacked consistency or rested upon skewed thinking and self-deception. To claim, as many did, that Chamberlain's policy in the wake of the Prague Coup *was* League collective security, was plainly stretching the facts to fit an ideal. Similarly, opponents often abused the British government alone for abandoning the League or killing collective security and then blithely extolled the virtues of multilateralism. Was it possible for one power to be responsible for destroying a system which was supposed to be collective? If only Britain would give a lead in the Assembly, some asserted, then the League could be revived and peace would be secure. But surely the concept of a collective security 'leader' was just a contradiction in terms?

By endorsing the League in this way, government critics merely demonstrated the weaknesses of the policy they were espousing. Were they blind to the realities of the day, caused by the beauty of the vision they so longed for? Support for the League rested upon the utopian ideals of the early 1920s, a decade far removed in its aspirations and hopes, if not in time, from the paranoid and dangerous world of the late 1930s. Indeed, the fact that the League had broadly been the way of things since the end of the Great War, and that so many people had adopted a 'never again' mantra, goes some way to explain why many supporters found it difficult to let go and accept Geneva's limitations. Peace through the League seemed a realistic proposition in 1919, a vision difficult to abandon later on. This also explains why it was so easy for the government to utilise the language of Geneva in an attempt to win support for its eventual pursuit of alliances. The League represented a convenient and attractive peg on which it could hang its other strategies.

Lack of universal membership hamstrung collective security from day one. As a famous *Punch* cartoon from 1919 testified, Wilson's America had built most of the bridge but then rested its head on the keystone and slept.[162] The fact that the three main aggressor powers of this era, Germany, Italy and Japan, had all left the League meant that it was impossible to work with them through Geneva in the quest for peace. The two leading member states, Britain and France, not only had different priorities and concerns, but also rival conceptions of the League's main purpose. The last of the world's major powers, Russia, was expelled in 1939 and was at best a lukewarm exponent of Covenant ideals. The League, therefore, had a marked lack of teeth. It rested upon economic sanctions as its main strategy to avert war and these failed dramatically in relation to Mussolini and Abyssinia. Nor did they prevent non-member powers trading with whomsoever they liked. Hitler looked on.

Collective security was only as strong as the collective will to make it work, and each member interpreted the system in its own way with its own interests paramount. In a League of such unequal powers, a sort of collective paralysis crept in. The small nations would not act unless they were confident of support from the big ones. The great powers, like Britain, were reluctant to take a lead for fear that the weaker ones would not join them. The repeated debacles over sanctions proved this, and a sort of 'after you' mentality took hold, especially in Britain and France. As Porter observes, 'the problem was a general one: that while every nation could conceive of some act of aggression somewhere which would affect it, very few nations could accept that every act of aggression everywhere would'.[163]

Collective security also forced otherwise hostile powers to work together as friends and broke up those traditional partnerships that had previously kept a fragile peace. Simply put, the collective security experiment dislocated much in Europe that worked in an effort to fix the things that did not. For example, the League put Britain and France in an awkward position with regard to Italy during the mid-1930s. Mussolini's Abyssinian venture meant that the League powers were forced to treat Italy as a Pariah, at exactly the same time as Britain considered reinvigorating the Stresa Front and needed to keep Italy and Germany apart.[164] The experience of the United Nations today suggests that collective solutions to global crises will always be hampered until such a time as traditional national interests have been abandoned in favour of true altruism. History suggests that such a development remains unlikely.

In the rapid-fire world of the late 1930s, the League was not suited to the decisive responses demanded by the latest foreign crisis. The fact that Chamberlain abandoned the League in favour of appeasement suggests that Geneva was widely felt to be a body to protect the *status quo*, at least on the big issues, rather than to make real and radical efforts to revise the Versailles settlement. All of these factors were driven home to Chamberlain by the vast majority of his party, by large sections of the Foreign Office and by most of his military advisers. The weight of government opinion against the League was huge. A Geneva-based policy in 1938 or 1939 would have been extremely divisive.

Were Churchill, Macmillan and Murray correct to state that committed support for the League would have averted war? The idea that the League could have stopped Hitler at the time of the Rhineland crisis is fraught with many doubts. While individual nations might have been able to check Germany at this time (though none of them felt moved to do so), a collective League response would have resulted in little more than ineffectual economic sanctions being applied, as Eden later suggested.[165] That 'Arms and the Covenant' would have deterred Hitler from war is similarly doubtful, certainly without a drastic, almost impossible increase in British armaments and without a drastic, almost impossible reshaping of the Covenant. All of this would have needed the backing of the other member nations. Would the threat of League sanctions have stopped Hitler invading Poland in 1939? They did not do so and were no deterrent to the *Anschluss* or his mobilisation against the Czechs in 1938. Cecil's claim at the time of Munich that collective security had deterred Hitler from war was delusional. His League 'collective' amounted to a possible *ad hoc* alliance between Britain, France, Russia and the Czechs, and this was, in fact, the antithesis of all the League stood for.

Much of this speculation is irrelevant anyway. The League did exist but did not avert war. Despite its various humanitarian achievements, its every diplomatic failure only encouraged the Fascists to chance their arm. It may even have accelerated the descent to conflict, its very existence a bone of contention for Hitler and Mussolini. For the League to have had a chance of averting the Second World War, all members would have had to deal with every minor incident that challenged international peace firmly and assuredly from the date of the League's inception. Given the condition of the world in the 1920s and 1930s, and the obvious predominance of national interest over multilateral impulses in these hungry, paranoid and uncertain times, this League could only have been carried on the back of a small band of traditional major powers. Peace might have been secured in this way, but it would not have been by a League of Nations at all.

4

ALLIANCES

If a number of states were assembled around Great Britain and France in a solemn treaty for mutual defence against aggression; if they had their forces marshalled in what you may call a Grand Alliance ... and if it were done in the year 1938 – and, believe me, it may be the last chance there will be for doing it – then I say you might even now arrest this coming war.[1]

(Winston Churchill, House of Commons, March 1938)

Introduction

A large body of Chamberlain's critics, amongst contemporaries and historians alike, have suggested that the National Government should have pursued a policy of alliances as an alternative to appeasement in the years before war. Indeed, Churchill's famous notion of the 'Grand Alliance', first advocated following the *Anschluss*, has emerged as perhaps the favourite rival strategy of those later appeasement detractors who like to imagine scenarios of what might have been. Whether envisaged as the spurned deterrent that could have driven Hitler away from war, or as the best means to have won the battle once it was joined, the option of an anti-Fascist bloc of nations is probably the most popularly explored alternative among scholars looking back on this period. It is, therefore, central to this study.

For the purposes of this chapter, an alliance or pact is considered to be a formal treaty between two or more powers, usually military in

character as a pledge to defend one another from attack. Such agreements as guarantees, blocs and fronts, however, will also be considered
under this broad umbrella. A guarantee could indicate a partnership
between two powers that did not quite constitute a formal alliance,
which were typically reciprocal in nature. A bloc or front could well
comprise a more informal grouping of many countries, often in close
geographical proximity and with several smaller alliances at its heart.
Calls for 'closer relations' between powers, moreover, need not represent any such binding arrangement at all. Many of these terms were
actually interchangeable at the time, as will become clear.

The pursuit of alliances was the alternative Chamberlain eventually
adopted, of course, some six months before war began, when Britain
guaranteed Poland on 31 March 1939 (which France also joined) and
similar agreements were extended to Greece and Romania in April,
and Turkey in May. Conversations with the Soviets, exploring the
possibility of a mutual assistance pact, were underway by this point,
while powers such as Holland and Denmark declined similar offers
in this period. Given that the government turned to this alternative
before war broke out, then, the time-frame for this chapter could
easily be different to others in this study. However, the failure of the
Russian negotiations and subsequent conclusion of the Nazi-Soviet
Pact on 23 August 1939 has emerged as another major criticism of
Chamberlain's tenure. Would not an alliance of Britain, France and
Russia have deterred Hitler from war in late 1939, and did not the
Prime Minister's reluctance to commit effectively force Stalin into
Hitler's arms? Such are the charges brought against the National
Government even today.

Almost all of the memoirs forming a large part of the orthodox
school of appeasement historiography have something to say on the
issue of alliances. For Churchill, the 1930s represented a series of
missed opportunities to have built an anti-Fascist coalition that would
have averted the Second World War. Germany could have been ejected
from the Rhineland in March 1936 by a firm Anglo-French stand.[2]
The Nyon Conference in September 1937 was proof that the combined
influence of these two countries was a powerful check on the Dictator
states, as it was widely accepted that this was a resounding diplomatic

victory over Mussolini.[3] It left Churchill 'breathless with amazement' that Roosevelt's Peace Initiative – 'the proffered hand stretched out across the Atlantic' – was waved away by Chamberlain in early 1938.[4] An Anglo-French guarantee of Czechoslovakia later that year might have 'deterred or delayed Hitler's next assault'.[5] It was, however, the spurned Grand Alliance of 1939 that most rankled:

> The alliance of Britain, France and Russia would have struck deep alarm in the heart of Germany in 1939, and no one can prove that war might not even then have been averted ... History might have taken a different course. At least it could not have taken a worse.[6]

Churchill's argument about the unmade alliance was taken up by numerous other anti-appeasers from the Chamberlain era. Anthony Eden asserted that he 'was convinced that close Anglo-French under-standing and coordinated action, endorsed as nearly as we could con-trive by the United States, was the only way to keep the peace'.[7] He attributed his resignation to Chamberlain's rejection of the Roosevelt Peace Initiative in January 1938 and the Prime Minister's persistence in bowing to Dictators.[8] Alfred Duff Cooper felt Britain 'should have retained the friendship of Italy' in the 1930s, 'and the Axis ... would never have formed'.[9] The Roosevelt Peace Initiative represented for him 'an immense opportunity which ... might have proved one of the turning points in European history and would probably have averted the coming war'.[10] Leo Amery, casting off his former isolationist cre-dentials, suggested that 'it was at all costs essential to build up a com-bination of powers prepared to keep Hitler in check'.[11] To his credit, however, he reminded the reader that Churchill's Grand Alliance would have relied upon a Russian army widely perceived to have been all but crippled by Stalin's purges.[12] The 1935 Stresa Front of Britain, France and Italy emerges as the deterrent spurned for Amery.[13] This point is echoed in Vansittart's memoirs, where he described such a grouping as 'the only real bulwark of peace' available at the time.[14]

Not all of Chamberlain's contemporaries were critical of the Prime Minister on this issue. Lord Strang offered a comprehensive defence of his own record at the head of the failed Moscow negotiations and puts the reason for their collapse squarely at the door of the Soviets. He claimed that while Poland would never have consented to Russian troops crossing their borders *en route* to fight the Nazis, the hard-line Soviet Foreign Minister, Vyacheslav Molotov, consistently upped his demands in light of every concession offered by the British delegation, making an agreement all but impossible. Indeed, Strang was suspicious that the cautious Stalin was only ever playing for time with Britain, in order to secure the best possible deal with Germany.[15] Samuel Hoare launched a similar defensive rearguard. Chamberlain 'had good reason to be sceptical of grandiose proposals' such as the Roosevelt Peace Initiative, coming as it did in a vague form from an ultra-isolationist power, far removed from the affairs of Europe.[16] Again, the Russian side of the alliance negotiations in 1939 was, for Hoare, the more destructive of the two. Stalin's intransigent refusal to sign anything other than a deal which would mean partitioning Poland and the extension of Soviet control in the Baltic all but killed the talks.[17]

Other loyal colleagues rallied to the Prime Minister's defence. Nevile Henderson reiterated that Soviet duplicity was the main reason that no Grand Alliance was ever made. Of the talks in the summer of 1939, he asserted: 'Stalin and Molotov kept putting the price up … I still believe that from the outset Moscow never meant them to terminate in agreement with us.'[18] Both Simon and Halifax emphasised how unattractive even Britain's best alliance options were in this decade. The former asserted that 'the French Air Force was deplorably weak' for the duration of the 1930s.[19] The latter claimed that even when America showed most willingness to help Britain in its mission for peace, in January 1938, the results of such a scheme would have been far from certain:

> I am satisfied that on neither count is it possible to maintain the argument … either that the President felt resentment at the reception accorded to this initiative, or that this initiative, if differently handled, might have had the effect of preventing the war.[20]

Many orthodox historians took up the theme of alliances. Both Sir Lewis Namier and A.L. Rowse wrote critical accounts of Chamberlain's tenure of high office, the former indicating that the Prime Minister could have halted Hitler's march 'without excessive effort or sacrifice' if only he had adopted a tougher line and acted in accord with others.[21] Rowse took the Churchillian view that a Grand Alliance was 'the only way to contain Hitler and keep Europe safe'.[22] Among revisionists, however, A.J.P. Taylor largely exonerated the Prime Minister from blame for the coming of war and saw appeasement as a realistic strategy given the harsh conditions of the day. Taylor was, however, critical of Chamberlain's failure to secure an alliance with the Soviets after the Prague Coup. Once it became clear in March 1939 that all other alternatives were dead, the government should have pursued alliances with far greater vigour.[23] This line was echoed by F.S. Northedge. In view of the weakness of existing alternatives, such as League collective security, Northedge felt the traditional notion of a balance of power would have been the best option to pursue: 'It has its faults, but it may have fewer faults than any alternative upon which the world could agree.'[24]

A host of later historians continued the debate by taking a more charitable view of the appeasers and their policies. Paul Kennedy addressed the long-term strained relations between Britain and its potential allies: Soviet Communism was widely seen as a bigger threat than Nazism in the 1920s and much of the 1930s; America was viewed as an aloof and unpredictable partner, while relations with France grew increasingly problematic as the decade progressed.[25] John Charmley was quick to point out that all these constraints weighed heavily upon Chamberlain's mind and mitigated against a Grand Alliance – something that was easy to suggest by those on the sidelines with no responsibility for actual events.[26] 'His was the only policy which offered any hope of avoiding war,' Charmley concluded.[27] Peter Neville concurred: 'The Grand Alliance was an impressive concept, but its component parts seemed to be defective. It also reminded Chamberlain of a pre-war Entente.'[28]

Among post-revisionists, Parker revives many of the classic criticisms of Chamberlain and maintains that Churchill's Grand Alliance was both popular and realistic in the years before war.[29] In his 2000 work, *Churchill and Appeasement*, he states his case more bluntly:

> Churchill could have prevented the Second World War. If Churchill had controlled British foreign policy, he would have made a 'Grand Alliance' ... It might have stopped Hitler or caused moderate Germans to stop him. Churchill might even have managed to make Britain and France seem to Stalin to be safer collaborators than Nazi Germany ... We shall never know ... It is, however, hard to imagine that any conceivable alternative chain of events could have been worse than what happened in 1939–1945.[30]

Parker's work has influenced other historians to readdress the issue of alliances as an alternative to appeasement, both those in favour of Chamberlain's policies and those against. Roy Denman argued that war might have been averted had Eden's detestation of Mussolini not driven the *Duce* irretrievably into Hitler's camp.[31] David Dutton is keen to point out that Chamberlain felt alliances would only provoke a war when he in fact sought to avoid one.[32] Would not a Russian agreement cause Hitler to lash out against perceived encirclement, or make the bellicose Japanese government think the Western powers were trying to gain a stranglehold in the Far East?

Anglo-Soviet relations in the late 1930s have been an area of active research in recent years and this trend will doubtless continue as new evidence is uncovered from the Soviet archives. Much of this work has revived old charges that Chamberlain never really wanted a deal with Russia in the first place and, therefore, drove a powerful ally into the Nazi camp. This, his critics say, made war all but inevitable when, in fact, he could have worked with Stalin to avoid it. Thus, while David Kaiser echoed Strang's anti-Soviet position by claiming that the Russians were never interested in making an alliance with Britain – 'they were merely stalling until Hitler would submit a bid of his own' – Geoffrey Roberts argued that Stalin only stumbled into the Nazi-Soviet Pact at the last possible moment.[33] There was no devious, long-term plan on Russia's part, and it only took the Nazi option late in the day in face of perceived Anglo-French reticence.[34]

Michael Jabara Carley and Louise Grace Shaw have both recently offered similar, charitable interpretations of Russian intentions with regard to the failed alliance. The former explained that Stalin only did the obvious, most sensible thing during August 1939 for his own country's safety, and, moreover, that anti-Communism constantly permeated the hesitant British efforts during negotiations.[35] Shaw was even more damning of Chamberlain and in many ways took the argument back full circle to the position first championed in *The Gathering Storm*: 'An alternative existed to the policy of appeasement – namely an Anglo-French-Soviet Alliance.'[36] This, she maintained, would have 'posed serious, and very possibly, successful resistance to Germany in 1938 and 1939'.[37] Where the blame lies for the failure to secure this deal is clear – with a Prime Minister enveloped in anti-Soviet prejudice: 'It was Neville Chamberlain, alone, who … repeatedly rejected Soviet proposals. Consequently, it was ultimately Neville Chamberlain who drove away the one ally who could have made a significant difference to Britain's experience of war.'[38] The historical consensus today, therefore, points towards the conclusion that Chamberlain could have done much more in the pursuit of allies than he ever did, regardless of the attractiveness, or otherwise, of his various options.

There was no 'one' policy of alliances suggested in the late 1930s. Appeasement critics from different political parties, at different times and in different circumstances, envisaged a swathe of variously constituted pacts and blocs which, they hoped, could deter Hitler from war. Advocates of one alliance could fiercely oppose those of another. Leo Amery enthusiastically backed an Anglo-Franco-Italian stand against Germany but vehemently opposed an Anglo-Franco-Soviet one. The links demonstrated in the previous chapter between alliances, collective security and the League of Nations serve only to muddy the waters further. However, some common trends emerge that merit brief discussion here. While many people suggested that Britain should improve relations with one country or draw closer to another – not necessarily advocating a formal alliance as such – several key powers were regularly considered as potential allies. France was widely viewed as Britain's closest friend and most important neighbour and was the one country that was almost always considered a constituent member of any alliance system envisaged. The USA was committed to isolation during the interwar years. It was, however, the world's most powerful nation and shared cultural, historical and political links with Britain. It was another frequently advocated partner in solving world disputes. After all, it had fought alongside Britain and France during the Great War. The Soviet Union did not enjoy so many bonds with Britain, but it was one of the foremost world powers and influenced strategic considerations in both Europe and Asia. The obvious ideological antipathy between it and Nazi Germany also suggested that Russia could be a potential ally in restraining Hitler. While Italy was considered more as a probable enemy than a friend during the late 1930s, a number of influential figures suggested a return to the 1935 Stresa Front as a deterrent to Germany. Driving a wedge between Mussolini and Hitler also played an important role in Chamberlain's early policy.

Thus, this chapter will focus extensively on British relations with a small number of key powers. The concept of a Grand Alliance, which had Britain, France and Russia at its core, but could also be supported by the USA, Czechoslovakia, Poland and whoever else cared to join its ranks – a whole host of small European powers were touted at one point or another – will also be addressed.

Origins and Nature of the Alternative

Huge alliance systems had been widely discredited in Europe by the mid-1930s, many believing they had played a major role in causing the Great War. The League of Nations was designed to supersede such pacts and blocs and maintain stable relations on the continent. Those that existed now were typically limited arrangements featuring two or three powers banded together. The Stresa Front, established by Britain, France and Italy in April 1935, and designed to safeguard the borders of Austria, or the Franco-Soviet Mutual Assistance Pact, concluded in the same year, offer good examples.

Ominous new developments in German foreign policy during the early part of 1936, however, caused rumblings of discontent within Britain at the League's ineffectiveness and prompted a few calls to revisit old partnerships and alliances designed to deter or contain a

German renaissance. Labour's Hugh Dalton suggested that Britain should move closer to the Soviet Union during a series of Commons debates in February 1936.[39] Such calls only increased and solidified in the wake of the Rhineland crisis. National Labour's Harold Nicolson was among many who suggested that the traditional close relationship with France should be cemented through a formal military alliance.[40] Conservative MP Henry Raikes argued that the crisis demonstrated the many frailties of the League and called for a system of regional pacts in Europe to supersede the existing, impotent, collective security.[41] The most concrete and radical proposals in parliament came, however, from Communist MP William Gallagher, who advocated the 'peace encirclement of Germany' through an Anglo-Franco-Soviet pact and called for the government to 'associate British foreign policy with the peoples who want peace rather than making any capitulation to Hitler and the Nazis of Germany'.[42]

While figures from the political Left backed closer relations with the Soviets, calls for alliances in general tended to come from those on the Right of the political spectrum. As the previous chapter has shown, Labour and the Liberals were staunch supporters of the League for almost the entirety of the interwar period, as the supposed antidote to the unpopular, old diplomacy of 1914. Nevertheless, the signature of the Anti-Comintern Pact between Germany and Japan in November 1936 solidified relations between the three Fascist powers and brought the issue of allies into sharper focus for the mainstream political parties. In a series of Commons debates in early 1937, several Labour MPs seemed to be concerned about their official party line, expressing a desire to draw closer to European friends and particularly the Soviet Union. Whilst largely couching his demands in collective security terminology, Stafford Cripps castigated the government for failing to conclude a definite 'pact or arrangement' with France and Russia.[43] James Walker felt that the Soviets offered 'the best help we could have as an Empire' in the event of increased Japanese militarism in the Far East.[44] From the Tory benches, by contrast, Churchill underlined his desire for a closer, more definite union with the French.[45] Viscount Astor felt it was to the USA that Britain should look for aid in the search for peace.[46] Liberal Geoffrey Mander's contribution on 18 February was particularly striking, seemingly amounting to a call for a Grand Alliance against the Fascists. Again, while he was careful to use the language of the League, the deeper meaning was pure *Realpolitik*:

> I suggest that if the government were to make it clear that we are willing to go all-out with our forces ... we could rely upon a system of alliances. After all, the League of Nations is only an alliance of all loyal nations against a potential aggressor. We could rely upon France, Belgium, Russia, Poland, the Little Entente countries, the Balkans, Turkey, Holland, and the Scandinavian countries. One would hope that all the others would come in, and Germany and Italy too. If they did not, they would rightly be encircled. Any aggressor deserves to be encircled.[47]

In a private memorandum at this time, Conservative MP Robert Boothby seemed to concur with this strategy: 'A catastrophe can still be averted', he wrote, if Hitler could only be made to fear the 'united opposition of the whole of the rest of Europe'. He continued: 'The three great powers, Great Britain, France and Russia ... if they stand together ... are more than strong enough to preserve peace.'[48]

By the time Chamberlain assumed the premiership, then, a small but significant band of MPs from across all parties was advocating the exploration of a range of alliances and pacts with various constituent members as a replacement for the ailing League. One or two even wanted to deter the Fascist powers from war through a coalition of major states such as Britain, France and Russia. Others, however, usually on the Right of the political spectrum, who were less ideologically disposed to look to the Soviets for assistance, felt that Italy could still be used as a partner against Germany. At various points during 1937, several MPs advocated attempting to revive the Stresa Front as Chamberlain's early conversations with Mussolini progressed and drew international publicity. Liberal National Robert Bernays was one figure who resented the way in which recent events had all but wrecked a beneficial arrangement for Britain. As he had noted in his diary as early as 5 November 1936, 'I do not see how we can possibly face the future unless we buy Italian friendship'.[49]

Leo Amery felt that if isolation was rejected, a return to Stresa would provide the best chance of averting war. Shortly after the Rhineland crisis he had asserted that 'the great thing I urged was to be patient and restore the Stresa Front'.[50] A letter to Chamberlain towards the end of 1937 confirmed that this intent remained. Here Amery advocated trying to drive a wedge between Britain's two most likely enemies by officially recognising Mussolini's conquest of Abyssinia:

> I would say that our first effort should be to get back to the Stresa position in which case we bring together not only France and Italy but their various client states in the Danubian Basin ... Stresa was the high water-mark of success of our diplomacy in Europe.[51]

* * *

The trend towards advocating alliances continued after Chamberlain took office and gathered momentum through the rest of that year. Former Liberal Prime Minister David Lloyd George declared on 25 June that 'if the great powers France and Russia ... and ourselves, talked quite frankly, brutally if you like, these three great powers together have such a force that there is no one in Europe could stand up against them'.[52] Even the Liberal leader Archibald Sinclair, supposedly a firm advocate of collective security, appealed to Chamberlain to make every effort to strengthen ties with the USA, as an additional measure should the League continue to flounder.[53] The perceived success of the Nyon Conference in September also emboldened those who favoured trying to deter Hitler and Mussolini. Churchill congratulated Eden on his success there, underlining the vital importance of a united Anglo-French stand against the Fascists.[54]

Calls for increased American cooperation grew after Roosevelt's famous 'Quarantine Speech' in October 1937. This seemed to suggest that America now favoured a tougher line against the Dictators, the President intimating that aggressive states in breach of international law and order should be isolated. Sinclair, again, felt this was a 'clarion call to action', offering a chance to draw the USA into the British

sphere: 'Let us not fail to seize with both hands this ... glorious opportunity of lining up the United States in the defence of the ideals of
peace and justice, which are common to our two countries, to France
and to all the great democracies.'[55]

The March 1938 *Anschluss*, by bringing the issue of Czechoslovakia
into sharp focus, provided renewed momentum to the idea of alliances
as an alternative to appeasement. The subsequent well-publicised offer
from the Soviets to Britain and France for talks with a view to 'the
organisation of collective resistance to the aggressor' also resulted in a
flurry of new calls for Russia to be an integral part of any anti-Fascist
bloc.[56] Following Churchill's dynamic lead, a range of figures from all
parties joined his campaign for a Grand Alliance. Again, despite being
officially opposed to alliances, and taking care once more to voice their
demands in League terminology, senior figures from the opposition
parties argued that a system of pacts and blocs might just keep the
peace. Philip Noel-Baker asserted that, while Labour did 'not believe
in power politics or in alliances of the old kind', war could be averted,
'if they were to make a definite, concrete, binding alliance with France,
Czechoslovakia and Russia'.[57] A few days earlier Sinclair had asked,
'What then should we do? Let us resolve to support France ... draw
more closely by all means in our power to the government of the USA,
and let us not forget ... the folly of leaving Russia out of account.'[58]
Former Liberal leader Viscount Samuel admitted to the *Manchester
Guardian* that, given the current state of the League, 'pacts, agreements and understandings, first with France, and then with others,
were the right policy'.[59]

The Tories advocated a wide variety of agreements in response to
the crisis. Sir Henry Croft felt that the 'finest line of policy we could
adopt' would be to draw closer to friends outside of Europe: 'There
are 500 million people in the British Empire and we have great
strength behind the Empire.'[60] His colleague Viscount Wolmer, however, called for 'a definite and specific alliance by which the Danubian
and Scandinavian states, and England and France will pledge themselves to go to each other's assistance'.[61] Perhaps surprisingly, Harold
Macmillan even talked privately of a 'London-Paris-Madrid axis' as 'the
best chance of avoiding a general war'. If Franco could be won over to

the democratic powers, 'such a compact geographical grouping would provide the maximum security and the minimum of provocations'.[62] Labour's Thomas Fletcher, however, thought in more general terms:

> If a man has an idea to hit me on the head, I certainly will fight for the idea of not being knocked on the head, and I try to find some friends who agree that I ought not to be knocked on the head. That is not a contest of political theories: that is common sense.[63]

There were many variations on the Grand Alliance theme over the coming weeks and months. Almost all of them envisaged a central core of Britain, France and the Soviet Union, with whoever else would come in around them. Unsurprisingly, now that Austria had been absorbed into the Reich, calls for a revived Stresa Front fell away sharply. As the Czech crisis gathered momentum through the summer of 1938, Chamberlain's appeasement policy came under increasing attack from the various pro-alliance camps. In May, Churchill wrote an article for the *News of the World* in which he appealed for greater Anglo-American cooperation as an urgent necessity, though he recognised that an all-out alliance was still unrealistic:

> If Britain and the United States were agreed to act together, the risk [of war] would be slight. These two great kindred powers, in collaboration, could prevent – or at least localise and limit – almost any quarrel that might break out among men ... almost certainly without any resort to force themselves, by moral, economic and financial power ... It is a union of spirit not of forms that we seek.[64]

On 4 July, Sinclair announced that the Liberals 'strongly dissented' from the Prime Minister's appeasement strategy and once again bemoaned Britain's neglected relations with France and America.[65] Independent MP Eleanor Rathbone talked of Russia being 'essential' to the anti-Fascist coalition and decried 'the selfishness of our present policy', through which 'we have been left practically alone'.[66] Labour's Josiah Wedgwood was even more critical. His alternative was obvious: 'Every time you sacrifice one of your potential allies to this pathetic desire to appease the tyrants you merely bring nearer and make more inevitable that war which you pretend you are trying to avoid.'[67]

*　　*　　*

A brief summary of wider opinion offers further evidence of the increasing popularity of alliances as war drew closer. Unsurprisingly, Far-Left groups such as the Independent Labour Party almost universally supported closer relations with the Soviet Union and were particularly keen on an Anglo-French military alliance with Russia from March 1938 onwards.[68] In fact, as early as January 1937, the British Communist Party had favoured 'opposing the warmongers by a policy of peaceful cooperation with Socialist Russia, the government of France supported by the People's Front, and the small states of Europe'.[69]

Whilst regularly advocating closer relations with the USA, the League of Nations Union tended to resist calls for alliances, for obvious reasons.[70] But clear evidence of the Union's crumbling conviction in the League's ability to deter war can be found from as early as 1938, particularly in the wake of the *Anschluss*. Senior figures such as Gilbert Murray gave approval for regional pacts at this time, which actually undermined the true ideals of collective security in favour of older, more limited measures.[71] By the summer of 1939, and despite the persistence of the usual collective security rhetoric, the Union had moved over to seeking 'a Peace Front too formidable to be challenged' as its solution to the Fascist march. This would be made up of Britain, France, Russia, Poland and anyone else in Europe wishing to join in.[72]

Even pacifists could take a similar line. For example, as the Czech crisis reached its climax in September 1938, the International Peace Campaign announced that 'the people's answer to the Dictators is collective security'. It went on, however: 'Britain, France and Russia can defend Spain and Czechoslovakia, defend Europe and defend peace.'[73] Their 'collective' amounted to an alliance of three great powers here, one of which had repeatedly flouted the ideals of Geneva.

Many elements of the press supported alliances at various points during Chamberlain's premiership. The *Manchester Guardian* felt that the *Anschluss* could have been averted with a determined and united stand by Britain and France: 'If Mr Chamberlain said in the House of Commons today that the British and French governments would not tolerate any further intimidation of small countries there would be no reason for gloom.'[74] Shortly afterwards, the *News Chronicle* greeted Churchill's rallying cry for a Grand Alliance with hearty approval.[75] A few months later, it felt confident that the Munich Conference need never have occurred, had a similar strategy been adopted in May or June 1938:

> The truth is that common and resolute action by Britain, France and Russia in the summer would...have saved us from ever coming to the brink of war, and would have marked a turning point – perhaps decisive – in the hitherto aggressive career of the Dictators.[76]

The *Yorkshire Post* was a vehemently anti-appeasement paper and its editor, Arthur Mann, a long-term advocate of alliances as the best strategy to pursue. During August 1938, he wrote privately of his desire to see Roosevelt's 'moral and implied material support' against the Dictators grasped by Chamberlain with both hands.[77]

The March 1939 Prague Coup marked a watershed in press calls for alliances as an alternative to appeasement. Indeed, demands for a Grand Alliance were almost universal across the main dailies from now on. The *Yorkshire Post* promptly advocated a pact with Russia, Mann believing that the possibility of a two-front war for Germany would deter Hitler from taking any further steps.[78] The *Daily Express*, which, as a pro-isolation paper, had traditionally urged closer relations with no one other than the USA or Dominions, now felt that France's borders were effectively Britain's own. In late March 1939, it called for the Empire to be turned into 'a vast, mighty and flexible instrument capable of offering instant and overwhelming resistance to any who may dream of attacking our heritage'.[79]

Unsurprisingly, the *Daily Herald* had favoured closer relations with the Soviets after Munich, but now came round to advocating a formal military alliance with France and Russia, as well as the closest cooperation with the USA.[80] The *News Chronicle* felt that strategically important smaller power such as Holland, Romania and Yugoslavia should be targeted first.[81] Even traditionally pro-appeasement papers like *The Times* felt that Prague had effectively killed this policy and now urged drawing closer to other powers in a large anti-Fascist coalition.[82]

Examples abound of the general public writing to newspapers and MPs in favour of alliances during the Chamberlain period. The *Anschluss* provided an initial spur for such letters, many of which demanded that Britain now draw closer to the Soviets or the USA. Others were more creative in the measures they suggested. F.W. Balch of Stockton wrote to Harold Macmillan on 22 March 1938, advocating not only guarantees to Poland and Romania, but also that 'Roosevelt should be asked to take temporary charge of all our interests in the Pacific'. Moreover, he thought that a late effort should be made to rebuild the Stresa Front through inducements to Mussolini: 'We should offer Italy ... if she comes in on our side ... £100 millions in cash ... and further French territories on the Moroccan coast.'[83] Events in Prague one year later produced another flurry of similar letters on foreign policy issues. On 20 March 1939, 'W.E.M.' of East London told the *Daily Telegraph* that now 'surely the time has come for a close military alliance between all the Western democratic countries ... A combination of Sweden, Denmark, Norway, Holland, Belgium, France and Great Britain would be a formidable obstacle to tackle'.[84]

Gallup Poll data clearly indicates where public opinion now stood. Asked in April 1939, 'Are you in favour of a military alliance between Great Britain, France and Russia?', a colossal 87 per cent responded in the affirmative, with only 7 per cent against.[85] These figures represent the highest levels of approval for any suggested alternative to appeasement in the years before war – more even than support for the League of Nations a year or two earlier.[86] Indeed, given these figures, alliances were surely *the* policy Britain now demanded.

*   *   *

Mainstream politics followed suit. In partial response to this groundswell of demand, the government effectively abandoned the concessionary dimension of appeasement after events in Prague, in favour of a much more deterrence-based strategy. Chamberlain announced the Polish Guarantee on 31 March and then talked of a 'new epoch in the course of our foreign policy'.[87] Many anti-appeasers felt that the Munich Agreement had been a wake-up call for Britain to marshal its defences in close accord with others, the cold-shouldering of Russia during the crisis being particularly criticised in both houses during the October 1938 debates.[88]

Approval for the government's tougher line in the spring of 1939 was, therefore, widespread and wholehearted. While still couching their words in collective security terminology, Labour and the Liberals now came over to the Grand Alliance strategy. On 3 April 1939, Greenwood welcomed efforts 'in establishing a formidable and insurmountable barrier against future aggression ... a new chapter which I entitle "Mutual Aid"'. In this front, 'the military value of the USSR ... might well prove to be the final, decisive and smashing factor on the side of keeping the peace in the world'.[89] Sinclair, stated that 'we shall, of course, support the policy ... of gathering together the friends of peace and order ... as the only way of stopping war'. He went on to express the 'supreme importance' of Russia to this new bloc and hoped the government would try 'to rally Romania, Turkey and other Balkan powers to the common cause'.[90] In the House of Lords, Labour peer Lord Snell welcomed the government's new policy but bemoaned the lack of consideration so far given to Russia: 'The key to this situation seems to us to be an Anglo-French-Soviet declaration of peace and intention to resist aggression.'[91] Similarly, Lord Lothian backed the Grand Alliance as his favoured policy, to which, he felt, the inclusion of Russia 'may be absolutely vital'.[92]

Loud criticism of the government soon resurfaced, therefore, over its perceived reluctance to include Russia in the new Peace Front, especially when guarantees were given to Greece and Romania in April. The Soviets had again approached Britain, this time with the suggestion of a six-power-conference, including France, Poland, Turkey and Romania, as early as 18 March 1939 and tentative talks duly began. It was not until 24 May, however, shortly after the Anglo-Turkish agreement was announced, that the Cabinet sanctioned negotiations for a

full blown Anglo-Soviet pact. Attlee underlined his party's conversion
to alliances, 'the best hope of preventing war' now being, in his view,
'a firm union between Britain, France and the USSR as the nucleus of
a World Alliance against aggression'. He also derided Chamberlain's
progress so far as 'dilatory and fumbling', blaming Tory mistrust of
Communism as the main sticking point.[93] This attack was echoed in
the Lords, where Liberal peer Lord Davies accused the government of
being 'obsessed with the notion that there is a "Bolshie" behind every
bush', and of being 'frightened to death of Communism'.[94] Churchill,
likewise, asserted that the new Peace Front could function 'only with
the effective support of a friendly Soviet Russia'.[95]

William Strang from the Foreign Office was duly dispatched to
Moscow in June to advance discussions further. The opposition parties
were by now furious, believing that Chamberlain's new policy needed
a rapid change of pace. In July 1939, Sinclair questioned the wisdom
of sending such a relatively obscure figure to Russia while Halifax
remained at home.[96] Anthony Eden, meanwhile, asserted that 'no other
policy' than an Anglo-Russian alliance stood any chance of averting
war.[97] His wishes were never to be fulfilled.

Consideration of the Alternative

As Chamberlain eventually adopted a policy of alliances at the expense
of appeasement – or at least the 'classic' appeasement of wide-scale
concessions to the Fascist powers – the links between the two strategies need not be considered here. It is clear that the Prime Minister
came to see blocs and pacts as the next best option available to him.
The following section will, therefore, ask why Chamberlain resisted
calls for alliances so vehemently until after the Prague Coup and
always had serious doubts about closer relations with France, America
and Russia throughout his premiership. In short, when did alliances
become viable for the government and why were some seen as realistic
when others were not?

The widespread hostility to alliances during the mid-1930s was
shared by the National Government. In the sort of statement that
was common at this time, Viscount Cranborne, Under-Secretary for

Foreign Affairs, claimed in February 1936 that a policy of alliances would not 'save us'. He continued: 'Already that has brought us to the greatest catastrophe in the history of the world.'[98] As has been shown, however, important government figures favoured regional pacts as a halfway house between collective security and alliances during much of 1936. Others considered a revival of the Stresa Front to be the more attractive policy. Eric Phipps, then Ambassador in Berlin, told Eden at the start of the year that it was 'essential to reform the Stresa Front'.[99] Sir Thomas Inskip, Minister for the Coordination of Defence, echoed these views in Cabinet during November,[100] while Vansittart remained the driving force for this policy within the Foreign Office.[101] Samuel Hoare, moreover, claimed in his memoirs that the infamous Hoare-Laval plan of December 1935 was just one part of a long-term British strategy to maintain and, later, revive Stresa.[102] Indeed, a *rapprochement* with Italy became an important part of Chamberlain's appeasement policy in 1937 and early 1938.

The conclusions of an important memorandum sent to the Cabinet by the Chiefs of Staff in December 1937 shed more light on the issue of alliances in general, and the revival of Stresa in particular. It suggests that, as time went on, the idea of winning Italy back to the Anglo-French sphere declined considerably as relations between the three Fascist powers became entrenched:

> We cannot foresee the time when our defence forces will be strong enough to safeguard our territory, trade and vital interests against Germany, Italy and Japan simultaneously. We cannot therefore, exaggerate the importance, from the point of view of Imperial defence, of any political or international action that can be taken to reduce the numbers of our potential enemies and to gain the support of potential allies. Of course, it would be possible to make an effort to detach one of the three Powers from the other two and it might even succeed. This, however, could only be done at the cost of concessions which would involve humiliations and disadvantages to this country by destroying the confidence of other nations. No-one would suppose, therefore, that we should try and bribe one of the three nations to leave the other two.[103]

The March 1938 *Anschluss* provided another serious blow to hopes of reviving the Front. Chamberlain, however, never ruled it out as a possible, if unlikely, part of his wider strategy.[104] As late as July 1939, figures from the Southern section of the Foreign Office considered attempting to win Italy over to a tripartite pact with Britain and France through extensive colonial inducements.[105]

Anglo-French relations are central to this chapter, as the failure to form a bold and united front with Britain's closest neighbour on the continent before the war is often attributed to Chamberlain. An ingrained mistrust of the French and a perception of Gallic weakness and instability all weighed heavily on the government during this period. Despite the usual lip-service paid in public statements to Anglo-French unity – Eden and Halifax regularly spoke about keeping in step with France – relations were normally quite poor.[106] Adamthwaite describes Anglo-French diplomacy as characterised by 'bickering and backbiting' during these years.[107] Despite a vague understanding that Britain would fight to protect France in any coming war – as Director of Military Operations, General Sir Henry Pownall put it, 'if France crumbles we fall' – no formal military alliance existed between the two powers until early 1939.[108]

Mutual suspicion had clouded relations for years. Disagreements over strategy during the Great War carried on into the Versailles settlement and were exacerbated by Imperial rivalries through much of the 1920s.[109] The effects of the Great Depression and subsequent French political instability led to growing discord, which came to the surface in 1935 over Abyssinia and the Anglo-German Naval agreement, widely perceived in France as undermining the Stresa Front. Glyn Stone points out that there were considerable tensions over coordinating policy with regard to the Spanish Civil War.[110]

Personal rancour increased during the Popular Front era, with the Tory-dominated National Government having to deal with a wide range of unpopular left-wing counterparts. Figures such as Joseph Paul-Boncour and Georges Bonnet, both French Foreign Ministers during this period, were widely disliked by most of Chamberlain's Cabinet, many of whom held latent anti-French prejudices.[111] Indeed, many British politicians felt that France was as much to blame for the state of Europe in the 1930s as Hitler, wedded as the former was to maintaining the Versailles *status quo* and ardently opposing a *rapprochement* with Germany.[112] Yet late as 1 November 1938, Halifax confided to Phipps, now Ambassador in Paris, that he thought the 'defeatist' French might actually renege on Britain and sign a non-aggression pact with Germany.[113] The feeling was mutual. Edouard Daladier, French Prime Minister for much of Chamberlain's premiership, described Chamberlain as a 'desiccated stick', Eden as a 'young idiot', the King as 'a moron', and England in general as 'feeble and senile'.[114]

Long-term political and economic chaos in France gave Chamberlain's government little confidence in its closest neighbour. It is a popular truism that there was no French government in place at the time of the *Anschluss* and some have even seen France as being on the verge of civil war in the late 1930s, with industrial turmoil and social tensions rife.[115] When a member of the French government asked Phipps to do what he could to organise talks between Ministers in the wake of the *Anschluss*, he replied testily that 'such meetings seemed to me quite useless until the days of transitory French governments were over; when a strong and durable government appeared here they would, on the other hand, be very useful'.[116]

Although the British hoped that France could hold out in any future war, the military picture was perceived to be equally bleak.[117] Defeatism was thought to be rife in the upper ranks of the French army, the Generals of which commanded a force suited only to a defensive conflict, hidden behind the outdated and crumbling Maginot Line. The Cabinet gloomily pondered what effective aid France could offer in a war to save Czechoslovakia during the summer of 1938, and, after Munich, Halifax urged the Foreign Office to harass their Gallic counterparts to put their military house in order.[118] Given all this, then, perhaps the biggest fear for the government, which militated against a formal alliance until so late in the day, was that a weak France could draw Britain into a war it was not prepared for, by its Soviet agreement or pledge to assist Czechoslovakia in case of attack. In its *Review of Imperial Defence* on 22 February 1937, the Chiefs of Staff ominously warned: 'If France becomes involved by a decision for which we should have no part, we, owing to our geographical and strategic position, are in danger of being drawn into a general European war.'[119]

*   *   *

Described by a close colleague as 'temperamentally anti-American', Chamberlain made a series of unfortunate statements about the USA which have been used by historians to characterise the nature of Anglo-American relations in the mid- to late 1930s.[120] Perhaps the most telling of these came in October 1934 when he claimed that the 'real trouble with Yanks' was that they 'never can deliver the goods'.[121] Always a realist, Chamberlain, like many of his fellow countrymen, believed that America, struggling to set its affairs in order in the wake of the Wall Street Crash, its public wedded to isolation and its Congress committed to successive Neutrality Acts, would never be able to offer substantial assistance in the search for a lasting peace. As with the French, Anglo-American relations were bedevilled by long-term tensions and personal rancour. Indeed, it has been argued that the two nations 'acted more like selfish, suspicious rivals' than partners at this time, 'materially reduc[ing] their effectiveness in confronting the challenge of Hitler in Europe – to say nothing of the Japanese threat in the Pacific'.[122] Many Britons resented that America had remained aloof from the League of Nations and yet continued to posture grandly during the Manchurian crisis in the early 1930s. The World Economic Conference in 1933 had been effectively destroyed by Roosevelt, when he refused to yield on the issue of fixed currencies. During the Chamberlain premiership, a personal frostiness between the two leaders, distrustful of one another's economic policies – the New Deal sat as uneasily with the Prime Minister as Imperial Preference did with the President – was matched by a wider suspicion between the two administrations in general.[123] David Reynolds even characterises the Anglo-American relationship as one of 'competitive cooperation' at this time, with economic rivalries as important to the respective administrations as the bigger question of how best to maintain peace.[124] Roosevelt's personal emissary, Harry Hopkins, thought the problem was a wider one of national and historical tensions, once telling a meeting of British MPs that 'there always has been and always will be' about a quarter of Americans who disliked Britain.[125]

Troubles in the Far East during the summer of 1936 set the tone for relations over the coming years. Despite it being the theatre in which America was most willing to act in partnership with Britain and where it had most direct interests to protect, Roger Makins of the Western Department of the Foreign Office confirmed that Roosevelt was 'unwilling to enter even into the shadow of a commitment' in this region.[126] Speaking in New York later that year, Cordell Hull echoed Jefferson's historic claim that American foreign policy rested upon the fundamental tenets of 'peace, commerce, and honest friendship with all nations, entangling alliances with none'.[127]

Despite the obvious signals that an Anglo-Franco-American pact was not on Washington's agenda, Chamberlain appealed to America for help in averting war shortly before assuming the premiership. Encouraged by figures such as Vansittart, who argued that 'we must act and state our case in such a way as to retain American sympathy at all times', Chamberlain deputed Orme Sargent to write to Roosevelt in March 1937.[128] In a lengthy memorandum, Sargent suggested that 'the greatest single contribution' America could make to world peace was to amend its existing neutrality legislation. He also called for the USA to help in any way it could to stabilise the Far East.[129] The response was lukewarm. Over six weeks passed before Hull and the Under-Secretary of State, Sumner Welles, even sent a reply. When they did so, they insisted that the Neutrality Acts did not encourage Fascist aggression and promised help on the Orient only 'within the limits of our general policy'.[130]

Chamberlain assumed the premiership, therefore, with little hope of concrete American assistance. Roosevelt's famous 'Quarantine Speech' in October 1937 – which later prompted Chamberlain to respond acidly, 'it is always best and safest to count on nothing from the Americans except words' – was followed just weeks later by virtually no response to the attack on the USS *Panay* by Japanese gunboats on the Yangtze.[131] Chamberlain complained at this time to Lord Tweedsmuir, the Canadian Governor General and a close friend of Roosevelt, that 'I have gone out of my way to encourage those sections of American opinion that seem to have welcomed the President's Chicago speech', but all to no avail. 'Nevertheless', he continued, 'I am very conscious of the differences that have still to be overcome by the President before it can be said that he has his people behind him.'[132] Despite some Foreign Office figures advocating renewed efforts to secure American help in the Far East, a memorandum from Ronald Lindsay, British Ambassador in Washington, exasperated government officials still further.[133] It warned that Cordell Hull wanted British Ministers to be careful about the language they used when talking in the press about Anglo-American cooperation, lest it have a misleading effect on public opinion there: 'As Mr Hull put it, "you may talk about parallel or similar action, or about constant or even close collaboration" but never use the word "joint" '.[134]

The Roosevelt Peace Initiative of 12 January 1938 has been presented by some critics of appeasement as the President's great effort to secure an Anglo-American partnership. Its collapse was one of the causes of Eden's resignation in February and it has been labelled as one of the missed opportunities to avert war. Unsurprisingly, much has been written, not all of it accurate though, about this secret proposal made for a peace conference to be held in Washington in early 1938. It is important to note that Chamberlain never actually rejected the plan outright as is often claimed. More accurately, he greeted the proposal with limited enthusiasm – albeit described by Welles as 'a douche of cold water' – and asked that it be postponed for a period of time because the majority of the Cabinet felt it was too woolly and vague and would cut across their own talks with the Dictators.[135] Moreover, it might even provoke a 'Mad Dog' act from Germany or Japan, lashing out against a perceived hostile front. Chamberlain was said to have penned: 'Eden's policy to line up the USA, Great Britain and France: Result war' on his notepad during a Foreign Policy Committee meeting at this time.[136] Nevertheless, the Prime Minister actually gave the proposal his backing on 21 January and then again on 12 February, but Roosevelt was away from the White House for most of this month and thereafter announced the scheme's indefinite postponement. There would have been little to stop the President going ahead without Chamberlain's blessing had he been determined to do so.

The allegation that this represented a rejection of the last chance to line up Britain and America in a firm alliance against Hitler is similarly flawed. The initiative was for the USA to host the conference, rather than to contribute actively to discussions, as Roosevelt himself spelt out at the time.[137] Only the states earmarked to attend would make any concrete decisions and these included powers such as Sweden and Switzerland, hardly likely to have been able to enforce any grand agreement on Germany, Italy or Japan. Moreover, the conference would have been designed for peace and not for war. Issues scheduled for discussion included arms limitation, the distribution of raw materials and other economic measures – that is, initiatives akin to Chamberlain's own appeasement and not of some great stand against Dictators. After all, the President said that he hoped the plan would run in parallel with Chamberlain's efforts.[138] Roosevelt's later warm reception of the Munich Agreement – indicated by his famous 'Good Man' cable to the Prime Minister – would suggest that he was himself more of a dove than a hawk. Rock even argues that he might have been relieved that his initiative failed, as this let him 'off the hook' from a hastily prepared and, in truth, rather vague proposal.[139] The results of such a conference, had it gone ahead, are also very uncertain. It seems unlikely that a plan of this kind would have met with Hitler's approval, or that it would have averted the *Anschluss* a short while later. Even Eden later admitted that it was unlikely anything concrete would have come from the scheme in the short term, but felt the general effects on Anglo-American relations made it worthwhile pursuing.[140]

Shortly after the Peace Initiative approach, Chamberlain privately outlined his wider thoughts on such issues. Despite optimistic flourishes, the Prime Minister's deep frustration is apparent:

> I am just now in closer relations with the American government than has been the case within my recollection. I have made more than one attempt, while I have been Prime Minister, to draw them even closer still and have had more than one disappointment ... The trouble is that public opinion in a good part of the States still believes it possible for America to stand outside

Europe and watch it disintegrate ... In spite of my disappoint-
ment, I intend to keep on doing everything I can to promote
Anglo-American understanding and cooperation. Not because
I want or expect America to pull our chestnuts out of the fire
for us; in any cooperation we shall always do our part, and perhaps more than our share. But I believe that Americans and the
British want the same fundamental things in the world.[141]

The next few lines are even more significant. They explain not only
why Chamberlain was prepared to give Roosevelt's plan his blessing,
despite believing it too vague, but why he would maintain contact
with the Americans throughout his premiership, regardless of his continued disappointments. The tone is almost Churchillian:

The United States and United Kingdom in combination represent a force so overwhelming that the mere hint of the possibility
of its use is sufficient to make the most powerful of Dictators
pause ... Cooperation between our two countries is the greatest
instrument in the world for the preservation of peace.[142]

Thereafter, the government's alarm at the deteriorating international
situation, which demanded closer American involvement, meant that
Chamberlain continued to keep the USA in his thoughts. This was
despite his personal doubts about concrete assistance from America,
more often than not later confirmed. The Anglo-German Agreement
signed at Munich was, according to Lord Home, Chamberlain's one
time Parliamentary Private Secretary, designed with America in mind.
If Hitler kept his word, all would be well and good; if he broke it, then
world opinion, particularly in the USA, would see how untrustworthy
the *Führer* really was – and where the blame lay for war.[143] But hopes
of increased cooperation were dashed soon after Munich, when former
President Herbert Hoover made a well-publicised speech, once more
singing the praises of isolation. This was attended by Roosevelt and
well received.[144]

The January 1939 war scare, when British intelligence incorrectly
warned of an imminent German invasion of the Low Countries, again

provoked panic in the Foreign Policy Committee and once more seemed to necessitate new contacts with America. Notwithstanding his ongoing reservations, Chamberlain agreed to share intelligence with the USA and sound out Roosevelt about making a public declaration on the subject.[145] Government ministers hoped that this sudden jolt, following on from the Prague Coup in March, would encourage a more positive response from America, with efforts to move closer to the Western democracies. Roosevelt was known to be greatly disturbed by *Kristallnacht* in November 1938, after all. Again, however, Chamberlain's scepticism seems well founded. A paper forwarded to the Foreign Policy Committee by Halifax on 20 April 1939 indicated that, should war break out, Roosevelt had offered little more to Britain and France than 'the most beneficial possible neutrality'.[146]

* * *

Government consideration of the Grand Alliance as an alternative to appeasement was most acute after the *Anschluss* and Churchill's subsequent rallying cry. Hitherto, it had only been discussed seriously prior to the Nyon Conference in September 1937. Here, Orme Sargent suggested 'the formation of a bloc of states in Europe which would be sufficiently powerful to deter Germany from taking the offensive', but felt it would have little effect unless Germany could be isolated from Italy and Japan.[147] Others feared it would only provoke conflict by splitting Europe into ideologically hostile camps, especially if the Soviets were included on one side against the Fascists on the other. As Cadogan noted, 'I hate the French-British-Russian party – it does exactly what we don't want – emphasises split in Europe'.[148]

Events in Austria and the subsequent Russian offer to Britain for a conference aimed at pooling security roused the government to readdress the Grand Alliance. While there is some evidence from Eden's memoirs that Chamberlain had been considering 'the encirclement of Germany and a possible alliance with Russia' in late January 1938, 'the mood did not last'.[149] It was not until German troops marched across the borders that it gripped the Prime Minister again. As Cadogan noted, 'Went to PM's room where I found H[alifax]. We had a short discussion: They rather on the line of Winston's Grand Alliance. I don't know about that'.[150] Cadogan's uncertainty about such a venture was exacerbated only a few days later when the first Soviet offer of talks came in. This, he felt, would only 'aggravate the tendency to divide Europe into two opposed groups of nations' – 1914 all over again.[151]

A letter from Chamberlain to his sister on 20 March 1938 illustrates his concerns:

> As a matter of fact the plan of the 'Grand Alliance' as Winston calls it had occurred to me long before he mentioned it. I was thinking about it all last weekend. I talked about it to Halifax and we submitted it to the Chiefs of Staff and the Foreign Office experts. It is a very attractive idea; indeed there is almost everything to be said for it until you come to examine its practicability. From that moment its attraction vanishes. You only have to look at the map to see that nothing that France or we could do could possibly save Czechoslovakia from being overrun by the Germans.[152]

Halifax's paper for the Foreign Policy Committee a few days earlier is similarly illuminating on why appeasement was thought to be preferable:

> The Grand Alliance ... is an attractive proposal, and there is a good deal that might be said both for and against it: but there is one decisive objection against it for our present purposes: In order to achieve it, it would be necessary to draw up a formal instrument in Treaty form, and this would be a long and complicated matter ... [which] would afford both a provocation and an opportunity to Germany to dispose of Czechoslovakia before the Grand Alliance had been organised ... It may be argued that in order to prevent such developments the two great democracies must rally their forces and make a stand at an early date before the position deteriorates still further ... I would say that we should not be justified in taking whatever risk there might be in trying to deter Germany from making war on Czechoslovakia.[153]

The geo-military factors Chamberlain alluded to in his letter of
20 March were echoed in military circles a day later. The Committee
of Imperial Defence produced a paper assessing the reliability of some
of the suggested constituent members of a pact. It asserted that 'the
alliance with Yugoslavia, Romania, Hungary, Turkey and Greece
would be of limited assistance to Great Britain and France, and they
might ultimately constitute an additional embarrassing commitment'.
It went on: 'Our association with allies, many of whom are of doubtful
military value against Germany, might precipitate a definite military
alliance between Germany, Italy and Japan.'[154] Chamberlain voiced
similar concerns in the Commons a few days later:

> The value of such alliances ... as a deterrent to possible aggression,
> must obviously depend upon their military efficiency, upon the
> numbers and equipment of the forces that can be mobilised, on
> their distribution in relation to the arena in which they might have
> to be employed and on the amount of preparation and coordination
> of plans which it might be possible to achieve beforehand.[155]

* * *

The perceived success of appeasement in averting war at Munich led
to a temporary abatement in government consideration of alliances as
an alternative policy. Appeasement was generally the order of the day
until the war scare in January 1939, which prompted immediate consideration of an Anglo-French alliance with the Low Countries.[156] The
Prague Coup, however, brought a Russian alliance on to the table for
serious consideration as never before. Frequently presented by appeasement critics as one of the best opportunities to deter Hitler from war,
the failed Anglo-Soviet negotiations of the summer of 1939 are central
to this discussion. As a power that affected Britain's strategic position
in both Europe and Asia, and, therefore, influenced relations with
Germany, Italy *and* Japan in a way that France or the USA did not,
the Soviet Union could not be ignored by the British government.
The Russian offer of a six-power conference in the wake of Prague (the

second such approach in a year) gave rise to widespread demands for an alliance from many pro-Soviet elements in Britain.

Anglo-Soviet relations had been characterised by over two decades of ignorance and mutual suspicion. Diplomatic contacts between the two countries were suspended for long periods. For the majority of the interwar years, Russia was seen as by far the biggest threat to Britain and world peace, Communism as the dark spectre on the horizon – especially loathed by Tories and the Tory-dominated governments of the 1930s. Indeed, 'Better Hitler than Stalin' was a prevailing sentiment among many Britons for most of this decade. Britain had, of course, fought against the victorious Bolshevik armies during the Russian Civil War in the early 1920s and the resulting acrimony lasted well into the following decade. As late as 1937, the Labour Party expelled the Socialist League from its Annual Conference as a result of that group calling for an alliance with Russia. Even Churchill, one of the foremost advocates of such a pact during 1938 and 1939, had made fiercely anti-Soviet speeches as late as 1936. Hugh Dalton talked of Britain's 'mad fixation about Russia', holding that many politicians, especially on the Right, would rather lose a war without Soviet assistance than win one with it.[157]

In February 1936, Eden warned his colleagues of the dangers of 'hugging the bear too closely' and claimed that many Germans were particularly apprehensive about an Anglo-Soviet *rapprochement* presenting them with a strategic dilemma on two fronts and fuelling Hitler's claims of anti-Fascist encirclement.[158] Fear of provoking Germany, and particularly Hitler, by closer union with the great ideological enemy of Nazism was a recurring factor in British calculations. 'Rab' Butler, Under-Secretary of State in the Foreign Office from 1938 to 1940, claimed during the negotiations that an Anglo-Soviet pact would have 'a bad psychological effect on Hitler'.[159] During the Commons debates that followed the Munich settlement, Inskip warned those Labour MPs bemoaning the lack of Russian involvement that they were pursuing 'the policy of the encirclement of Germany and [that] is one which offers no remedy for the disease'.[160] Chamberlain and Simon both denied that such a strategy existed when the Polish Guarantee was announced in March 1939.[161]

The great fear of British Ministers at this time was that alliances would lead to hostile blocs throughout the world akin to the pre-1914 era. Might not an alliance with Communist Russia provoke Franco's Spain to move into the Axis camp, or cement relations within the Anti-Comintern Pact? A Foreign Office paper from March 1939 warned of such risks: 'The conclusion of any consultative pact with Russia would no doubt merely encourage those powerful circles in Japan which are pressing the Japanese government to agree to German and Italian proposals for an alliance.'[162]

The perception of limited Soviet military capability played an important role in British considerations. While Churchill, with the benefit of hindsight, later claimed that pre-war calculations of Soviet weakness were excessively pessimistic, it is clear that Russia in the late 1930s was far from the colossal Superpower that emerged during the Cold War when Churchill was writing.[163] The effects of Stalin's cull of the officer class of the Red Army during the summer of 1937 (later reckoned by Hoare to be 3 out of 5 Marshals, 13 out of 15 Army Commanders, 30 out of 58 Corps Commanders and 110 out of 195 Divisional Commanders killed or imprisoned) were consciously noted in Britain.[164] Lord Chilston, British Ambassador in Moscow, informed the Foreign Office that the main effect would be to render the surviving officers devoid of any initiative. Many of these were now joined by new, inexperienced colleagues, described by his Military Attaché as little more than 'party dogs'.[165] At the end of the year, the Ambassador in Rome, Lord Perth, recorded that his Polish counterpart in Moscow believed the Red Army to be in such a state of chaos that 'he doubted if it would be capable of any except purely defensive operations for a period of three to four years'.[166]

Gloomy estimates such as these dominated British perceptions of the Red Army for most of Chamberlain's premiership and militated against alliance talks until May 1939, when the Chiefs of Staff finally recommended such an approach.[167] Lamentable Soviet infrastructure – especially poor road and rail networks – would also have been 'seriously inhibiting' to effective assistance for the Czechs at the time of Munich. As a result, many believe that Stalin would never have authorised Russia's inclusion in any war during the autumn of 1938, despite the agreement with France to defend Czechoslovakia in case of attack.[168] The French government shared many of these concerns about Soviet capabilities and intent.[169]

All these various fears played on Chamberlain's mind in the weeks before he sanctioned alliance talks. On 26 March 1939, he wrote of his 'profound mistrust of Russia' and of having 'no belief whatever in her ability to maintain an effective offensive, even if she wanted to'.[170] He spoke in Cabinet on 5 April of his scorn for the Left's 'pathetic belief that Russia is the key to our salvation',[171] and privately lamented the 'enormous irritative power' conversations with the Soviets had on friend and foe alike.[172] Given these personal doubts, then, it was only the enthusiasm of many of his senior colleagues and Foreign Office personnel, combined with growing pressure throughout the country, which led him seriously to consider the Soviet option.[173] When the Chiefs of Staff came round to supporting an Anglo-Soviet alliance on 16 May, and the majority of the Cabinet followed suit, the Prime Minister bowed to pressure, and conversations for a 'full-blown guarantee of mutual assistance' began later that month.[174]

Foreign Policy Committee papers from March and April 1939 illustrate an important factor in understanding why the talks ultimately failed. It was widely believed by senior government figures that adding Russia to the front currently being constructed – of Britain, France, Poland, Romania and Greece – would only lead to its eventual collapse and drive away other potential allies who might otherwise join them. Chamberlain's comments on 27 March are telling:

> We had received communications both from Poland and Romania that any public association of Russia with the scheme would greatly diminish and weaken the authority of the common front. Similar intimations had been received from Finland, Yugoslavia, Italy, Spain and Portugal.[175]

The Prime Minister pointed out that Poland also offered the opportunity to force Germany into a war on two fronts, whilst avoiding the provocative ideological effects on enemies and disruptive influence on friends that Russia alone would bring. Hence, Chamberlain felt that one option might be to approach the Soviets in secret so as not to

alienate other members of the front.[176] Only a few of his more junior colleagues objected to this proposal, while Halifax wholeheartedly
supported the strategy of keeping Russia subordinate to its smaller
neighbour in British strategic planning: 'If we had to make a choice
between Poland and Soviet Russia, it seemed clear that Poland would
give the greater value.'[177]

Poland, which was seen as the most senior of the Eastern European
powers, and to whom a guarantee had already been given, thus became
central to government planning during the Peace Front negotiations.
That country had endured hundreds of years of Russian occupation
during its history and greatly despised its larger neighbour. Foreign
Minister Jozef Beck's early-stated opposition to allowing Soviet troops
to cross Polish territory in the event of war with Germany – for fear
they would remain there at the end of the conflict – hindered alliance
talks throughout March and April and became one of the main stumbling blocks to an agreement by June and July.

A delicate balancing act was, therefore, needed during the Anglo-
Soviet negotiations and this was undermined only by the frosty nature
of relations between the two delegations throughout that spring and
summer. As early as 12 April 1939, Halifax announced in the Lords
that there were 'great difficulties' surrounding the early talks, 'and
those difficulties most certainly are not of *our* making'.[178] This sort
of sniping set the tone for conversations. Above and beyond such well
known factors as the aggressive tough-talking which characterised
Soviet diplomacy when Molotov succeeded Litvinov as Soviet Foreign
Minister in May, or the painfully slow ship journey transporting the
British military experts to meet their Russian counterparts in August,
it was clear that mutual suspicion abounded.[179] Each side believed the
other to be in no hurry to sign a deal. From the British point of view,
repeated Soviet intransigence on specific issues, as well as the raising
of new demands when others had just been met, were major points
of antagonism. They merely convinced Chamberlain that his earlier
suspicions were correct and that a deal was unrealistic.

Discussions in May were dogged by Soviet insistence on a No
Separate Peace Clause, designed to stop Britain or France agreeing its
own terms with Germany in any war and leaving Russia to carry on

the struggle alone. The British delegation eventually conceded this point and agreed to insert such a caveat into the pact, but was greeted in return with a blank refusal to have a League of Nations framework erected in support of the deal – a move Chamberlain was particularly keen on in view of world opinion.[180] In June, the issue of Polish consent for Soviet troops to cross its borders reared its head and then arguments over definitions of 'Indirect Aggression', one trigger for any pact to be activated, muddied waters still further. It was feared in Britain and Poland alike that Russia might annex certain territories itself under some fabricated minor disturbance. Britain eventually agreed to the Soviet definition of 'Indirect Aggression' but the new blueprint was again rejected by them.[181] Such wrangles prompted Cadogan's complaint: 'The Russians are impossible. We give them all they want, with both hands, and they merely slap them.'[182]

Later that month, Molotov demanded that the names of all the smaller states which would be guaranteed under any pact should be published for all to see. These provisionally included Poland, Romania, Turkey, Greece, Belgium, Finland, Latvia and Estonia. The British government was much less keen on this proposal – many of these states feared that being publicly linked with Russia might just provoke a German attack – but it conceded the point once more in order to advance discussions.[183] But the Soviets responded by calling for the removal of all other powers from the arrangements and a return to a more straightforward tripartite agreement with Britain and France. On 4 July, Chamberlain again conceded to Molotov's demands and reluctantly accepted this more simple formula. Then, just as it seemed that a deal was to be concluded, the Russians countered with more new requirements for detailed military conversations to commence before the general political agreement was finalised.[184] Again this was reluctantly conceded by Britain, but the frosty and complicated staff talks in early August only delayed matters further and led Chamberlain to call off discussions later that month.

The inconsistencies, uncertainties, opportunism and delays which characterised Russian diplomacy during the alliance talks seemed, to the government, to epitomise all that they believed about Russia. In fairness, this was no doubt also felt about Britain on the Soviet side. Both parties only wanted an alliance with the other on their own terms, but the Soviets were in the much stronger bargaining position and could afford to play for time. Stalin and Molotov knew, not only that the British political Left and general public were pressing the government to make a quick deal, but that Germany had been waiting in the wings since May to open its own talks. Yet, there was a general assumption in Britain that a Nazi-Soviet Pact was extremely unlikely. Russia could, therefore, afford to play it tough in conversations with Britain and France, periodically raising the stakes to get the best possible agreement. By contrast, Chamberlain's government felt that it could, at best, secure a pact that had a multitude of drawbacks and which would only undermine the existing Peace Front, and, at worst, lead to its tacit acquiescence in Soviet troops marching into an ally's territory. Large regions of Eastern Europe and the Baltic might follow. The negotiations duly collapsed in mid-August and the Nazi-Soviet Pact was concluded a few days later.

*　*　*

Opposition to alliances in Britain before the Prague Coup was widespread and underpinned Chamberlain's cautious strategy. Even Churchill, the most ardent advocate of the Grand Alliance, seemed genuinely convinced in the early 1930s that the League was a better alternative, and only later began to use its rhetoric as a cover for a policy of pacts and blocs. Despite its later conversion to the cause, the Labour Party was officially opposed to all alliances for the vast majority of the interwar period. Unsurprisingly, given its ideological distaste for Fascist Italy and that country's attack upon the authority of the League in Abyssinia, Labour strongly opposed the notion of reviving the Stresa Front, in particular, during 1936 and 1937. The Liberals were of a similar mind, officially supporting Geneva ahead of a return to alliances, but were slightly less ardent in their opposition to the latter, as evidenced by their regular statements about the importance of renewed Anglo-American relations.

Conversely, it was the Tories who tended to be amongst the most committed opponents of the Left's drive to rehabilitate Anglo-Soviet relations. This move was described as 'producing a red rag to a bull' by John Sandeman Allen in the wake of the Munich Agreement.[185] Furthermore, it was from Conservative ranks that most concern was voiced when alliance talks with the Soviets began in the last months before war, although the vast majority did support Chamberlain's new direction after Prague. The Earl of Mansfield questioned the moral and military character of Russia in a speech in the Lords in April 1939 and pointed out that Soviet inclusion in any bloc would greatly disturb both Poland and Romania, as well as pushing Spain and Hungary closer to the Dictators.[186]

Political prejudice thus played as important a role in the opposition to certain alliances as it did in generating support for others. Leo Amery backed a revival of the Stresa Front and yet hoped Britain would keep Russia 'out of the picture' in the wake of the Rhineland affair.[187] Writing to Chamberlain in November 1937, he described the Anglo-Franco-Russian combination as 'for us, at any rate, the far most dangerous conceivable'.[188] A day after the Nazi-Soviet Pact was concluded, he attacked Soviet duplicity in a letter to Lloyd George: 'Doesn't it look rather as if Stalin, from the first, was only concerned with cheap territorial expansion, and simply played off one side against the other in order to see which would give him what he wanted?'[189]

Many members of the smaller political parties were also opposed to alliances. Socialist MP Rhys Davies was scathing of the perceived weakening of Labour on this issue after Munich. In an article for the *Glasgow Forward* from November 1938, he questioned the wisdom of their continued support for closer relations with the Soviets: 'When she is engaged in a major war, she is likely to break up from within. If Russia is so powerful, why does she not give a helping hand to the poor Chinese, who are being slaughtered right and left by Japanese militarism?'[190]

Groups such as the League of Nations Union tended to reject alliances until after the Prague Coup, for obvious reasons. Gilbert Murray was convinced that the USA in particular could never be relied upon as a committed ally. To an LNU colleague in April 1938, he claimed that Roosevelt had warned a mutual friend that pressing his country to act in conjunction with Britain in the Far East 'was just the way to make the Americans say no'.[191] It appears that this view was popular in Britain at the time. Hugh Dalton claimed that Chamberlain himself told him something very similar: 'The surest way, said the Prime Minister, to lose the Americans is to run after them too hard.'[192] Was the best way to win American sympathy in the long term to leave it alone in the short? This was certainly the opinion of many political figures.

The national press was overwhelmingly hostile to alliances as an alternative to appeasement for most of the late 1930s, even those papers that did not back Chamberlain's strategy. The pro-isolation *Daily Express* was particularly vehement in this respect, stating that the Munich Agreement had killed 'once and for all the old plan of putting a ring round Germany, of encircling her with hostile states'. It went on: 'That plan was always dangerous, always wicked. It sought to perpetuate in Europe a fixed antagonism between one state and a group of other states.'[193] The press turned almost universally pro-alliance, however, after the Prague Coup. This was clearly a media watershed as well as a political one.

While Gallup Poll data has already shown that the general public enthusiastically backed a Soviet agreement in the final months of peace, no direct questions were asked about alliances prior to events in Prague. But extremely high public support for the League of Nations at the end of June 1937 must indicate much lower enthusiasm for the old diplomacy of blocs and pacts.[194] Asked in August 1939 whether or not they felt the government was doing its best to secure a deal with Russia, 50 per cent of those questioned responded in the affirmative, with only 30 per cent against. This would suggest that the general public thought failure to secure an alliance was not the result of limited effort on Chamberlain's part, but owed more to Soviet actions.[195] Given this widespread lack of faith in alliances among all sections of politics and society, it is understandable that the government sought to avoid them for so long.

Conclusion

The pursuit of alliances, variously formed and constituted, had limited support in Britain in the mid-1930s. One or two advocates then emerged as the Rhineland crisis caused concern about the new menace to European peace. By the time Chamberlain assumed the premiership, a small number of political figures, recognising that the League was inadequately suited to these dangers, favoured alliances as an alternative to the Prime Minister's policy of appeasement. Calls were heard for Britain to 'move closer' to other powers including France, America and Russia and a rehabilitation of the Stresa Front became the pet project of a small band of Tory enthusiasts.

The *Anschluss* and the Prague Coup were crucial events in the consideration of alliances as an alternative to appeasement. Though people disagreed amongst themselves over the precise formula required, a sizeable group of politicians rallied around Churchill's call for a Grand Alliance in early 1938 as the future of Czechoslovakia became the key issue in Europe. In the final six months of peace, an Anglo-French alliance with Russia became the most-favoured policy of all sections of politics and society. Indeed, Chamberlain adopted the Peace Front as his strategy in April 1939. One cannot escape the conclusion that the majority of Britons now felt that it was not a case of 'if', but 'when', war would erupt and alliances were increasingly discussed as a means to prepare for this conflict, rather than deter it.

The verdict of history suggests that alliances were the most promising of all the alternatives to Chamberlain's policy. First trumpeted by Churchill, the charge that the government should have formed a Grand Alliance has been reiterated by Parker and Shaw at the beginning of the twenty-first century. Inevitably, hindsight substantially influences this judgement. Why, then, did Chamberlain ultimately resist alliances until so late in the day? His was a generation scarred by the impact of the Great War and he entered high politics at a time when alliances were widely believed to have been one of the main causes of the catastrophe. It was not until after the Prague Coup that they ceased to be the unpopular policy of a radical minority. For Chamberlain, the sheer practicalities of the situation militated against a Churchillian Grand Alliance in the summer of 1938. Its defective component parts only added to the widespread view that dividing the world into camps would hasten a war, especially when dealing with such volatile figures as Hitler, so opposed to Soviet Bolshevism. The balance of risk between allies strengthening the British hand and yet increasing the likeliness of conflict occurring was a constant problem with which the government had to grapple. On the face of it, this would seem to matter less after March 1939. Alliances, however, were felt to be a policy for war and Chamberlain was ever a man for peace, still believing it could be saved long after most of his colleagues had abandoned hope. After Prague, he reluctantly accepted alliances as necessary but distasteful, hoping, in his own words, for the best but preparing Britain for the worst.[196]

Chamberlain is often accused by his detractors of having a provincial mind and lacking the capacity to think beyond short-term goals, regularly ignoring the long-term repercussions of his initiatives. The Polish Guarantee is one example of such a knee-jerk reaction, which could not, in fact, be implemented with any great chance of success. Yet there is evidence that some of the Prime Minister's reluctance about alliances with Russia and America derived from lucid and far-sighted concerns about the future, which few of his contemporaries shared. Chamberlain clearly realised that a victorious war against Fascism with the Soviets on Britain's side would more than likely end in a shabby, dangerous peace for whole swathes of Central and Eastern Europe. As Orwell stated in 1940, 'we cannot win the war without introducing Socialism', and the Prime Minister greatly feared this eventuality for large parts of the continent as well as Britain.[197] 'We must pay him a carefully assessed tribute for keeping his eye on the dark monster at the horizon,' noted Robert Sencourt in 1954.[198] Poland's fears about Russia in 1939 were fully realised during the Cold War when Soviet occupation became an unwelcome substitute for Nazi oppression. Towards the end of the Second World War, Churchill became haunted by the fear that he had helped free Eastern Europe from Nazi tyranny only to hand it over to Soviet barbarism. But this is something he and others appear not to have considered when clamouring for an alliance in the spring of 1939.

Where America is concerned, Chamberlain saw that limited assistance in the short term might cost Britain more in the long term, with a post-war challenge to the Empire and Britain's fragile pre-eminence in Europe.[199] Whilst becoming a victorious American satellite would be preferable to ending up a defeated Nazi dominion, neither option was at all attractive. Even after war had broken out, Chamberlain wrote to his sister: 'Heaven knows I don't want the Americans to fight for us – we should have to pay too dearly for that if they had a right to be in on the peace terms.'[200] The broad tide of events in the post-war world shows that many of Chamberlain's fears about Britain's place *vis-à-vis* the two emerging Superpowers were well-founded.

Would alliances or a Grand Alliance have averted hostilities? The Anglo-French union did little to deter Hitler from war in 1939. Reforming the Stresa Front was explored as an early part of Chamberlain's strategy but was doomed once Mussolini moved squarely into Hitler's camp. America would not enter the conflict until attacked itself at Pearl Harbour in late 1941. Its sympathetic isolation in the early months of war did nothing to slow the invasion of Poland or France. Even if the Roosevelt Peace Initiative had led to America and Britain standing together in some formal anti-Fascist front, there is little evidence to suggest that Hitler would have been deterred from his foreign adventures. A stronger line by the USA might have emboldened other anti-Fascist powers or put a seed of doubt in the *Führer*'s mind, but, as Rock points out, his estimation of the fighting qualities of what he regarded as 'a mass of immigrants' was extremely low.[201] Indeed, Hitler believed that 'the United States was incapable of conducting war' and only a few of the leading Nazis showed any concern at Roosevelt's increasingly vague statements about maintaining neutrality as 1939 progressed.[202] It is also to be remembered that Hitler himself declared war on America just days after the Japanese attack on Pearl Harbour.

If America's enthusiasm for war was so doubtful, could a Grand Alliance including the Soviet Union have avoided conflict breaking out? Such a pact in the spring of 1938 would have been unlikely to deter the Sudeten crisis unless the Allies could convince Hitler that they were really prepared to use force, and Britain and France were clearly not willing to bluff. Russia, of course, was treaty-bound to protect Czechoslovakia if France also did so and Hitler knew this – still he threatened to march. It is also far from certain that Russia would have stood by its commitments to the Czechs in September 1938.

Even if Britain, France and Russia *had* stood firm at this juncture, is there any indication that Hitler would have backed down without another Munich-style conference? He was known to be furious that Chamberlain had robbed him of his chance for a small, decisive war in September 1938.

It is also far from certain that a Grand Alliance including Russia could have been made in the summer of 1939, even if Chamberlain had wholeheartedly wanted it. This is something many critics of the Prime Minister, such as Parker, greatly downplay. Chamberlain, while personally reluctant, decided to pursue an alliance in May and even agreed to a straightforward tripartite pact between Britain, France and Russia in early July. At this juncture, yet another new demand was raised by the Soviet delegation. Indeed, many still believe that Russia never meant to sign any agreement with Britain and France at all. As Kaiser points out, Molotov may still have had more new demands to make of these two powers at the time when talks broke down.[203] Be that as it may, it is clear that the German offer, when it came in, was by far the more attractive to the ultra-cautious and opportunistic Stalin. It secured peace for Russia, at least in the short term, gained time to rearm and reorganise the home front, and afforded the chance to acquire large sections of Poland, carved up between the signatories of the Nazi-Soviet Pact. Chamberlain's hesitance may have played a part in the collapse of the talks, but these other, wider factors are at least as important in explaining their failure.

Chamberlain's policy of appeasement was designed to avert war and it is unlikely that even a successfully concluded Anglo-Soviet pact would have done this in the autumn of 1939. It might have influenced the precise timing or even the particular flash-point for conflict, perhaps putting off an invasion of Poland for a few months or temporarily moving Hitler's focus elsewhere. The fact that Germany invaded Poland little more than a week after concluding the Nazi-Soviet Pact is evidence that avoiding hostilities with Russia at that juncture was of high importance to him. It is doubtful, however, whether an Anglo-Soviet alliance could have averted war altogether. Indeed, given the ideological animosity between Germany and Russia, it might even have brought it closer or made the eventual catastrophe a certainty. Hitler attacked his former ally in 1941, after all, without much provocation.

Events showed that Soviet forces were best suited to a defensive struggle, as the Chiefs of Staff repeatedly stressed, and it is uncertain what concrete help Russian soldiers could have offered France as German tanks rolled across its borders. A simultaneous Soviet offensive on Germany's eastern front would have served as a distraction to the Nazi forces, but it is doubtful whether it would have been powerful enough – or come sufficiently quickly – to stop France falling. The attitude of Poland would again have been crucial. Would the Russians have been welcome on their soil or treated as invaders? Either way, with a successfully concluded Soviet pact, Britain and France would have been honour-bound to consider the defence of Russia in a way that they were not in 1939. This might have hindered their own defensive plans, or led France to fall more quickly. Would the Soviets have stood by their part of the agreement anyway, or merely concerned themselves with the defence of their homeland and acquiring local, vulnerable territories?

Finally, though critics of Chamberlain are quick to claim that the Prime Minister failed to understand Hitler's true nature, and suggest that he was immoral to appease a regime such as Nazi Germany, they cannot ignore the barbarous character of Stalin's Russia. In advocating an alliance with the Soviets as an alternative to appeasement, they are substituting the pursuit of better relations with one devil for the close embrace of another.

5

ARMAMENTS AND DEFENCES

They have too long delayed the rearming of Britain ... If you want peace you must prepare for war.[1]

(Viscount Wolmer, House of Commons, June 1936)

Introduction

According to many of its detractors, the National Government should have attempted to deter Hitler from war in the late 1930s by a programme of colossal rearmament. A large number of Chamberlain's critics believed that the only language the Fascists understood was force and that a huge arsenal of weapons would therefore be the best means to secure peace, or win the ensuing struggle if that mission failed. A number of later historians have shared this damning indictment of the government's record with regard to arms and asserted that Chamberlain left the country woefully under-prepared for the task which it eventually faced. In short, they accuse him of dangerously neglecting the country's defences – rearming too little and too late.

The orthodox school of appeasement literature had much to say on this topic. Some critics even began abusing Chamberlain's rearmament record before the war was over, seeking to apportion blame for the precarious situation the country now endured. Alfred Duff Cooper attacked his former Cabinet colleague as early as December 1939, accusing the Prime Minister of being 'sadly remiss in making adequate preparations for war'. He continued in no uncertain terms:

> As Chancellor of the Exchequer and the dominant figure in Mr Baldwin's Cabinet he never ceased to apply the break to expend-iture on armaments ... A year ago he preferred to put his trust in Adolf Hitler and to denounce as alarmists those who thought differently. And so he resisted the demand which came from his own colleagues in the Cabinet for the setting up of a Ministry of Supply and the introduction of conscription.[2]

The most famous attack on Chamberlain's rearmament record came in the form of *Guilty Men*, published in July 1940, which painted the soldiers at Dunkirk as the brave victims of a neglectful government: 'One infantryman said "Why didn't we send more planes? Why? Why? Why?" '[3] Cato likened Baldwin's choice of Sir Thomas Inskip as Minister for the Coordination of Defence to the Roman Emperor Caligula making his horse a Consul.[4] Cato concluded the work in stark terms: 'The soldiers of Britain had insufficient tanks and airplanes to protect them for the simple reason that insufficient money had been spent to buy them.'[5]

Rearmament, or the lack of it, figured prominently in Churchill's *The Gathering Storm*, the 'theme of the volume' being 'how the English-Speaking peoples through their unwisdom, carelessness and good nature allowed the wicked to rearm'.[6] 'It was a simple policy to keep Germany disarmed and the victors adequately armed', asserted Churchill, before detailing how his own repeated warn-ings about Nazism were ignored and how his calls for the govern-ment to make good its defensive shortages fell largely on deaf ears.[7] He even intimated that a different policy might have averted war: 'Much however could have been done to make us better prepared and thus lessen our hazards. And who shall say what could not have happened?'[8]

Anthony Eden presented himself as of one mind with Churchill on this issue, but also hit out at the opposition parties' hypocrisy on the question of arms:

I was convinced that we could only reach worthwhile agreements if we were strong in spirit as our rearmament made itself felt. The Labour and Liberal opposition, though detesting the Dictators, failed in their duty by voting and speaking against all measures to provide their country with the armaments to which alone the Nazis and Fascists would give heed.[9]

Clement Attlee inevitably responded to such attacks. To his credit, the former Labour leader acknowledged that moves such as voting against the introduction of partial conscription in April 1939 'probably wasn't awfully wise'.[10] But he was keen to point out that his party's opposition to the government's Defence Estimate Bills in the late 1930s did not necessarily mean that it opposed all rearmament *per se*, but disagreed with the government's specific methods: 'We wanted combined thinking on defence problems ... a combined doctrine with a proper allocation between the services based on a coordinated plan and not just on which particular service had a pull on the Chancellor of the Exchequer at the time.'[11]

Not all of Chamberlain's contemporaries were critical of the Prime Minister's rearmament efforts. Lord Home praised Chamberlain's farsightedness in significantly altering Britain's defence strategy during the late 1930s, a move which ultimately contributed to victory in the Battle of Britain:

Did Chamberlain ... fail to pursue rearmament with sufficient vigour? ... It has to be remembered that he and Lord Swinton [Secretary of State for Air] saw the absolute importance of air defence in any future war. The fighter planes, which they had authorised, which enabled Britain to survive, were only just in time. They were decisive in victory.[12]

Similarly, Samuel Hoare pointed out that there were significant factors militating against a mass rearmament drive, as well as measures such as the conscription of men and labour during peace-time: 'I doubt whether even Churchill, if he had been a member of the government, could have roused the country in the spring and summer of 1939 to an all-out war effort.' Indeed, 'even if we had possessed a great popular leader, I do not believe that the country would have accepted war conditions in the months before war started'.[13] Chamberlain's Secretary of State for War, Leslie Hore-Belisha, concurred: 'Neither parliament nor people was prepared to abandon peace-time methods and to gear the industrial machine of the country to war production, as in Germany.'[14]

As early as 1946, Chamberlain's official biographer, Keith Feiling, offered a stoic defence of his subject's rearmament policy. He credits Chamberlain as the Cabinet figure most conscious of the need to rearm during the mid-1930s, orchestrating scheme after scheme of defence expenditure in his time as Chancellor. Yet Chamberlain's was also a delicate balancing act: 'No man could feel more disgust at diverting all the national resources to destruction, or the peril to the financial stability which he had laboured to restore, yet ... the initiative and determinate decisions in rearmament were chiefly his.'[15] As Prime Minister, Feiling's Chamberlain was the driving force behind spending on the air force assuming priority over that on the army and navy, as well as on fighter planes rather than bombers – both bold and unpopular decisions which actually enabled Britain to survive in the war. Furthermore, Feiling noted that Chamberlain was the leading advocate of financial stability as a 'fourth arm of defence', where a strong economy was held to be as important in the long term as an efficient military machine in the short. Based upon the belief that Britain's economy could outlast Germany's in a prolonged war – and that all that was required was the ability to repel a 'knock-out blow' from the air, rather than win a decisive all-out victory – this strategy proved remarkably far-sighted and contributed greatly to British survival in 1940.[16]

While many orthodox appeasement critics wrote in the heyday of Keynesian economics, which held that mass rearmament was a good way to stimulate economic growth, historians from the revisionist period were more keen to stress the severe financial constraints under which the Prime Minister laboured. Above all, it was the importance of maintaining the economic recovery after the Depression that so restrained the government's rearmament efforts. Robert Shay adopted a more understanding tone than most. He explained how appeasement was born from the need to balance budgets and maintain low inflation in the fragile economic climate of the decade, to the detriment of huge arms spending. While the author acknowledged the risks Chamberlain was taking with this policy in such dangerous times, the overall result was a general success:

> It is a testimony to Chamberlain's abilities as an administrator that, despite the restraints he continued to impose on rearmament, Britain was better prepared for war when it came than she would have been had defence planning been allowed to continue as it had under Baldwin.[17]

George Peden took a similar line in his 1977 work *British Rearmament and the Treasury*, asserting that Chamberlain's cautious stewardship of the nation's finances actually helped rearmament efforts: 'Far from being paralysing, the Treasury's use of the power of the purse forced Ministers and military men to come to decisions about priorities, and thereby ensured that essential elements in Britain's defences were completed first.'[18] A follow-up journal article was even more generous, claiming that Chamberlain's 'fourth arm of defence' policy enabled Britain to win the war. There was no better alternative available:

> The balance struck between defensive strength and economic stability in 1937–1939 at least allowed Britain to survive the initial Nazi onslaught, and to have the financial credit to draw upon the considerable resources of the Empire and Commonwealth during the war.[19]

More generally, Paul Kennedy stressed the strong correlation between the outcome of major wars and the amount of productive resources mobilised by each side, seemingly vindicating Chamberlain's policy.[20] He also pointed out that where rearmament was limited during the late 1930s, this was not always the Prime Minister's fault. After nearly two decades of peace and massive popular aversion to rearmament, as well as the crippling effects of the Depression, 'industry itself could not adequately respond' to the new arms drive until well on into the war effort.[21]

Not all the works from the 1970s and 1980s challenged the critical *Guilty Men* thesis. J.P.D. Dunbabin conceded that though Chamberlain's preparations for war eventually proved adequate, they did not succeed in preventing that war – the very result the Prime Minister craved. Indeed, Chamberlain's cautious approach to rearmament only provoked Hitler: 'Insofar as British rearmament influenced him at all, it was to bring forward the time when he was prepared to risk war, not to deter him from war.'[22]

Many of the most important works from the post-revisionist period of appeasement literature have continued the debate on arms and defences. John Ruggiero fiercely criticised Chamberlain's record, asserting that he was far too slow in rearming, and that his resistance to doing so was explained by a 'prejudicial hidden agenda' to keep the Labour movement at bay and resist nationalisation throughout the industry.[23] Establishing a Ministry of Supply, for example, could have led to changes in the economy with potential benefits for the Left and this was precisely why he opposed such a move until so late in the day: 'Given the choice between Hitler and Labour, Chamberlain chose the former.'[24] Ruggiero concludes that things would have been better for the rearmament effort without this Prime Minister in charge:

> That Britain failed to rearm in a manner consistent with its international obligations in the 1930s was due largely to the baneful influence of Neville Chamberlain on the defence programme. Without his commanding presence in the National Government British defence (and hence foreign) policy would have taken a vastly different turn.[25]

Other recent contributors have revived older revisionist arguments and developed them further. In 1996, Scott Newton claimed that the government's arms programme was so limited due to its overriding concern to keep Britain from the economic woes it suffered during the 1920s. It was also feared that massive rearmament and peace-time conscription would turn the country into one with values more akin to Nazi Germany than those which were traditionally British. All in all, held Newton, the balance struck by the government was just about right:

> As a result of these preparations Britain was able to defeat the Luftwaffe in 1940 ... Overall, as Chancellor and Prime Minister, Chamberlain presided over an increase in the share of defence spending unprecedented in peace-time and which by 1939 compared well with the efforts of Nazi Germany.[26]

James Levy's 2006 *Appeasement and Rearmament* defended Chamberlain's position. Not only was the Prime Minister's arms record very solid given the conditions he inherited – especially with regard to R.A.F. improvements in 1939 – but an earlier drive than the one he sanctioned would have been counterproductive:

> A rush to rearmament in the mid-1930s would have frozen in place the production of weapons that would have been obsolescent in 1939–1940. Early attempts at arms build-ups by France, Italy and the Soviet Union seem to have hurt those counties early in World War Two, not helped them, because they were burdened with an abundance of weapons one generation behind the steep technological curve.[27]

Such varying interpretations suggest that the debate over Chamberlain and rearmament is still far from settled.

This chapter will attempt to examine the viability of the strategy of mass rearmament as an alternative to appeasement. This issue was never straightforward. Rearmament itself was not necessarily contrary to appeasement and the two were in no way mutually exclusive. Indeed, they could be seen as twin parts of the same strategy. Chamberlain presided over the largest arms programme in Britain since the Great War and it was not uncommon for appeasement supporters to call for much more to be done in this field. Put simply, rearmament was a central pillar of Chamberlain's strategy. This chapter is, therefore, more about advocates of greater and quicker rearmament, than of rearmament itself. The question is largely one of extent once again. The majority of government critics covered here felt that Chamberlain should have done much more than he did – and faster.

Rearmament is defined as increasing the size, power and capabilities of the three service departments – the army, navy and air force. In addition to basic issues of manpower, the quality and quantity of weapons and equipment will be considered. Improving Britain's defences – its anti-aircraft guns, bomb-shelters, radar stations, and so on, was also very important. Issues of supply and national service – that is conscription of wealth and industry as well as men – will also be addressed. The idea of limiting the arms of other nations merits some consideration too. Churchill is the most obvious example of someone who argued that if only the government had acted to keep Germany disarmed, war might never have occurred. That country was, of course, prohibited from maintaining anything but the smallest of forces by the Versailles Treaty. Despite conflicting intelligence reports about the precise extent to which Germany was rearming – a problem for the entire decade as a whole – it was well known that Hitler was doing so.[28]

Origins and Nature of the Alternative

While rearmament was generally unpopular in a country with recent memories of the Great War and suffering the economic hardships born of the Depression, the international arms situation nevertheless caused increasing alarm during the late 1930s. Churchill had been talking about Hitler's illegal rearmament programme for several years and, shortly after the Rhineland crisis, ominously warned of 'the great wheels revolving and the great hammers descending day and night in Germany, making the whole industry of that country an arsenal'.[29] This, however, was not so much a call to arms for Britain – he advocated collective security as his favoured policy now – but a rallying cry for the Western democracies to consider how best to reduce the weapons produced by other countries.

There were, however, a few demands for Britain to make good the gaps in its own defences, largely neglected during the interwar

period, in face of the increased militarism and closer alignment of
Germany, Italy and Japan. These tended to come almost exclusively
from the Right of the political spectrum, as Labour generally opposed
all arms expenditure in the 1930s, unless it was to enable Britain to
play its part in collective security. The Liberals advocated a middle
way between these two positions, opposing government foreign policy
and mass rearmament in general, yet recognising the need for limited
arms in order to make the League an effective instrument for peace.
In a debate about defence spending on 9 March 1936, Liberal Leader
Archibald Sinclair admitted that 'differences of opinion are bound to
arise when we come to discuss the methods, but on the principle that
we must have adequate and efficient defences there will be none'.[30]
Churchill, however, sniped that 'this work should have been begun in
vigour three years ago'.[31] A few weeks later, Tory rebel Robert Boothby
suggested that League sanctions against Italy over Abyssinia could
not be adequately pursued by Britain in its current state of weakness:
'We have not at the present moment defences in any field sufficient to
enable us to carry out the foreign policy we are at present attempting
to follow.'[32]

That summer, Viscount Wolmer made a stinging attack on the
government's defence record, part of which is quoted at the head of
this chapter. However, he added that it was the Labour Party which
had 'constantly denied the policeman his truncheon' by refusing to
support the last new arms bill the government had tried to initiate.[33]
This quarrel escalated when Paul Emrys-Evans accused the opposition
of being 'the greatest sinners' with regard to rearmament, espousing collective security and yet opposing any defence improvements
the government tried to make.[34] Labour's Hugh Dalton responded to
this attack, arguing that his party's position had been misrepresented
by the government and that it was not pacifist, resisting every arms
increase in all instances.[35] Instead, Labour opposed so many of the
bills to register its disapproval at the lack of clarity and coherence
which characterised government foreign policy.[36]

The Defence Loans Bill debates during February and March
1937 were an important catalyst in the discussion of mass rearmament, coming as they did in the wake of the government's proposed

expenditure of £1,500 million over the next five years, £400 million of which would be raised by loans. As Chancellor of the Exchequer, Chamberlain had moulded this policy. Taking such a move as evidence of a new resolve on the government's part, Tory advocates of increased rearmament rallied to the cause. On 4 March, Churchill, by now espousing 'Arms and the Covenant' as his favoured policy, welcomed the proposal but called for even more to be done, especially regarding the R.A.F. and bomber aircraft: 'Financial sacrifices alone will not suffice; the whole nation must pull together.'[37] Sir Thomas Moore backed increased rearmament, 'not only for the safety of this country, but for the peace of Europe and the general appeasement of the tense situation existing in the world today'.[38] This emphasised that appeasement and rearmament were not incompatible. Meanwhile, Robert Boothby privately noted, 'let us admit at once that we started to arm two years too late ... A catastrophe can still be averted ... We must arm and arm and arm again'.[39] Even a Labour MP, Josiah Wedgwood, spoke in favour of the government's bill and advocated the stockpiling of huge reserves of ammunition for future use. He claimed that many of his colleagues would oppose such initiatives, not because they were unprepared to fight for Britain, but because they had no faith in the precise nature of government policy.[40] In the end, Labour abstained. The Liberals opposed the bill, to no avail, although they concurred with the general need for a limited increase in arms.

By the time Chamberlain assumed the premiership, then, a small but significant group of politicians was calling for much more to be done in the sphere of rearmament. These were mostly Tories, although one or two Labour and Liberal MPs came on board in recognising the essential needs of the day. Following the success of the Nyon Conference and President Roosevelt's 'Quarantine Speech' in September and October 1937, Tory MP Commander Archibald Southby adopted an almost Churchillian tone. Arms rather than appeasement was the line he demanded:

If you review the whole course of history since the war I do not think there is any fair-minded or impartial person who would not agree that had our policy as regards armaments been different we should be in a position to speak with much greater authority throughout the world.[41]

The March 1938 *Anschluss* provided a new spur for rearmament calls on a scale as yet unseen. From the Conservative benches, Boothby begged the government to make 'a substantial addition in the very near future to our first line air strength'. He then demanded 'parity with Germany, whatever the cost; even if it involves some form ... of industrial conscription'.[42] By this, Boothby meant imposing strict controls on those factories manufacturing planes or the materials used in their construction, in order to force rearmament at a greater pace and with a clearer sense of priorities. Leo Amery called for 'whatever preparations may be necessary' to make Britain secure, while the Duchess of Atholl advocated a scheme of national military training to be introduced for all men of service age.[43] A week later, Churchill even mooted the idea of creating a Ministry of Defence, to coordinate rearmament efforts. He concluded: 'We should lay aside every hindrance to endeavour, by uniting the whole force and spirit of our people, to raise again a Great British nation.'[44] Even the Archbishop of Canterbury, Cosmo Lang, admitted that 'necessity is laid upon us' as far as arms were now concerned.[45]

The Liberals continued their twin policy of opposition to mass rearmament and appeasement, alongside a cautious acceptance of the need for limited arms production. Sinclair stated that 'of course we should rearm ... but rearmament is not enough', before reiterating his belief that faith in the League was the best means to avert war.[46] Even a few Labour MPs admitted that more arms were needed if Britain was to be safe in the future, although this never equated to the party's support in the lobby for government initiatives. At its Edinburgh conference in October 1937, Labour had endorsed a limited rearmament effort and this allowed some speakers the freedom to call for such moves more openly in parliament. Subsequently, Attlee announced that Labour believed in 'the maintenance of force', but only for the pursuit of collective security and not to buttress the 'uneasy equilibrium' currently existing in Europe, created by Chamberlain's appeasement.[47] Lord Snell also welcomed such measures and attempted to clarify Labour's position as he saw it:

> It has always been a part of our advocacy that we could not
> indulge in unilateral disarmament ... We have always expressed
> our wish to give what arms were required to the nation to enable
> her to take her proper place and fulfil her proper responsibilities
> as a part of a great international undertaking for peace.[48]

But this did not go far enough for some. Lord Lothian, in an uncharac-
teristically bellicose outburst, called for 'some form of national service'
and the compilation of a register of all men fit for conscription as the
necessary first step.[49] He also advocated far-reaching improvements to
the R.A.F. and Britain's air defences. Lothian, as has been noted, was
a committed isolationist for much of the decade, but many advocates
of this policy were vocal in their demand for greater armaments, for
obvious reasons.

The consideration of some form of national service, along with vast
expenditure on the navy, was also mooted by Admiral of the Fleet Sir
Roger Keyes.[50] Alongside the suggestions of industrial conscription,
national training programmes and a Ministry of Defence, this marked
a new highpoint in calls for massive rearmament and defence measures
as an alternative – or, at the very least, a supplement – to Chamberlain's
appeasement strategy. By the spring of 1938, not only were calls to re-
equip and improve the three defence services becoming widespread, but
some also advocated bolder measures akin to establishing a peace-time
war economy, thereby creating a radically different type of society. Much
of the Labour Party even came on board. Hugh Dalton recorded that he
had told Vansittart he was 'deeply disturbed by the failure of the British
air rearmament programme' at this time. He also impressed upon Attlee
'that this failure of the Air Ministry and of private enterprise to give us
aircraft was the biggest single issue at the present moment'.[51]

*   *   *

The Sudeten crisis only magnified such trends. When the Czechs mobilised their army in response to rumoured German troop movements

on the border, resulting in a war scare during May 1938, Liberal National Robert Bernays wrote: 'If only we can impress upon Germany our potential strength, then we can negotiate with them on any grievances that there may be.'[52] For Bernays, appeasement should follow the primary need to deter aggression through the force of arms. Tory MPs Leo Amery and Edward Grigg began to coordinate support for national service in parliament, collecting 174 signatures between July and October supporting a motion to this effect.[53]

Following the Munich Conference, a good deal of stocktaking about British foreign policy took place. For some, the immediate future seemed to offer hope that Britain could build upon the Anglo-German declaration brought home by Chamberlain. But for others, the crisis had demonstrated serious flaws in Britain's defensive preparations which greatly alarmed the pro-rearmament lobby and won many new converts to this cause. 'There is a real feeling in the country that we were grossly unprepared', wrote Bernays, a sentiment which troubled many figures over the coming weeks and months.[54] For example, Eden launched a broadside against his former Cabinet colleagues on the first day of the Munich debate:

> There is surely no excuse for our failing to take every precaution in our power, in every sphere of national defence and national life ... None of us ever wants to find himself in this position again ... Our rearmament has been, and is, too slow ... [We need] a national effort in the sphere of defence very much greater than anything that has been attempted hitherto.[55]

Nor did other leading Tory rebels hold back. Churchill spoke on 5 October and lambasted the 'gross neglect and deficiency in our defences' which had been revealed by the crisis, urging the immediate attainment of 'that supremacy in the air which we were promised, that security in our air defences which we were assured we had'.[56] Members of what would become known as the Eden and Churchill Groups joined the attack and demanded improved arms and defences ahead of further appeasement measures. National Labour's Harold Nicolson recorded the general feeling at the height of the crisis: 'Meeting at WC's

flat: We discuss plans. If Chamberlain rats again ... We shall press for
a coalition government and the immediate application of war measures ... then national service, even if it entails conscription of capital.'[57]
Leo Amery, with a foot in both camps, called for a wide range of
measures including 'some scheme of national registration and national
service' as well as 'military training for all', whatever the costs.[58] 'No
doubt', he noted privately, 'the real blame lies on the nation as a whole,
or on our national character, but still that is not the complete excuse
for the successive drifting of Baldwin and Neville over the whole field
of foreign policy since 1935'.[59]

Other Conservatives, less opposed to appeasement, also spoke out
about the wake-up call provided by Munich. Captain Sidney Herbert
referred to the famous remark of Thomas Inskip from late 1936 about
'the years the locust hath eaten' in Britain's rearmament programme:
'I was led to suppose that the locusts had stopped nibbling about two
years ago, but I can hear their little jowls creaking yet under the front
bench.'[60] John Sandeman Allen succinctly summarised what would
become a regular line of criticism of the government's policy over the
coming months: 'An air force cannot win a war, but the lack of an air
force might very well lose a war. For that reason we must increase,
improve and further strengthen our air force.'[61]

There was now also considerable support for rearmament from the
opposition benches. In the Lords on 4 October, former Liberal leader
Viscount Samuel expressed the growing conviction within his party
that 'we must be armed and be prepared if occasion absolutely requires
to make great sacrifices'. He continued: 'This country cannot yet be
relieved of the enormous expense and cannot yet relax the tremendous
effort which it is making for its own protection.'[62] Even most of the
Labour Party now came on board. Herbert Morrison opened the debate
on 4 October by giving credit for the breathing space Chamberlain had
gained at Munich but warned him not to waste it: 'You have some further time for rearmament and the development of Air Raid Precautions
[A.R.P.]; but remember that the enemy has further time, too.'[63]

Another Commons debate later that month clarified a number of
positions on this issue, now that the immediate danger of war had
passed. The specific topic of discussion was whether or not a Ministry

of Supply should be established in peace-time to coordinate rearmament efforts. A precursor to the Ministry of Defence which Churchill had mooted after the *Anschluss*, a supply ministry would provide a central body orchestrating the national rearmament effort and heavily regulating the arms industry. Politicians from all parties and with varying opinions on Chamberlain's policies called for such a body to be set up. From the Conservative benches, Churchill claimed that he had been making demands for the better organisation of arms production for three years now, all with limited response:

> I submit that these evil tendencies, this lamentable lag, will continue ... unless new efforts are made to lift the whole process to a higher and more efficient basis of organisation and production ... More than ever there is a need to establish without delay one supreme controlling authority over the whole field of supply ... Now we have 'adequacy'. What is adequacy? Adequacy is no standard at all ... Is not this the moment when all should hear the deep, repeated strokes of the alarm bell?[64]

Labour and Liberal MPs also backed the establishment of such a body. Accusing the government of always being 'behind the needs of the time', Sinclair claimed that setting up a Ministry of Supply now would mean it would be firing on all cylinders in a year or so, by which time Britain might need it to be. Introducing it at the start of a war itself could be too late.[65] Attlee felt such a body should be just one part of a wider Ministry of Defence, both of which could help organise the better location of arms factories and depots. Constructing new factories in specially selected areas would increase supply efficiency and decrease the vulnerability to aerial bombardment of civilians living near major industrial centres. A new ministry would also provide a check on the huge profiteering of arms manufacturers, a practice widely condemned in such a vital yet distasteful industry.[66] Attlee's colleague Major Owen, moreover, was keen to explore the wider effects of such a move on the overall economy:

> If a Ministry of Supply is set up and it finds in the carrying out of its task that nationalization of the whole armaments industry

is necessary, we on this side of the House will not quarrel with
that conclusion. We have been urging it for years. If armament
production is nationalized, the Ministry will be able to control
and mobilise it with real efficiency.[67]

*   *   *

The evolution of opinion within the wider community mirrored that
among the political elite. It is no surprise that for most of the decade
a group with so many pacifist links as the League of Nations Union
was hostile to rearmament and supported the League Disarmament
Commission's grand vision of a world free of all weapons.[68] As major
events in the approach to war made it apparent that a degree of rearmament was a vital necessity, many within the Union, however, came
to accept the inevitable. Though still keen to resist amassing a huge
Churchillian arsenal, LNU Chairman Gilbert Murray pointed out
during May 1938 that some rearmament was nevertheless essential:
'It is not necessary to create an "overwhelming force" capable of utterly
crushing any aggressor or group of aggressors, but merely a force so
strong and so determined that war against it will obviously not pay.'[69]
   The brutal realities of the Czech crisis forced Murray to rethink
his position further. In a letter to a constituent he admitted that 'to
preserve our skins but to lose our souls seems to me a terrible choice,
but the conditions of modern wars are such that a grave responsibility
rests on any government which allows a country to be involved unless
fully prepared'. He went on to recommend that 'each one of us should
do what we can in regard to A.R.P. or any other national service'.[70] By
December 1938, the Union Executive even demanded that the government rearm far more than it was doing, specifically in anti-aircraft
weaponry to protect the civil population from German bombers.[71] The
LNU had travelled full-circle on the issue of arms. Angry with the
Chancellor for arming in the first place, it now attacked Chamberlain
the Prime Minister for not doing so sufficiently in the months after
Munich – all within a period of two years.
   The national press demonstrated a diverse range of opinions on the
question of rearmament. One or two newspapers were particularly

keen on a huge arms drive irrespective of their wider views on foreign policy. The *Observer* was generally enthusiastic for appeasement but nevertheless had a strong pro-arms bias. It wanted greater armaments as part of the policy and its editor J.L. Garvin was particularly strident on the issue. He wrote to Amery during the Czech crisis: 'The peril will come again unless we turn out guns and planes with might and main for the next six months. Hideous deficiencies with respect to preparedness have been revealed.'[72] Much less keen on appeasement, the pro-isolation *Daily Express* also backed intensive rearmament, declaring in March 1937 that 'war can be fended off as flood and fire can be fended off – with wise and strong precautions'.[73] In response to the *Anschluss*, the *Express* backed rearmament even at the expense of the wider health of the economy. 'What', it asked 'is our business? To build up our air strength to the level of our most formidable neighbour ... If this vital requirement interferes with present trade no matter. We must face it, tackle it, and pay for it'.[74] Likewise, the *Daily Telegraph* was sceptical about Chamberlain's policy and felt that the *Anschluss* ought to occasion a mass A.R.P. drive: 'The more efficient our precautions the less likely will be the emergency which would call for their use.'[75]

Most other papers shared the general mood of hostility towards rearmament prevalent in the country for most of this decade. The *Manchester Guardian* sneered at '£400 million for death' in response to the Defence Loans Bill in February 1937.[76] The *News Chronicle* initially backed rearmament 'to the full' in its panicked response to the *Anschluss*, but then insisted that 'rearmament alone is no sort of answer'.[77] Indeed, the government's arms programme was then deemed too far-reaching for a country with other urgent priorities: '£3 on Armaments for Every £1 on Health and Education.'[78] The *Chronicle* even felt that the Munich Agreement heralded a new opportunity to campaign for universal *dis*armament:

> Disarmament is the one issue on which all peoples would agree ... What is required above all else is the discovery of a technique which will harness the wills of these peoples and so influence their governments in a new drive for disarmament, military, economic and mental.[79]

Even papers like these, however, were forced to change their long-term policies and support Chamberlain's rearmament programme as the international situation worsened. Indeed, many began criticising the government for its tardiness in respect to the nation's defences. The *Daily Herald* welcomed rearmament efforts after the Munich Conference, stating that 'we cannot remain unarmed or supine against future aggressions'.[80] By February 1939, it had come out in favour of mass rearmament: 'In the coming financial year we will spend a total of £580 million on the defence of our country ... It is a grim business for democracy. But as things stand today it is an inevitable business ... and the government is right to spend the money.'[81]

The *News Chronicle*, after calling for universal disarmament following Munich, responded to the Prague Coup six months later in almost Churchillian terms: 'A great effort of physical preparation and of will is called for ... Peace may yet be secured by strength and firmness; but peace or war, the one supreme necessity is preparedness of armed power on a scale to match whatever may challenge us.'[82] Thereafter, support for intensified rearmament in the press was universal and wholehearted.

There is no doubt that public opinion was utilised by politicians as a justification for the rearmament policies they espoused, despite the inconsistencies in views expressed. Leo Amery noted during September 1936 that 'whatever may be said by way of formal opposition in parliament, I believe the people in England are united today in recognising the necessity of adequate defence on seas or land and air'.[83] Yet, shortly after the *Anschluss*, Lord Halifax told the Foreign Policy Committee that, on the question of rearmament, 'the great majority of responsible people in the country would be opposed to any new commitments'.[84]

There is strong evidence, however, that public opinion broadly followed suit – or perhaps even led the way – in opposing rearmament early on, and then demanding a massive arms drive as events progressed and the skies darkened. Notwithstanding Baldwin's huge election victory in 1935 on the platform of no great arms, or the seemingly incontrovertible findings of the 'Peace Ballot' just a few days later, the infant Gallup Polls of the era once again give the most accurate indication of public opinion.[85] Asked in January 1937, 'Do you favour compulsory military training?' exactly three quarters of those surveyed did not.[86] Asked in December 1937, 'Are you in favour of the all-round reduction of armaments by international agreement', 49 per cent answered in the affirmative, more than double the 24 per cent who said they were not.[87] It seems clear, then, that in the year Chamberlain became Prime Minister, the nation was not only firmly against any form of national service but also favoured disarmament over rearmament by a ratio of around two to one.

Again, the tide of events dramatically shook this conviction. Immediately after Munich, 72 per cent of those polled favoured increased expenditure on arms, with an even larger 78 per cent agreeing that the government should compile a national register of all men fit for service.[88] By February 1939, only 21 per cent expressed satisfaction with the government's A.R.P. programme, with 70 per cent demanding the construction of deep air-raid shelters in all towns and cities.[89] In April, a slim majority of those asked now supported the immediate introduction of compulsory national service – 48 per cent in favour, as opposed to 45 per cent against.[90] In little over a year, then, the British public had gone from backing universal disarmament and opposing military training to calling for vast rearmament and conscription, and being wholly unimpressed by Chamberlain's defence programme. This is a powerful indication of the rapidly changing lines of criticism the National Government had to face and the swift flow of events with which the country had to contend.

The Prague Coup also provided a new spur for rearmament calls in parliament, of course. Indeed, Chamberlain now effectively abandoned his policy of major concessions in favour of alliances and rearmament on a hitherto unprecedented scale. Calls for the conscription of men and labour were widespread, demands for improved A.R.P. and a Ministry of Supply even more so. In the Commons, politicians from all parties now urged the government to redouble its efforts in arms construction, especially aircraft. On 6 April 1939, Amery questioned the extent to which Chamberlain was truly committed to the cause, viewing his recent decision to double the size of the Territorial Army as being far from adequate.[91] Lloyd George had described himself as 'not at all satisfied with our own preparations' just a few days earlier.[92]

Coming from the British leader during the First World War, these words carried considerable weight. A number of peers also joined the clamour, with Viscount Astor, the Earl of Mansfield, Lord Mottistone and Lord Lothian – three Tories and a Liberal – each calling for conscription, military training and the reorganisation of the economy to facilitate the arms effort. For example, the first demanded that the government 'mobilise the whole industry, the whole manpower, and the whole wealth of this country' in a new drive to prepare for war.[93]

The government's decision to introduce a Ministry of Supply and partial conscription later that month did little to quell the criticism, despite 310,000 men now being called up for service for the first time ever in peace-time. A feeling that conflict was now all but certain gripped both Houses. By May 1939, Churchill was calling for urgent improvements to 'aeroplanes, tanks, artillery, ammunition and equipment', and subsequent speakers talked less and less about preventing war and more about the means to survive the coming onslaught.[94] Nevertheless, Lloyd George felt peace could still be saved by 'the strengthening of our own military forces to prepare for any emergency'.[95] In June, the Liberal peer Viscount Elibank urged not only the improvement of Britain's own defences but also those of its various interests overseas. He was particularly keen to buttress the forces garrisoned at Shanghai and to reinforce Britain's Far East naval presence in general.[96] Labour's Josiah Wedgwood announced that the position was now so dire that old party loyalties no longer held: 'We are all united on one other point – rearmament.' His concern was not just with that on land, sea and air, however, but with 'a moral rearmament of the people' – waking the masses to their grave responsibilities in the coming struggle.[97] They did not have to wait for long.

Consideration of the Alternative

As the National Government rearmed substantially as part of its appeasement policy, and yet also regulated arms expenditure in a carefully controlled manner, there is frequently confusion over how much it actually did. The highlights in Chamberlain's arms programme are often overlooked and there is an enduring myth that this Prime

Minister was always vehemently anti-rearmament. All this is made even more confusing when such radically contradictory accounts as those of Ruggiero and Levy are written just a few years apart, both enjoying access to the same relevant archives.

It is clear that in the mid-1930s the vast majority of people thought the government was rearming on a colossal and excessive scale. It was common for critics to talk alarmingly about the huge arsenal Chamberlain was sanctioning, Labour's Philip Noel-Baker deriding the government in 1935 for rearming 'to the edge of lunacy'.[98] And yet, by the 1950s, with the passing of war and the benefit of hindsight, the majority of commentators felt that Chamberlain had woefully under-prepared Britain for the challenge it had to encounter. Few would now contest that the Prime Minister could have done substantially more in the field of arms and defence had he really wanted to, certainly in the earlier part of his premiership. At the same time, it must be acknowledged that Chamberlain presided over the greatest increase in peacetime rearmament that this country has ever seen – easily the largest arms effort in the 20 years since the Great War.

Chamberlain felt that rearmament needed to be given more emphasis in the mid-1930s, impressing upon his colleagues the necessity to place arms and defences near the centre of the 1935 election campaign.[99] As Chancellor, he sanctioned spending on the first major R.A.F. expansion scheme for many years, production of military aircraft nearly doubling between 1934 and 1935 from 740 to 1,140.[100] Long before he became Prime Minister, Chamberlain had demonstrated that he recognised that radical defence spending was required, despite finding it personally distasteful, not least because of its impact on more congenial spending priorities in the social arena. In the spring of 1937, Chamberlain not only engineered the spending total of £1,500 million over five years for rearmament, but also went against the majority of his own party in proposing the establishment of a new tax for defence. The National Defence Contribution became one of Chamberlain's pet projects but was buried under the weight of Tory opposition. Nevertheless, it demonstrates that he was more alive to the need for rearmament at this time than many of his peers. The highest spending on the army since the Great War was also sanctioned in 1937.[101]

Chamberlain's rearmament programme gathered pace in 1938, with total GNP on military expenditure climbing to 8.1 per cent – from 5.6 per cent in 1937 and 4.2 per cent in 1936.[102] In March, the Cabinet also voted to cancel the rule that defence expenditure could not impinge upon normal trade levels, and, by the end of the year, Chamberlain had shifted spending priorities on the R.A.F. to fighter planes from bomber aircraft. This flew in the face of conventional wisdom and ruffled the feathers of figures such as Churchill, who favoured the construction of more traditional bombers ahead of fighters. There were also great improvements in radar stations and anti-aircraft weaponry, all despite the apparent success of appeasement at Munich.

It was 1939, however, when the most startling rearmament improvements were made by the government and vast expenditure was sanctioned, particularly after the Prague Coup. Partial conscription and a Ministry of Supply were both accepted in April as well as a doubling of the Territorial Army in March. Parker observes that industry delivered 3753 aircraft in the first half of 1939, compared to 1045 in the same period of the previous year.[103] GNP spending on the military shot up nearly threefold to a huge 21.4 per cent in 1939, almost on a par with Nazi Germany itself, and a feeling that Britain was becoming strong again spread amongst many people.[104] Even critics of Chamberlain's arms record within the Foreign Office, such as Oliver Harvey, Private Secretary to both Eden and Halifax, could happily proclaim that 'our own air rearmament is going ahead by leaps and bounds'.[105] Overall, as Chancellor of the Exchequer, Chamberlain presided over an increase in defence spending from £136 million in 1935, to £186 million in 1936, and £197 million in 1937. When he was the Prime Minister, this increased to £254 million in 1938 and soared to a colossal £626 million by 1939 – more than a fourfold increase in little over as many years.[106] *Guilty Men* does not record these figures.

So why did Chamberlain adopt the apparently contradictory strategy of carrying out a huge rearmament programme while also carefully regulating arms spending, periodically resisting calls from opponents to do much more? Why did the National Government not view a truly colossal arms effort – which some of its critics claimed might have prevented war – as a viable prospect until so late in the day? For the vast majority of his tenure, the Prime Minister supervised an arms effort in which every two steps forward were accompanied by one step back. He tended to authorise what was necessary given the global developments of the day, yet cautiously reined in any other measure he deemed too provocative or damaging to the wider national interest. There was considerable conflict within the government between those who wanted to accelerate rearmament in a Churchillian frenzy and those who sought to keep a tight check on defence spending. As early as December 1935, Chamberlain privately claimed, 'If only our defences were stronger I should feel so much happier but though we are working night and day they aren't what I would like'.[107] Yet in the same month, he turned down a recommendation from the Defence Requirements Committee to increase armament spending by around two-thirds over the next five years. This seemingly contradictory approach characterised the Prime Minister's attitude to rearmament over the next few years.

The National Government had been created to deal with the economic consequences of the Depression, and Chamberlain, as Chancellor since 1931, had had primary responsibility to ensure that recovery took precedence over unpopular activities such as rearmament. On this policy Baldwin admitted in November 1936 that 'I cannot think of anything that would have made the loss of the election from my point of view more certain'.[108] Chamberlain loathed war and saw himself primarily as a social reformer, as evidenced by two successful spells as Health Minister in the 1920s, where he forged his political reputation. Unemployment had fallen year on year from 3.0 million in 1932 to a low of 1.7 million in 1937 and the Chancellor was not about to upset this welcome trend if he could help it.[109] Hence, while Churchill sniped from the sidelines and Vansittart complained that 'for fifteen years we have starved our fighting services and made a virtue of it', the Chancellor's loyalty to Treasury objectives remained steadfast.[110] A diary entry from October 1936 outlined his main concerns:

If we were to follow Winston's advice and sacrifice our commerce to the manufacture of arms, we would inflict a certain injury to our trade from which it would take generations to recover. We should destroy the confidence which now so happily exists, and we should cripple the revenue.[111]

Chamberlain assumed the premiership, therefore, recognising the need to rearm significantly but retaining clear spending priorities. The conflicting interests within his Cabinet merely added to his woes. A few weeks before assuming office, he wrote:

> No-one is more convinced than I am of the necessity for rearmament and for speed in making ourselves safe. But the Services, very naturally, seeing how good the going is now and reflecting that the reaction is sure to follow, want to be 100 per cent or 101 per cent safe on everything.[112]

In addition to the Defence Ministers, there was also pressure for accelerated rearmament from within the Foreign Office. Vansittart was a constant thorn in Chamberlain's side and, at the end of 1936, lambasted 'the years the locusts hath eaten', bemoaned that 'we have begun the cure full late' and called for a 'really impressive display of strength on our part'.[113] Other figures shared these concerns. In February 1937, Oliver Harvey made little secret of his desire to see the pace of rearmament increased substantially.[114] Eden advised the Cabinet in July that a demonstration of Britain's strength in the Mediterranean would be advantageous from the point of view of relations with Italy.[115] Cadogan, however, advocated the dual approach to rearmament that Chamberlain himself so favoured. On 10 May 1937, he recommend that 'our armaments must, of course, go on at all speed'.[116] Yet only a fortnight later, he wrote of an impending Vansittart paper: 'I hope it won't be another in his usual German-scare style, simply urging rearmament and disclaiming the complete bankruptcy of our foreign policy.'[117] For Cadogan, like Chamberlain, rearmament was only one part of the main strategy and not a substitute for it.

*　*　*

By mid-1937, government military experts were fully alive to the urgent need to rearm and improve Britain's defences. In February, the Air Raid Precautions Department of the Home Office called for sweeping reforms to overcome the chaos in Britain's defence programme.[118] The Defence Plans Sub-Committee of the Committee of Imperial Defence, in close consultation with Secretary of State for Air, Lord Swinton, warned in October that aircraft production was far from adequate. Britain remained in 'a position of grave inferiority to Germany in effective air strength'.[119]

The *Defence Expenditure in Future Years* paper, presented to the Cabinet on 22 December 1937 by Inskip, was to have a major impact on rearmament policy for the remainder of Chamberlain's premiership. One important passage stated:

> We must therefore confront our potential enemies with the risks of a long war, which they cannot face ... It is true that the extent of our resources imposes limitations upon the size of the defence programmes which we are able to undertake ... Seen in its true perspective, the maintenance of our economic stability would more accurately be described as an essential element in our defensive strength: one which can properly be regarded as a fourth arm in defence, alongside the three defence Services, without which purely military effort would be of no avail.[120]

Neatly encapsulating what became known as the 'fourth arm of defence' thesis, this paper set down as policy a measured rearmament drive based upon the twin pillars of a long, defensive war and general economic stability. Given strong support by Hore-Belisha and his former military adviser Sir Basil Liddell Hart, this theory advocated a policy of limited liability, with the size and role of the British Expeditionary Force greatly curtailed. The idea was to be strong enough to be able to survive the feared German 'knock-out blow' from the air in the short term, and then to rely upon the greater financial strength of the British Empire to win any war in the long term.

This calculated gamble remained at the heart of Chamberlain's strategy, more or less, until the coming of war: 'You don't need offensive forces sufficient to win a smashing victory', he claimed. 'What you want are defensive forces sufficiently strong to make it impossible for the other side to win except at such a cost as to make it not worth while.'[121] Assisted within the Treasury by his successor as Chancellor, John Simon, and the Permanent Under-Secretary, Sir Warren Fisher, Chamberlain held that economic strength should remain paramount over short-term rearmament efforts. Support from industry and important financial bodies outside the government, favouring a cautious appeasement strategy over a Churchillian call to arms, buttressed this line. It was widely reported that the City of London backed concessions and vehemently opposed increased arms expenditure.[122]

The radical theories of the economist John Maynard Keynes were thus supported by many within the Foreign Office such as Vansittart, but were all but rejected by the Treasury. Keynes advocated mass rearmament, as well as a cap on borrowing from the Empire, as a way to stimulate the domestic economy and create jobs. Chamberlain and Fisher, however, favoured the more cautious approach of maintaining financial stability.[123] Growing tensions between the Foreign Office and Treasury over defence policy came to a head at the end of the year when Chamberlain and Eden clashed over the government's rearmament priorities.[124] Such disputes no doubt contributed to the latter's resignation.

The March 1938 *Anschluss* tested Chamberlain's resolve on the issue of massive rearmament; however, it ultimately reinforced his dual approach. A few weeks before the crisis, he wrote with concern that 'our own armament programme continues to grow, and to pile up our financial commitments to a truly alarming extent'.[125] In response to the Austrian affair, however, the Cabinet decided to cancel the rule that defence expenditure could not impinge upon normal trade, while Halifax called for the 'acceleration and intensification of our military preparations in every sphere, coupled with measures for the reorganisation of national life for war purposes'.[126] The Prime Minister responded on 24 March by announcing in the Commons:

> If Britain is to make a substantial contribution ... she must be
> strongly armed for defence and for counter-offence ... In the

present circumstances acceleration of existing plans has become essential and, moreover … there must be an increase in some parts of the programme, especially in that of the R.A.F. and the anti-aircraft defences … Rearmament work must have the first priority in the nation's effort.[127]

Despite these words, the government did not embark upon a colossal rearmament drive of the kind demanded by Churchill, but instead only moved production up through several gears at this point. There would certainly be no military effort to defend Austria and the Committee of Imperial Defence's frank assessment of German strength only underlined the 'fourth arm of defence' thesis: 'The weak point in Germany's defensive position is that she cannot face the prospect of a long war with confidence.'[128] Chamberlain could still find many supporters for his measured approach. In April 1938, Simon told his colleagues that a greatly accelerated rearmament programme was impossible, 'unless we turned ourselves into a different kind of nation'.[129] Cadogan, now safely ensconced in Vansittart's former post, noted that the 'parrot-cry of "Rearmament" is a mere confession of failure of foreign policy'.[130] This emphasised the distance now opening up between two rapidly-forming camps on the issue of rearmament: one judging arms *and* appeasement as the best strategy; the other calling for arms ahead of appeasement as the preferred option – and arms to a much greater extent.

*   *   *

The Czech crisis spurred both further rearmament efforts by the government and increasing calls from its critics for yet more to be done. Munich provided a wake up call because Britain had come so close to war and its defensive weaknesses had been illuminated under a fierce spotlight. Chamberlain announced on 5 October 1938 that 'there has been an awakening on our own side'.[131] Just one day later he stated even more boldly: 'We must arm ourselves to the teeth'.[132] Predictably, voices within the Cabinet stepped up their demands to make good the deficiencies so graphically demonstrated, with Samuel Hoare joining the Defence Ministers in calling for rapid A.R.P. improvements. Within the Foreign Office, generally more restrained figures including Strang and Jebb called for an intensified rearmament drive in their post-Munich review of policy.[133] Even the cautious Cadogan felt that a 'vitally necessary first step' was 'to get on more equal terms ... at least put our defences in order'.[134]

Yet the Sudeten crisis also presented a quandary. An intense arms drive now would run counter to the new mood signified by the Anglo-German declaration accompanying the Munich Agreement, and risk jeopardising the apparent success of appeasement. Viscount Cranborne attempted to address this issue in parliament by exploring the finer subtleties of Chamberlain's policy: 'Appeasement is no alternative to rearmament, and conciliation is no alternative to firmness. They are complementary. They must go hand in hand, because one is no use without the other.'[135] Munich thus witnessed a further acceleration of the government's rearmament effort. Chamberlain, however, was still concerned enough to tell his Cabinet on 3 October that he felt 'oppressed with the sense that the burden of armaments might break our backs'.[136] Economic concerns were still important to him and would retain a decisive influence on the measured pace of the rearmament drive.

A fortnight later, Chamberlain wrote that 'something will have to be done about national service'.[137] The issue of a national register as a preliminary step was therefore debated in the Foreign Policy Committee during November. While Halifax, Hoare and Lord Runciman, the Lord President, all backed the compilation of such a list, as well as military training schemes and an acceleration of the A.R.P. programme, Chamberlain and Inskip were more circumspect.[138] Economic factors were again decisive in slowing these improvements. The Prime Minister was 'in favour of any acceleration that we could obtain', but also felt that it must be coupled, 'with the warning which the Federation of British Industries deputation had given' in an earlier meeting with Inskip.[139] The Federation, which contained representatives from leading industrial groups within the country, had observed that there would be severe labour difficulties involved in speeding up the programme. These included the costs for lodging allowances and extra wages needed for workers to complete the longer shifts required. According to Inskip, 'the effect of any such arrangements on cost would of course be devastating, but if we were determined to go all-out, to pay attractive wages and to work three shifts we could, in a comparatively short time, greatly increase production'.[140] Runciman suggested that measures of labour control such as these, as well as the introduction of a national register, would be difficult to implement, given Labour's opposition to government policy. The Trade Unions also needed consideration.[141] Accordingly, a decision on this matter was delayed.

Further evidence that Chamberlain still sought to protect the health of the economy and resist labour control measures, even to the detriment of the defence programme and in face of Cabinet unrest, came in the Commons debate on a Ministry of Supply later that month. Again, Inskip and the Prime Minister made the key contributions. Both stressed that many industrialists opposed the establishment of such a body at this juncture, as it would impose authoritarian controls on their practices and only cause more delays and bureaucracy. Inskip noted that it 'would not be helpful, but would be definitely harmful' to the arms effort, while Chamberlain felt it would only mean that 'you would now have two people to consult instead of one'.[142] He also stressed that a Ministry of Supply could never completely eradicate profiteering within the arms industry, something the Labour Party was particularly keen to address.[143] Inskip went on to explain that the rearmament programme had so far made only slow progress because of the technological complexities of the new weapons being produced, as well as years of inactivity in arms factories during the 1920s and early 1930s. 'Productive capacity was allowed to fall into arrears' during this period, he conceded.[144]

The January 1939 war scare led to even more demands for an accelerated rearmament drive and for more efficient defensive preparations. A.R.P. spending was increased again and the Foreign Policy Committee considered organising black-out drills for many areas of London.[145] Still the advocates of massive rearmament urged greater action on the part of the Prime Minister. Though his influence had now waned considerably, Vansittart announced his dissatisfaction with the limited liability formula and called for Britain's contribution to the defence of France and Belgium to be, 'let us say at least 20 divisions'.[146] Hore-Belisha wrote privately of his deep frustrations with the rearmament process as a whole: 'The great difficulty always has been the financial control. I don't blame the Treasury in the very least but it has slowed down everything, almost, that has been done.'[147]

Prompting the government to authorise both partial conscription and a Ministry of Supply, the Prague Coup led to a rapid acceleration in Chamberlain's rearmament policy, as outlined above. The Treasury shackles were now all but removed from defence spending as the Prime Minister sought to couple arms with alliances in a last, desperate bid to deter Hitler from war. Whereas in the past Chamberlain had sought to keep his rearmament as low key as possible, so as not to provoke Hitler or jeopardise appeasement, he now boldly flouted his defences in an attempt to scare the Dictators from making further trouble. However, accelerated rearmament, conscription and a Ministry of Supply were all 'designed not to wage war but to prevent it'.[148] Chamberlain had, according to Cadogan, considered making a speech in February announcing: 'Come the three corners of the world in arms, and we shall shock them!', but did not do so for fear of provoking a new Nazi outrage.[149] After Prague, his approach was different. In the Commons on 31 July 1939, he proudly announced that 'our defences are now indeed of a formidable character'.[150] In little over a month they would need to be.

*   *   *

While not necessarily always favouring universal *dis*armament, root and branch, as many pacifists did, wider critics of the government's rearmament policy provided a further complicating factor and another body of opinion to consider. Most early opposition to rearmament came from the ranks of the Labour Party, of course, convinced that huge spending on weapons detracted from the social and economic recovery programme necessitated by the Depression. For example, in the run-up to the 1935 General Election, Herbert Morrison condemned Chamberlain for his readiness to 'spend on the means of death, but not on the means of life'.[151] This was a far cry from his position shortly after the Munich Conference, covered above, where he warned Chamberlain not to waste the time he had secured for further rearmament.

The Defence Loans Bill debates in February and March 1937 provided a key platform for those most opposed to the government's strategy. Stafford Cripps condemned the vast spending now proposed: 'It is the poor housewife and her family who will feel the pinch as wages crawl up far behind the price rise in the next few months and years.'[152] Attlee addressed the bigger issues, however: 'It is clear that what we have now is the organisation of this country permanently on a war basis. The government have absolutely no policy for peace.'[153]

A year later, in February 1938, Labour's George Ridley accused Chamberlain of creating the 'mad arms race' which now existed in Europe,[154] while, on 24 March, his colleague Major James Milner decried the 'arms, arms and more arms' ethos of the National Government.[155] After Munich, despite the party line now being reluctantly to accept the need for limited defence improvements, the government's biggest critics on the question of arms were still often found within Labour ranks. Cripps attacked Chamberlain directly on 5 October, sneering that 'our new-found dove of peace seems to insist upon a sharpening of the claws as the most vital factor'.[156]

Both Labour and the Liberals voted against the introduction of peace-time conscription in April 1939 following the Prague Coup, with Cripps, again, describing it as a 'method fit for servile and suppressed people but not for free people'.[157] Viscount Cecil chided the government for what he saw as its unimaginative and warlike policy: 'Merely to say we are going to pile up arms and pile up alliances and leave it at that is not enough.'[158] In June, Lord Ponsonby abused Chamberlain for 'disturbing the life of this country with rearmament, with A.R.P., with various activities all over the country, straining the nerves of the people and straining the resources of the country'.[159] This was just three months before the outbreak of war.

Elements of the extreme Left also opposed rearmament for much of this decade. A British Communist Party pamphlet from late 1936 asked: 'Can the strengthening of those very forces which are the most powerful factors making for war hold back the outbreak of war itself?'

It went on: 'To argue this way is as dangerous as to argue that the piling up of armaments in the hand of imperialist governments is the best way to secure peace.'[160] While the Communists campaigned for a better A.R.P. strategy through much of 1938, the announcement of peace-time conscription in early 1939 again provoked hostility among their ranks. It not only amounted to the enforcement of 'industrial slavery on the British workers', but was tantamount to making Britain as brutal and authoritarian a state as Nazi Germany itself: 'We oppose conscription because it would mean a defeat for democracy and a strengthening of the powers of reaction in Britain.'[161] Assailed from both sides by fiercely pro-rearmament and anti-rearmament camps, the government seemingly could not win on this delicate and complex question.

Conclusion

The idea of massively increased rearmament as an alternative to appeasement during the late 1930s is clearly very complicated. Not only was rearmament part of Chamberlain's strategy itself, but it was also suggested by government critics as a policy to pursue in its own right, at a much greater pace and volume than appeasement afforded. Advocates of increased rearmament were very few in number in the mid-1930s, though there were one or two people greatly concerned at the illegal Nazi rearmament drive, with Churchill the obvious example. Supporters of a huge arms effort tended to be from the Right of the political spectrum, although one or two Left and Centre-Left figures also came on board. By the middle of 1938, wider issues like A.R.P. became talking points and measures to ready the nation for war, such as conscription of wealth and manpower, also acquired new supporters. After Prague, almost everybody came to advocate intensive rearmament as part of the strategy to stop Hitler, viewed now less as a policy to deter war and more as a means to survive it. The press and the public overwhelmingly concurred, though the attitude of the opposition on this issue remained inconsistent and at times contradictory.

The government rearmed hugely set against the norms of inter-war Europe. Much of this was very unpopular with large sections of politics and society. It is an enduring myth, propagated by the *Guilty Men* school, that Chamberlain was always vehemently 'anti-arms', although for the majority of his premiership he did attempt a delicate balancing act between economic stability and national defence. Nevertheless, there were many within the government machine who found Chamberlain's balancing act dangerously uneven. They demanded that he quicken the pace of rearmament as a means to make good the gaps between Britain and Germany. As a consequence, fierce political infighting on the question of arms and defence priorities characterised most of Chamberlain's tenure. It was only after Prague that such infighting diminished, although it never disappeared altogether.

A plethora of historians and many of Chamberlain's contemporaries, writing later on with the benefit of hindsight, asked why the National Government did not do much more in face of such an obvious threat. Intensive rearmament was personally repugnant to Chamberlain, though he was not alone in this view. It is, however, easy to forget how economic stability was such a priceless commodity when he inherited the premiership, and many thought that a huge arms drive would only provoke further hostility and similar action from the Dictator powers. It seemed a safer and less provocative plan to steer a middle course between doing just enough to ensure that Britain could survive an attack and maintaining an economy and society so rocked by war and the Great Depression. Chamberlain's original mandate was to save the economy, not to churn out weapons. He feared a massive rearmament drive would turn Britain into a state beset with those problems it had endured after the Great War – or, worse, into a country well on the way towards Fascism itself. The fear that an intensively rearming Britain would have to become more like the very countries it was preparing to oppose haunted the government constantly. It also partially explains the reluctance to introduce conscription or seemingly draconian labour control measures such as a Ministry of Supply in peace-time.

Not all the reasons for rearmament being slower than many critics demanded were down to Chamberlain. Germany had a massive head start due to the nature of its government, while, in Britain, almost two decades of relative inactivity in the sphere of rearmament could not be transformed overnight into full military preparedness. The Ten Year

Rule, which operated in government defence planning until the early 1930s, dictated arms spending and military strategy on the basis of no war being fought for the next ten years. This was only revoked in 1932 so that *1942* was the earliest date at which Britain might be prepared for a major war. Nor has Chamberlain's own personal contribution to the rearmament effort been given sufficient credit. His was the driving force behind the decision to switch air spending priorities from bombers to fighters. The Spitfires and Hurricanes that won the Battle of Britain were built in the year's grace secured between Munich and war and under his specific instruction. It is difficult to believe that a Churchill-led government would have constructed so many fighter planes in the years before war.

Was Chamberlain correct, then, to view massive rearmament as viable only within the careful parameters of a 'fourth arm of defence' framework? What might have happened had he sanctioned a Churchillian arms drive, rearming faster and in far greater magnitude than he actually did? Chamberlain did just about enough. Events proved that his vision of surviving the 'knock-out blow' turned out to be eerily prescient in 1940. If his defence policy, inextricably linked to the notion of limited liability, contributed to French defeat, it also allowed Britain to survive Germany's initial onslaught and soldier on long enough for America's economic and material assistance to swing the war back in the Allies' favour. The fact that Nazi Germany adopted a lightening-quick, *Blitzkrieg* strategy in the early phases of the war would suggest that British perceptions of German economic weakness and its inability to fight a long struggle were not entirely inaccurate.

A pacific, total disarmament policy would have been disastrous in the conditions of 1930s Europe. Had Chamberlain joined a huge arms race with Germany, as Churchill suggested, Britain may have lost fewer lives in the early stages of the war, but it would almost certainly have made that conflict inevitable, or actually hastened the outbreak itself. Furthermore, the lives saved in the first instance by being more heavily armed might have been outnumbered by those lost towards the end of the struggle, had the British economy been under even greater strain by that time. Britain's economic position and world status after victory in the Second World War was bad enough as it was – one can only imagine the effects had the arms budget been bigger.

The arms Chamberlain sanctioned were sufficient for Britain to survive and the economy he maintained allowed the country enough credit to borrow from the Empire until American Lend-Lease entered the picture. Admittedly, it was a very close run thing. Would increased rearmament have deterred Hitler from war? It might have affected the timing of his assaults but it is doubtful that even a heavily armed Britain could have deterred Hitler from launching attacks in Central Europe – geographically remote from any new tanks, planes or ships. Hitler declared war on both Russia and the USA during the conflict, irrespective of the vast resources and arms capacity these two giant nations possessed. There seems little likelihood that a Britain as strong and determined as Germany was in 1939 – assuming that were possible given the fundamental differences in the type of states they were – would have deterred Hitler from war. Furthermore, reaming too early, as Levy has recently pointed out, might only have produced an outdated arsenal, insufficiently suited to the war that eventually came. All of this would have met with fierce resistance in Britain, of course – from the political opposition as well as the general public.

All in all, then, it seems likely that massive rearmament as an alternative to appeasement would have caused as many problems and offered no better solutions than the path that was actually taken. Indeed, the position might have been worse had the ultimately successful balance between sufficient arms and a strong economy that Chamberlain struck been overturned.

6

WAR AND THE THREAT
OF WAR

The Prime Minister has believed in addressing Herr Hitler through the language of sweet reasonableness. I believed that he was more open to the language of the mailed fist.[1]

(Alfred Duff Cooper, House of Commons, October 1938)

Introduction

Perhaps the most obvious alternative to appeasement in dealing with the menace of Nazi Germany in the late 1930s was war. Indeed, Chamberlain abandoned his policy of reconciliation in favour of conflict in September 1939 – not soon enough, according to some critics. With the benefit of hindsight, many later writers claimed that Hitler could have been stopped in his tracks at the time of the Rhineland affair in March 1936, or at least during the Czech crisis of 1938, but some contemporary observers also urged this option. While most talked in vague terms of 'standing firm' – or more usually of the *threat* of military action being required to deter the Dictators – a few, such as Alfred Duff Cooper, who resigned from the Cabinet in protest at the Munich Agreement, openly advocated war itself as the only means to deal with the Fascists long before Chamberlain reached the same conclusion.

Historians and political figures from the orthodox school of appeasement literature, who lived through the bleak events they later dissected, sometimes argued that an earlier war could have been won at a lower cost than the one actually fought. Churchill was convinced that the Abyssinian and Rhineland crises represented lost opportunities to put the Dictators in their place early on and thereby dramatically divert the course of history: 'If ever there was an opportunity of striking a decisive blow in a generous cause with the minimum of risk, it was here and now' he wrote of events in Africa during 1935.[2] But it was the 1938 Czech crisis which afforded Churchill most ammunition with which to attack his predecessor. Of the Munich Agreement he wrote: 'There is no merit in putting off a war for a year if, when it comes, it is a far worse war or one much harder to win.'[3] The cold-shouldering of the Soviets at Munich was, for Churchill, a fatal error which alienated a potential ally that would have swung the balance decisively in the Allies' favour during a war in September 1938.[4] Churchill believed that the year 'saved' by the Agreement was no such thing, an irrelevance because Germany also rearmed substantially during this period, maintaining its predominance over Britain. While acknowledging the progress in aircraft production made by Chamberlain during this year's grace, he also noted that the Allies lost the assistance of the Czech army, the huge Skoda munitions works, several million potential Sudeten soldiers and labourers, and freed German forces to operate in other areas of Europe.[5] All in all, for Churchill, Britain entered the war far worse off in 1939 than it would have been had it fought alongside the Czechs one year earlier.

Many contemporaries rallied to Churchill's flag and aligned themselves with him. While admitting that 'there was not one man in a thousand in the country at that time prepared to take physical action with France against a German reoccupation of the Rhineland', Eden came to realise that Britain and France should have called Hitler to order in early 1936.[6] Duff Cooper agreed: 'In the light of after-events, a light that is always denied to us, this was undoubtedly the moment when Great Britain and France should have taken a firm line and insisted upon withdrawal ... Germany was not ready for war and had no allies.'[7] Keen to justify his own resignation two years later, Duff Cooper claimed that a stand in the autumn of 1938 would have led to eventual Allied victory, by way of a possible revolution in Germany:

> I thought I was right then. I know it now. Every fact of which
> we were ignorant at the time and that has come to light since,
> such as the inadequacy of German preparations and the deep
> discontent and even conspiracy of the German Generals against
> Hitler, has confirmed the view that I took.[8]

Harold Macmillan held views similar to Churchill with regard
to the Rhineland crisis. He thought the main problem lay with the
French, but that both they and the British should have considered a
counter-occupation of the heavily-industrialised Saar region in order
to convince Germany to leave without conflict.[9] In a detailed analysis
of events two years later, Macmillan conceded that the Chiefs of Staff
had no confidence at any stage in the military position and that France
was weak and Russia an uncertain quantity. For Macmillan, however,
a war in 1938 with Britain at the Czechs' side would have meant a
two-front war for Germany against a well-armed and determined foe,
all of which would have significantly hampered Hitler's capability to
attack Britain from the air later on.[10] He concluded: 'At the time ... I
thought we ought to have fought at Munich. Since then, after study of
much that has been written on both sides, I see no reason to change
this view.'[11]

The 'both sides' Macmillan referred to here was established with
the stoic defence of Chamberlain's policy launched by some other contemporaries, who maintained that appeasement had been the best
option available. Both Halifax and Simon agreed with the action taken
at Munich, although with the benefit of hindsight they conceded that
the Rhineland was a missed opportunity to have checked the Nazi
march.[12] Of September 1938, Halifax observed that the British people
were simply not ready for war. By contrast,

> When war did come a year later it found a country and
> Commonwealth wholly united within itself, convinced to the
> foundations of soul and conscience that every conceivable effort
> had been made to find the way of sparing Europe the ordeal of

war, and that no alternative remained. And that was the big thing that Chamberlain did.[13]

Simon rounded on the folly of those who would have gambled with peace at the time of Munich when it was well known that the country was still weak:

> There are critics who, after the event, are disposed to say that Britain should at that moment have "called Hitler's bluff". However attractive in retrospect, this is not a wise course to adopt unless you are sure that you are really dealing with a mere bluffer, or that, if he persists, there is ready, there and then, an adequate, united force which will go to all lengths to deal with him.[14]

Simon maintained that the year gained by Munich was preferable to war at this time, as it allowed Britain the space to build up its air force – which was to prove so essential – notwithstanding the fact that Germany was also rearming. He concluded that the cause as well as the military position was far from certain in 1938:

> Then what could Chamberlain do, other than what Chamberlain did? Threaten to declare war forthwith, when the *casus belli* arose out of a claim to adjust a boundary which had worked injustice and to rescue people of German race who were suffering under an alien jurisdiction? There is no ground whatever for imagining that this would either have rescued Czechoslovakia or led to a united front.[15]

Even Vansittart criticised the overly simplistic Churchillian version of history with regard to the so-called missed opportunities of 1935 and 1936:

> He said that 'we could have fought Italy with a minimum of risk'. Yes, if one could exclude the German war, and he could not. Failure to fight, he wrote, 'played a part in leading to an

infinitely more terrible war'. And if a few easy targets had been torpedoed at Alexandria we should have lost it. I still think Winston was mistaken. Germany *might* have been deterred if every valid member of the League had attacked Italy. Of such action there was never the least prospect ... If we had attacked alone and suffered loss, Germany would not have been deterred but incited.[16]

Lord Balfour, second in command at the Air Ministry during these critical years, boldly proclaimed 'thank God for Munich' and rounded on Churchill's claims that a 1938 war would have been better for the Allies. According to Balfour, Chamberlain's successor would have been 'the bravest hero of a defeated country'.[17] Notwithstanding his enduring scepticism about the Soviets, Lord Strang admitted that they should not have been cold-shouldered at Munich. There was still a chance Russia would have fought for the Allies in 1938. Against this, however, he asserted that while the will of the British people was undoubtedly for war in 1939, it had been deeply divided a year earlier.[18] Strang concluded: 'In the war that followed, the aggressor was indeed destroyed ... It is still difficult to assert with any confidence, nor equally can it be disproved, that these results would have been achieved if we had gone to war in 1938.'[19]

Many professional historians have sustained this debate through to the present day. Keith Robbins' influential work *Munich 1938*, published to mark the thirtieth anniversary of the Agreement, tended to support the assertion that Chamberlain sanctioned little more than a tragic necessity. Noting that self-determination was clearly being denied to the Sudetendeutsch prior to the settlement, Robbins pointed out that the majority opinion among the Chiefs of Staff was firmly for appeasement. He also attacked the inconsistency of those such as Churchill who blithely advocated war in 1938 and yet also talked most loudly about the perilous state of Britain's defences.[20] Robbins concluded:

Munich was the necessary purgatory through which Englishmen had to pass before the nation could emerge united in 1939 ... In September 1939 there were few conscientious objectors. Britain went to war in September 1939 rather than 1938, not merely because there was greater confidence in the armaments position, but because it was agreed enough was enough.[21]

Arnold Offner concurred that Chamberlain's decision not to call Hitler's bluff in 1938 could only be understood in light of the over-whelming mood of the era:

> The disillusioning aftermath of the First World War ... the effect of the Great Depression, the popular desire to resolve difficul-ties peacefully ... the widespread legitimate revulsion in the face of warfare's horrors, and belief that at least some of Germany's grievances were real.[22]

Writing in 1972, however, Peter Calvocoressi and Guy Wint brushed aside many of these claims and breathed new life into the Churchillian argument. While conceding that Britain was not ready for war in 1938, they pointed out that neither was Germany. Moreover, the small but efficient Czech army, fighting for its very existence, would have given a good account of itself if supported by Britain and France. Though earning a year's peace for Britain, they continued, Munich lost the war for Europe. They concluded with the telling observation that many of the tanks and weapons which lay waste to France in 1940 were Czech built, in the lands and factories transferred to the Reich as part of the Agreement.[23]

Robert Kee's *Munich: The Eleventh Hour* concluded that Chamberlain had probably made the correct decision 50 years earlier. Putting aside the wider debate about Britain's responsibility to protect Czechoslovakia and France, Kee noted that the majority of Spitfires and Hurricanes which won the Battle of Britain were built in the year the Prime Minister secured at Munich. Moreover, the fact that Hitler broke the terms of the Agreement less than six months later demon-strated to the world where the real blame for war lay, when it eventu-ally came. Long-term American neutrality was certain in any war in 1938, whereas Britain at least had Roosevelt's sympathy in the conflict that erupted a year later.[24]

After Kee, a succession of hard-hitting books published over the following decade restated some of the older arguments and brought the balance of judgement back in favour of the anti-appeasers. For example, Richard Lamb claimed:

> The archives reveal Munich was a disaster, because Hitler completely bluffed Neville Chamberlain over German military potential. If the British and French had declared war on Germany in October 1938 Russia would have joined them, and the result must have been an ignominious defeat for Germany.[25]

Williamson Murray's various works on the balance of power in Europe during the 1930s have provided a compelling case that Britain should have fought in 1938 rather than in 1939. In a detailed counterfactual exploration of how a 1938 war might have developed, Murray, while accepting the inevitable uncertainty surrounding his conclusions, asserted that Germany was substantially weaker in almost all areas in 1938 than in 1939, and that the losses it would have taken in defeating the Czechs would have significantly hampered it in any ensuing struggle against France and Russia. Moreover, the economic effects on Germany of a war in 1938, with no Russian ally to provide supplies as in 1939 and 1940, would have seriously undermined the whole war effort. In short, Germany would have fought itself to a virtual standstill against the French, akin to the stalemate of the Great War, after taking heavy losses against Czechoslovakia in the autumn of 1938. It would therefore have been in a diminished position to attack Britain from the air during 1939. All in all, there would have been no Battle of Britain and even the Holocaust might have been prevented.[26]

While conceding that Britain missed its opportunity to stop Hitler during 1936, Roy Denman has recently argued that he was not bluffing during the Czech crisis two years later. Nor, he insists, would eventual Allied victory in a 1938 war against a state that had just absorbed the vast resources of Austria have been at all certain. Similarly, he claims that the German generals were in no position to launch a serious coup attempt against Hitler in 1938, as Duff Cooper and others speculated, all of which made Chamberlain's decision for peace at Munich a sound and sensible policy.[27]

David Dutton observes that the time secured by the settlement – 'in all the circumstances of September 1938, the best outcome that Chamberlain or anyone else could have hoped for' – resulted in British fighter command being almost ten times as powerful by the outbreak of war.[28] Moreover, he suggests that even if Churchill had been in charge during the Czech crisis, he too would have sanctioned a Munich-style agreement, as evidenced by the cynical way in which he bought off Stalin with Poland and other spheres of influence at Yalta in 1945.[29] Finally, the recent work of Hugh Ragsdale suggests that Stalin would never have sanctioned a struggle to defend Czechoslovakia in 1938. Even if he had, the prospects of reasonable military support were 'not very bright'. The weakness of the Red Army, Soviet transport and infrastructure chaos, as well as Polish reluctance to allow Russian troops across its soil would all have contributed here.[30] Doubtless this debate will take a few more twists and turns over the coming years.

In what follows, special attention will be paid to the key year of 1938. This was the peace-time year when the option of war was most widely considered in the wake of the *Anschluss* and during the dark months of the Czech crisis. It will also be shown, however, that Chamberlain and his government considered war at other times, when the public knew much less about the imminent threat, as in January 1939, when intelligence reports erroneously warned of an imminent German invasion of the Low Countries. Various ambiguities surrounding the idea of war as an alternative to appeasement will also be considered. In fact, very few critics ever mentioned the word 'war' itself. Instead, they tended to couch statements in deliberately vague language about 'standing firm' or 'drawing a line'. Obvious links with previous chapters will also be apparent, as many who backed war did so only on the assumption that certain alliances would follow, or with the proviso that the gaps in Britain's defences would be remedied. As this chapter is concerned with war itself – the ultimate final resort – wider opposition to that alternative is taken as given, and needs no further exploration here.

Origins and Nature of the Alternative

Despite the widespread revulsion towards war prevalent in Britain throughout the 1930s, events in the middle of the decade caused the first stirrings from a small band of political figures that a more robust response to the Fascist problem was required. The Italian invasion of Abyssinia in October 1935 inevitably led to increased foreign policy discussion in parliament. One or two League of Nations supporters, such as Viscount Cecil and Lord Lothian, mooted an Anglo-French blockade of the Suez Canal in late 1935 and early 1936, to cut supplies to the Italian army and force Mussolini to capitulate. This was somewhat ironic, given that League enthusiasts would be considered among the leading 'pacificists' of the era. Even some figures less enamoured with the League, such as Liberal National MP Robert Bernays, felt that 'if the British and French fleets took up their station in front of the Suez Canal, Mussolini would be powerless'.[31] This strategy would, of course, have run the serious risk of war breaking out with Italy.

The German remilitarization of the Rhineland broadened the debate. Though Robert Boothby did not feel that this specific breach represented a *casus belli*, he was nevertheless convinced that a clear line would soon have to be drawn, after which force should be actively considered:

> Are we at any stage going to take up a line and say, 'We are not going to let this happen'? I am sure that moment will come when the whole of the people of this country unitedly will say to Germany, sooner or later, 'you have got to stop'. I agree that the moment has not come now. Nobody feels that we can apply very strong or stringent measures against Germany because she has put troops into the Rhineland, but she must know at what point we intend to say 'enough'.[32]

His colleague Harold Macmillan elaborated on this theme in a letter to *The Times* a few days later. He referred to the lessons of the Great War, where it was popularly held that Britain's reluctance to state its position clearly beforehand actually contributed to the outbreak:

It is indeed quite evident that a previous clear commitment would have kept them out: If German statesmen had realised beforehand that a certain line of policy would involve the enmity of so vast a combination, that fatal policy would not have been followed, and there would have been no war. If, that is, it had been clear beforehand that the combatants would do what, at the last they were obliged to do, they would not have had to do it.[33]

The continuing Abyssinian conflict remained a live issue and led more politicians to speculate that the foreign adventures of the Dictators could be averted by the threat of war. On 6 April 1936, James Maxton of the Independent Labour Party stated that 'you are not going to get the League of Nations accepted by the Mussolinis or the Hitlers unless you are going to take armed force methods'.[34] Labour peer Lord Strabolgi concurred: 'We have to be prepared to resist force with force'.[35]

In June 1936, Conservative Viscount Wolmer summarised a growing mood in the Commons. Economic sanctions were no longer sufficient to bring the Fascists to heel:

The lesson to be drawn surely is that if the League decides to act against individual nations it must come to an act of war. There must be the employment of the policeman's truncheon against the gangster. Policemen do not deal with gangsters by sitting outside the house and preventing the baker calling. They have to deal with them by more forcible and speedy methods.[36]

While almost nobody in Britain advocated a full-blown conflict over Abyssinia or the Rhineland – though some were prepared to run the significant risk of it – the idea of using the threat of force as a legitimate tool of diplomacy had been suggested by a number of figures, from across all parties, by the time Chamberlain assumed the premiership. Most, however, only backed limited forms of conflict under a League of Nations banner, rather than an all-out continental war.

The *Anschluss* caused the next consideration of war, or the series of steps possibly resulting in war, on any sizeable scale. This event brought the issue of Czechoslovakia to the fore, leading to the imminent threat of war in the summer and autumn of 1938 and the Munich Agreement in late September. Eden had resigned as Foreign Secretary in February, calling somewhat vaguely for Britain to 'stand firm' against the Dictators, rather than continue along the road of appeasement.[37] In response, Sinclair and Churchill reflected on the chances Britain had lost. The former noted that 'the one occasion when the ruthlessness of the Dictatorship powers was temporarily checked, was when we stood up to them in the Nyon Conference'.[38] The latter bemoaned the lack of action taken against Hitler over the Rhineland two years earlier, something he now saw as a golden missed opportunity to check the Nazis.[39]

The events in Austria gave rise to a host of criticisms of appeasement, the majority of which were on the lines of Eden's demand for Britain to toughen its stance. Such calls were heard repeatedly in parliament over the coming months. In March 1938, Attlee announced that 'there must come a time when it is necessary to stand firm'.[40] This point was directly echoed by his colleague James Ede in the same debate.[41] As the crisis deepened in July, Sinclair joined the chorus by claiming 'now is the time ... to stand firm'.[42] His colleague Richard Acland used the same phrase just minutes later,[43] while Josiah Wedgwood rounded on appeasement with a call for Britain, once again, to 'stand firm'.[44]

But what did this vague term actually mean? War itself? Resistance to Hitler's likely next move in the form of an ultimatum? A guarantee of Czechoslovakia, which, if broken, would result in conflict? The strategy was rarely fully explained. It was as if many MPs felt that a much tougher line was needed but did not know what precise form it should take or what the potential results might be. They hoped the Nazis would back down in the face of increasing firmness but were unsure what to do if they did not. Many were afraid to utter the word 'war' itself – for *Hansard* shows that almost none did so – lest it trigger the unwanted explosion, or see them denounced as warmongers by their political opponents and the general public alike. Very few had concrete and clearly stated policies in the spring and summer of

1938, most stumbling through this uncertain period lurching from one position to another. A small number, however, did talk publicly of a Czech guarantee as the move by which the policy of 'standing firm' might be implemented. This would at least lay down a marker for conflict to Germany and the wider world. James Ede coupled his call to stand firm with a demand for a guarantee and he was joined in this by figures such as Vyvyan Adams from the Conservatives and Geoffrey Mander from the Liberals.[45] Leo Amery, meanwhile, put it in stark terms:

> Let us either make up our minds that we must stand out, and let everybody concerned know it or let us say to France, Czechoslovakia and Germany, in language plain and simple as we can make it, that the first German soldier or aeroplane to cross the Czechoslovakian border will bring the whole might of this country against Germany.[46]

A few days later, however, he admitted privately that 'the more I thought over it since, the more doubtful I have become, partly because we shall not get Dominion or home public opinion sufficiently united'.[47] This once again underlines the uncertainty surrounding considerations of war – where the heart often pulled for resistance, but the head favoured accommodation, and sometimes *vice versa*.

Nevertheless, Viscount Cecil, regularly presented as a pacifist figure, felt certain enough to echo Amery's public statement by claiming that the only sound policy now was to say to Hitler: 'If you insist on breaking the pie then you must find as your opponents the whole force of the British Empire.'[48] Churchill soon joined the ranks, coupling his rallying cry for a Grand Alliance with calls for an Anglo-French statement of intent to stand by the Czechs if they were attacked by Germany.[49]

* * *

The world lurched precariously on the brink of war during September 1938. As the Czech crisis reached its peak and conflict looked increasingly likely, a number of politicians settled on military action against Germany as their policy of last resort. Churchill wrote to Halifax on 31 August, urging fleet movements in the Channel to act as a deterrent.[50] By the end of the following month, when Hitler's new demands at Godesberg made war seemingly inevitable, this had evolved into the notion of a full naval blockade and had the support of small band of MPs who gathered at Churchill's flat. According to Harold Nicolson, they included Sinclair, Macmillan, Boothby, Cecil and Amery, all pressing for 'the immediate application of war measures'.[51]

Despite the widespread relief, freely acknowledged on all sides of the House, that war had been averted following the Munich Conference, many were still deeply unhappy with the outcome. Josiah Wedgwood wrote to Duff Cooper just after the latter's resignation, congratulating him on his principled stand. He added: 'I do dislike belonging to a race of clucking old hens and damned cowards.'[52] But the scale of opposition to the settlement – the final parliamentary vote on Munich was 366 in favour and 144 against – could hardly be viewed as nationwide backing for war or the threat of war as an alternative. Indeed, many of the fiercest critics merely lapsed into the vague 'stand firm' terminology so popular during the spring. Only a handful of speakers openly favoured conflict instead of appeasement and the majority of these felt that only the inference of war would be required to make Hitler back down. Whether or not they were prepared to make good their threats if Hitler did not blink first was another question entirely. Indeed, Tory MP Sir Thomas Moore rounded on the vague words of many appeasement detractors when defending Chamberlain's achievements at Munich:

The critics in this House ... have rather disappointed me ... One phrase has been repeated over and over again, the phrase of 'taking a stand' or 'standing up to'; but those who have used it have not developed, indeed they have endeavoured to avoid developing, that bellicose declaration to its logical conclusion. They know, though fearful of acknowledging it, that 'standing up to' or 'taking a stand' means fighting.[53]

Duff Cooper's resignation speech was, however, unequivocal. On 3 October, he opened the parliamentary debate by claiming that Britain should have opposed Hitler and taken a much stronger position: 'Our first duty was to make it plain exactly where we stood and what we would do.' He went on: 'All information pointed to the fact that Germany was preparing for war at the end of September, and all recommendations agreed that the one way in which it could have been prevented was by Great Britain making a firm stand and stating that she would be in that war.' He concluded that, unlike many of his former colleagues, 'I can still walk about the world with my head erect'.[54]

Churchill felt that threatening war in the form of a Czech guarantee would have saved peace as well as honour, although he admitted that he could not be certain of this: 'Between submission and immediate war there was this third alternative', he stated, and then claimed that the Czechs would have been able to make better terms with Germany alone, in battle, than those they had dictated to them at Munich.[55] Harold Nicolson claimed 'we ought to have resisted ... We still ought to resist ... I should have almost been prepared to go to the point of war to demonstrate, I hope, that it was not possible for one country in Europe, a large country, to crush another'.[56] How he could have resisted Hitler by *almost* going to war is unclear, although he presumably felt the German Chancellor would have backed down in response to an ultimatum. A day earlier, Josiah Wedgwood had hinted that he might have fought had he been in Chamberlain's shoes: 'To my mind the freedom of this country, the democracy of the world, is something that is worth fighting for.'[57] Lord Strabolgi agreed. Indeed, he was confident that the Czechs would have been able to resist Germany long enough for Britain to come to their assistance: 'I believe the best military opinion maintains that the Czechs could have held out on those magnificent fortifications which they are now surrendering as part of this "peace with honour" for about four months'.[58]

Despite widespread ignorance of the true state of Britain's military preparedness, a small group within the anti-Munich camp thus felt that resisting Germany would have been the right policy at this time. They would fight if they had to, but most were convinced that

Hitler would have backed down at the last moment. Yet many within this group, including Duff Cooper and Churchill, only abstained in the parliamentary division on Munich, rather than voting against the government's policy. Party loyalties no doubt played an important role here as many of the abstainers were Conservatives and could not easily vote against Chamberlain. Harold Nicolson, however, claimed that dissatisfaction within Tory ranks was much higher than suggested by the vote alone: 'The House breaks up with the Tories yelling to keep their spirits up. But they well know that Chamberlain has put us in a ghastly position and that we ought to have been prepared to go to war and smash Hitler.'[59]

* * *

Wider opinion on the question of war illustrates many parallels. The League of Nations Union seemingly favoured a hard line over the Czech crisis, with Gilbert Murray feeling sure that the threat of war would have been enough to pacify the situation without recourse to a humiliating settlement. On 7 October 1938, he noted privately, 'I believe that if we had told Hitler months ago not "that we very likely would be drawn in", but that we certainly would fight together with France and Russia, he would have drawn back'.[60] Some pacifists also took a similar line, perhaps surprisingly. The International Peace Campaign produced a leaflet at the height of the crisis, claiming that war could be avoided by the clear threat of war: 'The tragedy of the Great War of 1914 was that if those who went to war with Germany had been able to say beforehand that they would resist her, the war might have been avoided.'[61] That such groups, with a clear loathing for conflict, could advocate such a risky strategy suggests they must have been very sure that Hitler was only ever bluffing.

The national press was, in general, vehemently hostile to war for the majority of the decade, although some of those most critical of appeasement did advocate increasing firmness after Hitler's rise to power. Many papers adopted the vague 'stand firm' language popular in the wake of the *Anschluss* and the Munich settlement, but explicit calls for war itself were much less common. The *News Chronicle* was

one of the most militant British papers and in March 1938 backed a
Czech guarantee and collective security as its response to the *Anschluss*:
'Only one thing will make Hitler pause – his own weapon, the threat
of force ... What else should Britain do? Declare solemnly, and now,
before all the world, that if Czechoslovakia is invaded, and France
goes to her aid, Britain will be found by their side.'[62] In response to
Munich, the *Chronicle* backed the principled stand of the former First
Lord of the Admiralty:

> We believe Mr Duff Cooper was right. We have ourselves
> been urging for months past that British policy should be
> stated in unmistakable language. Had that been done earlier,
> Czechoslovakia would have been saved, Britain would have been
> spared the gnawing anxiety of these last days, and war would
> still have been averted.[63]

The Prague Coup led to even wider condemnation of Nazi Germany
and expressions of greater firmness on the part of many newspapers.
On 17 March 1939, the *Daily Telegraph* opined that 'only the threat
of a counter-offensive ... can deter a Dictator with the will towards
aggression'.[64] Even the largely pro-appeasement *Times* was moved to
state that 'there is nothing left for moral debate in this crude and
brutal act of oppression and suppression'.[65] However, it only favoured
the introduction of preparatory war measures, such as vast rearmament
and the pursuit of alliances, rather than a declaration of war itself.

Many members of the general public also felt that war or the
explicit threat of war was required when tensions were high. 'J.E.J.'
from Richmond wrote to the *Daily Herald* just after the *Anschluss* to
state that 'British statesmanship is bankrupt if it cannot say now to
Hitler, "So far and no further"'. On the same day, Paul Ingham from
Birmingham wrote: 'It is just August 1914 all over again ... For heaven's
sake let's tell Hitler where we stand now, instead of leaving it till it is
too late.'[66]

The Czech crisis evoked similar emotions. Mass Observation
recorded numerous colourful examples of such statements from inter-
viewees in the unnamed London borough of 'Metrop' as tensions

reached their peak. Following Chamberlain's return from Godesberg, when Hitler had threatened to march within days unless his new demands for the Sudetenland were met, the majority of responses were decidedly bellicose:

(Man of 30):   Yes I am prepared to go and fight. Hitler has gone too bloody far this time, he needs teaching a lesson ...
(Man of 24):   I don't want to fight but I will go ... Hitler is a big brag-gart ... We can still call his bluff. All my pals are war-minded now.[67]

Gallup Poll data suggests that the general public also seriously con-sidered war following the Prague Coup in 1939. A huge 76 per cent of those surveyed in July felt that Britain should stand by its guarantee to Poland if it was attacked by Germany, with only 13 per cent against.[68] The Russian negotiations were well underway by this point, of course, and there was now greater faith in the nation's defences.

The Prague Coup also gave rise to a general feeling in parliament that war was on its way. Even if few called for direct military action as a result of Hitler's violation of the Munich Agreement, the result-ant clamour for alliances and mass rearmament, as discussed above, was huge. In the Commons on 15 March 1939, Labour's Hugh Dalton asked the government whether 'a barrier will be drawn', whether 'it shall be said to the totalitarian states, "Thus far, but no further"?'[69] In the Lords a few days later, the Liberal Marquess of Crewe raged against Hitler's betrayal and demanded that Britain join those countries pre-pared to resist Germany, 'if necessary to any forcible extent'.[70] Even the Archbishop of Canterbury, who claimed that war was 'indescribably odious', conceded that 'there are some things that are more sacred even than peace, and ... these things must be defended'.[71]

Buoyed by the Prime Minister's tougher policy as represented by the Polish Guarantee, politicians increasingly talked of strategies to prepare for and win a future conflict, rather than how to prevent it. Again, this transcended party lines. Peers Lord Lothian and Viscount Astor delivered similar speeches on 13 April 1939, both advocat-ing 'superior power' as the only answer to the Nazi menace,[72] while National Labour's Harold Nicolson noted: 'I can now see no alternative between early war upon a false issue or the abandonment of the whole of Europe to Nazi domination.'[73]

By the summer of 1939, almost every politician backed the government's Peace Front policy, confident that the prospect of a two-front war with Britain and France to the West and Russia to the East would deter Hitler from any new outrage, or defeat him if battle was joined. Europe was no longer the only possible sphere of conflict, however. Cecil called in June for Britain to join the ongoing Chinese struggle against Japan: 'We ought to do everything to assist China to drive back the Japanese invasion from her shores.'[74] By late July, the mood in parliament was positively bellicose. 'We cannot afford any more appeasement', declared Josiah Wedgwood, 'we are determined to stand firm, whatever comes of it'.[75]

That parliament was overwhelmingly in favour of war when it eventually came is without doubt. Indeed, it was the furious mood of the Commons at the delays in enacting the Anglo-Polish Alliance on 2 September 1939 which ultimately dictated the final timing of the declaration. This mood in parliament left Chamberlain 'as white as a sheet', and convinced him that his government would fall unless he announced war the next morning.[76]

Consideration of the Alternative

Chamberlain eventually declared war in September 1939. To what extent, however, did the National Government consider this option before that point? Was it ever seen as a viable strategy in 1937 or 1938? Did the government agree that the Abyssinian and Rhineland crises were missed opportunities to stop the Fascists in their tracks? When Mussolini amassed troops on the Abyssinian border in the summer of 1935, Chamberlain himself speculated about one possible solution: 'If we and France together determined that we could take any measures necessary to stop him, we could do so, and quite easily. We could, for example, stop the passage of his supplies through the Suez Canal. If the French would play their part.'[77]

Chamberlain's initial response to the invasion suggests that he had it in him to be one of the most pugnacious figures within the government. On 29 November 1935, he recorded the course of that day's Cabinet discussions in his diary: 'I replied that if anyone else would give the lead, well and good, but in the last resort, if necessary, we ought to give the lead ourselves ... We should press Laval to tell Mussolini that, if he attacked us, France would at once come to our assistance.'[78]

The remilitarization of the Rhineland was not felt by the government to be a *casus belli*. While Chamberlain announced that 'this is a time when people should keep cool heads', the Ambassador in Berlin, Sir Eric Phipps, told Eden that the zone represented the sort of post-war grievance he was keen to get away from in efforts to pacify the continent:[79]

> Though Germany might be defeated in a fresh resort to arms today, the position in Europe would be no better. There would be no guarantee that the French would prove more reasonable at a fresh Peace Conference than they were at Versailles. In other words the seeds of fresh wars would be planted in a new peace treaty. Proof of this is the fact that France twenty years after the war is still clamouring for a one-sided demilitarised zone.[80]

Despite Eden's warnings that the integrity of France and Belgium were of vital importance to Britain, he gave no lead to his French counterparts with regard to military action during the crisis. Instead, he broadly looked for the opportunities that could be gained from the situation for better Anglo-German relations – that is, he favoured moves towards appeasement over moves towards war.

The Abyssinian hostilities were progressing comfortably in Italy's favour by the spring of 1936 and, again, several important figures within the foreign policy making elite contemplated action against Mussolini. Vansittart summarised the debate taking place within the Foreign Office during April:

> I do not think it is of any use at this stage to write of closing the [Suez] Canal. It is highly improbable that the government would consider it, and a very serious situation would certainly be

created for the government in the country, particularly if the war (for of course it would lead to war) did not go well in the opening stages. There would have been a great deal to be said for closing the Canal at the very beginning of this unhappy affair. But we were not in a position to do so and even now it would mean taking great risks.[81]

Prime Minister Baldwin seemed to indicate that Britain would not be involved in any conflict in the near future when he let slip in July to a delegation of senior Tories that 'if there is any fighting in Europe to be done I should like to see the Bolsheviks and Nazis doing it'.[82] Britain remained committed to non-intervention during the Spanish Civil War, which had just begun and served as an additional complication over the coming years. This decision clearly illustrates the government's basic position on European conflict at this time. In a review of foreign policy options at the end of 1936, Vansittart indicated that the broad aim was to avoid war for the next two years at least, while rearmament and the defensive position improved:

> It may be generally said that the year 1939 is the first in which we shall be able to breathe with even comparative relief, although much will yet remain to be taken in hand. We shall not even have reached safety. Germany is admittedly not yet ready for war on a considerable scale, either militarily, economically or politically ... To the Foreign Office therefore falls the task of holding the situation at least till 1939.[83]

When Chamberlain assumed the premiership in May 1937, his government had briefly considered, but ultimately rejected, the idea of war on several occasions. The fresh vigour with which the new Prime Minister approached foreign policy, however, led some within the Foreign Office to call for a tougher line towards the Dictators. For example, following conversations with his Austrian counterpart at this time, Eden suggested that 'a word of warning as to our interests in Central Europe expressed in general terms would suffice to hold German ambitions in check'.[84]

Echoing Vansittart's earlier reference to 'holding the situation at least till 1939', the Military Attaché to the British Embassy in Berlin, General Hotblack, stated in September that only by 1940 would German soldiers 'be in a position to carry out offensive action outside their frontiers', and that too 'provided they are not faced with the prospect of a very long war'.[85] This gave the impression that all-out war would not need to be contemplated, as a worst case scenario, for some time yet. Nevertheless, the success of the Nyon Conference later that month seemingly convinced Eden that appeasement should give way to firmness in any future dealings with the Fascists. In a memorandum produced shortly afterwards, he elaborated on his increasingly firm position:

> There are those who say that at all costs we must avoid being brought into opposition with Germany, Japan and Italy. This is certainly true, but it is not true that the best way to avoid such a state of affairs is continually to retreat before all three of them. To do so is to invite them to converge upon us. In any retreat there must on occasion be a counter attack and the correct method of counter attack is to do so against the weaker member of the three in overwhelming force.[86]

In November 1937, Laurence Collier, head of the Northern Department of the Foreign Office, agreed that it was impossible to 'fight all three robbers at once … though that is what is likely to come if the aggressors think we will always give way to them'. Instead, he proposed 'a state of armed truce based upon a balance of power'.[87] Unlike Eden, however, he did not favour any 'counter attack'. More cautious voices within the Foreign Office, such as Vansittart's successor Cadogan, urged restraint upon the Prime Minister. He warned that it was 'no good blustering unless we are sure we can carry out our threats'.[88]

As already noted, the key Chiefs of Staff report of December 1937 announced that 'we cannot foresee the time when our defence forces will be strong enough to safeguard our territory, trade and vital interests against Germany, Italy and Japan simultaneously' and this serves as one of the most concise statements of why appeasement was favoured over war for most of Chamberlain's premiership.[89] The report clearly had a profound impact. Eden adopted a more cautious tone over Christmas when asked whether he favoured League military sanctions against Japan in view of the conflict in China: 'I say deliberately that nobody could contemplate any action of that kind in the Far East unless they are convinced that they have overwhelming force to back their policy.'[90] Cold strategic realities weighed heavily here. Britain was too vulnerable and its commitments too numerous to send an armada on dangerous adventures far away from home waters. The attractiveness of even Britain's most likely allies was very limited at this time.

The events of March 1938, culminating in the Munich Agreement in September, led to the most serious contemplation of war by the government until the final declaration itself. Initial responses to Hitler's latest foreign policy coup were firm. Days before the German troops marched into Austria, Vansittart warned that 'we are incurring an enormous responsibility in not speaking to Hitler a great deal more firmly and explicitly than we have yet done in this matter ... If he is not checked ... he may carry himself and everyone else into disaster'.[91] A few days after the *Anschluss*, Oliver Harvey joined him in calling for a guarantee of Czechoslovakia as the best means to underline the point at which Britain would go to war.[92] Chamberlain himself conceded in a letter to his sister that 'it is perfectly evident, surely, now that force is the only argument Germany understands'.[93] However, even more combative figures, such as Vansittart, did not think the *Anschluss* was a good enough reason to declare war. As Cadogan noted of conversations in the Foreign Office,

> Van has been like a cat on hot bricks, but Halifax doesn't care. I had it out with Van. I said, 'It's easy to be brave in speech: Will you fight?' He said, 'No'. I said, 'Then what's it all about? To me it seems a most cowardly thing to do to urge a small man to fight a big if you won't help the former'.[94]

Halifax himself announced on 16 March that 'nothing short of war can put back the clock, and statesmen of the League are not prepared

to go to war on this issue', which seemingly ruled out direct military action.[95] The Foreign Policy Committee met over several days to
discuss strategy and decided against a guarantee of Czechoslovakia.
Military logistics were again the key issue in determining appeasement ahead of resistance. Chamberlain observed 'that the more one
studied the map of Central Europe the more hopeless was the idea
that any effective help could be swiftly brought to Czechoslovakia in
an emergency ... We were in no position from the armament point of
view to enter such a war'.[96] Halifax pointed out that any new military
commitment made to the Czechs would also 'involve considerable risk
in that there would be an element of bluff on our side'.[97] It made little
sense to threaten a war that nobody in the government wanted to fight
anyway.

A Chiefs of Staff report reinforced the Committee's decision. It concluded: 'We can do nothing to prevent the dog getting the bone, and
we have no means of making him give it up.'[98] Accordingly, when
Chamberlain addressed the Commons on 24 March, he ruled out a
Czech guarantee. But he did add an ominous general warning:

> There are certain vital interests of this country for which, if they
> were menaced, we should fight – for the defence of British ter-
> ritories and the communications which are vital to our national
> existence .... for our liberty and the right to live our lives accord-
> ing to the standards which our national character have prescribed
> for us ... Where peace and war are concerned, legal obligations are
> not alone involved, and, if war broke out, it would be unlikely
> to be confined to those who have assumed such obligations. It
> would be quite impossible to say where it would end and what
> governments would become involved.[99]

*   *   *

Tensions increased during the summer. Harvey speculated that
British involvement against Italian forces in the Spanish Civil War
might cause Mussolini to 'behave as he did over Nyon ... by effectively

withdrawing'. On the other hand, he admitted, it might just cause
him to 'go off the deep end'.[100] Accordingly, Britain kept out of
Spain and the primary focus remained Czechoslovakia. On 5 August,
Halifax conceded that 'I have always felt that to fight a war for one,
two or three years to protect or recreate something that you know
you could not directly protect, and probably could never recreate,
did not make sense'.[101] By contrast, Vansittart warned that one of his
intelligence contacts in Germany had told him that *only* by standing
firm and threatening war would Hitler be deterred from taking all of
Czechoslovakia in the next few weeks.[102] Assailed by such contradictory reports and recommendations, Chamberlain contemplated what
action he could take. Seemingly moving towards a firmer stand, he
told his Cabinet on 30 August that 'many people in this country
and in Germany took the view that if we made it clear now that, if
Germany used force, we should come in on the side of Czechoslovakia,
there would be no war'.[103]

Military experts continued to put forward their conflicting views.
Basil Liddell-Hart suggested that 'it is doubtful whether the Germans
are capable of conquering Czechoslovakia as a whole unless they
were free to concentrate the bulk of their forces against her – which
would hardly be practicable unless the French were neutralised'. This,
though, was a minority opinion.[104] Phipps, now based in Paris, sent
the Foreign Office an account of how Colonel Lindbergh had returned
from a tour of German bases, 'horrified at overwhelming strength
of Germany in the air and terrible weakness of all other powers'.[105]
This sort of information weighed heavily upon Chamberlain in early
September and, with a remarkable degree of foresight as to the future
historical debate about his reputation, he elaborated on his thoughts
in a letter to his sister. British military weakness was the crux of the
matter once again:

I fully realise that, if eventually things go wrong, and the aggression takes place, there will be many, including Winston, who
will say that the British government must bear its responsibility, and that if only they had had the courage to tell Hitler now
that, if he used force, we should at once declare war, that would

have stopped him ... But I am satisfied that we should be wrong to allow the most vital decision that any country should take, the decision as to peace or war, to pass out of our hands into those of the ruler of another country, and a lunatic at that ... You should never menace unless you are in a position to carry out your threats.[106]

After the Prime Minister's dramatic first flight to see Hitler at Berchtesgaden on 15 September, the Cabinet, including Duff Cooper, agreed in principle to cede areas of the Sudetenland to Germany in order to avoid war and allow self-determination for the Sudetendeutsch. Following meetings with Daladier and Bonnet, an Anglo-French proposal to this effect was delivered to the Czech government on 19 September and reluctantly accepted two days later. Britain and France had made it clear in the meantime that they would be unable to help resist any German assault.

Chamberlain then met Hitler at Godesberg, intending to inform him of the Czechs' grudging consent to the territorial transfers – the timescale of which he proposed should be decided by an international commission – only for the *Führer* to announce that delay was no longer possible and a solution must be found either by agreement or by force before 1 October. After several days digesting this new development, on 25 September the majority of the Cabinet, led by Halifax, overrode Chamberlain's inclination to accept the Godesberg terms. Duff Cooper, Hore-Belisha and Oliver Stanley were the leading voices here. Horace Wilson, Chamberlain's special adviser, was accordingly deputed to meet Hitler and deliver news of the British rejection. A day later, the German Chancellor announced to Wilson that their countries would be at war within days unless the transfer took place immediately. This was averted only at the eleventh hour by Hitler's acceptance, under pressure from Mussolini, of Chamberlain's final plea for a new summit. This was held at Munich. In the days before the conference took place, trenches were dug in British parks and gardens, gas masks were issued to the general public and the fleet was mobilised. Chamberlain, though horrified, accepted that war was imminent unless he could secure a late reprieve. The nation was overwhelmingly relieved when he did so. The scenes of popular celebration and the thousands of gifts which poured into Downing Street over the coming weeks are testament to this.

There is no doubt that Hitler's unreasonable new demands at Godesberg were the deciding factor in causing the Cabinet to reluctantly settle on war as an alternative to appeasement, in defiance of their Prime Minister's wishes. On 30 August 1938, Hore-Belisha wrote in his diary, 'I was against any threat being made that we would declare war if Germany attacked Czechoslovakia' and he voted with his Cabinet colleagues to accept the Sudetenland transfer on 17 September.[107] By 24 September, however, despite conceding that war now would be like 'a man attacking a tiger before he has loaded his gun', he wrote that 'it is quite clear that Hitler only understands one argument... Why should we not display the might we possess? Why should we not mobilise the fleet?'[108] The government's decision for war in late September was a bottom-up process, with Chamberlain pressured to reject the Memorandum by Halifax and the Cabinet, and Halifax in turn being stiffened by Cadogan in the Foreign Office. Ardently pro-appeasement since assuming his post, Cadogan nevertheless recorded:

> I was completely horrified – he [Chamberlain] was quite calmly for total surrender... Ye Gods! ... Pray God there will be a revolt... Drove him [Halifax] home and gave him a bit of my mind... I know we... are in no condition to fight: but I'd rather be beat than dishonoured.[109]

The National Government had, therefore, reluctantly accepted that war was necessary, but it was Chamberlain's determination that appeasement should win through which averted hostilities at the eleventh hour. This policy was always preferable to war in Chamberlain's eyes – indeed, avoiding conflagration was its central purpose. At Munich, Britain and France pledged to guarantee the new Czech borders, a strategically naive move, heavily criticised by Chamberlain's opponents and eventually swept under the carpet by the Prime Minister himself after Prague.

Reviewing foreign policy in the wake of the crisis, Cadogan noted soberly that, while he did not advocate fighting Germany in the near future, a tougher line was now clearly needed. 'The only alternatives', he noted, 'are: (A) Fight Germany; (B) Continue to do nothing. The former, I suspect, would lead to disaster, the latter has proved to lead nowhere else.'[110] The Nazi orchestrated *Kristallnacht* in Berlin shortly after, dented any mood of optimism about Anglo-German relations still lingering after the conference. Discussing potential responses in the Foreign Policy Committee, Halifax speculated that 'it was possible that a resolute attitude on our part, backed by a display of strength, might discourage the extremists in Germany and encourage the moderates'. Inskip, however, spoke for everyone present when he stated that 'the one thing that clearly we could not do was go to war on this issue'.[111] Chamberlain also resisted calls at this time, both from within the government and outside, to set up a peace-time War Cabinet, possibly taking Eden or Churchill back into the fold. Such a move, he felt, would only provoke Hitler into fury, as well as undermining his own appeasement efforts.[112]

In December 1938, Chamberlain addressed the Foreign Press Association, elaborating on the decisions he took at Munich:

> It seemed to me that only two alternatives were open to us. One was to make up our minds that war was inevitable and to throw the whole energies of the country into preparation for it. The other was to make a prolonged and determined effort to eradicate the possible causes of war and to try out the methods of personal contact and discussion ... There are some who sincerely believe that the first course was the one we should have taken. I believe that in this country they are a small minority ... We should rather remember what was the alternative which the Munich Agreement averted.[113]

He then went on to give an insight into his personal motives for pursuing appeasement. The death of his cousin Norman during the Great War had devastated him as a younger man, but any future war might be even more catastrophic:

War today differs fundamentally from all the wars of the past inasmuch as its first and most numerous victims are not the professional fighters, but the civilian population, the workman and the clerk, the housewife and, most horrible of all, the children ... It leaves behind a trail of loss and suffering ... Such consequences ought never to be incurred unless we can be satisfied and our people are satisfied that every honourable alternative has been tried and found impossible.[114]

* * *

The January 1939 war scare tested this resolve further. Cadogan claimed that it was 'vital that we should do what we can to resist a German invasion of Holland', something William Strang also mooted a day earlier.[115] The Foreign Policy Committee met on 23 January and decided upon immediate military conversations with France, Holland and Belgium, while also agreeing to share information with America. Chamberlain was keen to remind his colleagues of the weakness of the British Expeditionary Force, granted the policy of limited liability over recent years: 'Whatever might eventually transpire, it must be clear that at the outset there could be, in fact, no possibility of Britain landing a large army on the continent.' Halifax, however, suggested making a public statement about the integrity of the Low Countries, while the Dominions Secretary, Malcolm MacDonald, felt that 'even if there was very little that we could do in a military sense to save Holland from invasion ... we should have to intervene'.[116]

Accordingly, when the Committee met on 26 January 1939, despite the warnings of the Chief of the Air Staff, Sir Cyril Newall, that 'we could do little or nothing to prevent Holland being overrun', all present decided that Britain must fight if the Low Countries were invaded. Halifax declared that 'failure on our part to intervene would undermine our position in the world and would only mean that at some later stage we should have to face the same struggle with Germany with fewer friends and in far worse circumstances'. The minutes record that 'the Prime Minister said that this was also his opinion'.[117] Once again, intelligence turned out to be flawed and no invasion attempt was launched. But the government had clearly resolved for war in the event of a German offensive, a development not always noted by historians of the period.

The disturbing events of recent months had woken the government to the necessity to consider a full-scale war against Nazi Germany. Halifax had certainly adopted a firmer line since the Munich Agreement, described by him much later as a 'horrible and wretched business, but the lesser of two evils'.[118] As Harvey recorded in his diary during February 1939,

> He is almost unrecognisable from the Halifax of a year ago. He says bluntly "no more Munich for me" and I am sure he is convinced that now we are stronger we must stand firm. He felt in September that we were not strong enough to risk fighting unless it was absolutely vital to us – and that the Czech issue was not vital.[119]

Indeed, a gap clearly existed between Chamberlain and many of his senior colleagues in the last six months of peace. While most of the latter now viewed war as increasingly likely, the Prime Minister refused to do so – partly explaining why the Government chose not fight in response to the Prague Coup, despite its pledges at Munich. Just after events in the Czech capital, Chamberlain wrote to his sister: 'As always, I want to gain time, for I never accept the view that war is inevitable'.[120]

Nonetheless, the Prague Coup marked another decisive shift in the government's foreign policy, in that it now pursued alliances and rearmament with vigour and virtually abandoned the idea of major concessions to the Fascist powers. On 20 March 1939, Cadogan wrote privately: 'I am afraid we have reached the crossroads'. He continued, 'I always said that ... if Hitler proceeded to gobble up other nationalities, that would be the time to call "halt!" That time has come ... But of course we are not ready (nor ever shall be)'.[121] A week later, Halifax told the Foreign Policy Committee that while there was no way that Britain and France could prevent Poland from being overrun, he favoured going to war in this eventuality over doing nothing.[122]

The Polish Guarantee was announced on 31 March 1939. Criticised by opponents at the time and later for making little military sense, especially without confirmed Soviet cooperation, Cadogan described it as Chamberlain's attempt to make 'a signpost for himself', the real value of which lay less in the aid Britain and France could render and more in the deterrent effect it might have on Hitler.[123] After all, Chamberlain coupled the Polish Guarantee with the statement in parliament that war, 'wins nothing, cures nothing, ends nothing'.[124] In contrast to the guarantee of rump Czechoslovakia given at Munich, which Britain had evaded a few weeks earlier on the dubious technicality that that country had broken up from within, it seems that Chamberlain intended the Polish Guarantee to be the first in a series of steps removing his own hatred of war from the picture, whilst also forcing Hitler to face the real possibility of a major conflict on numerous, simultaneous fronts.

In April, Greece and Romania were offered similar guarantees and tentative conversations for an alliance with the Soviets began shortly after. However, despite its increasing pessimism about the chances of maintaining peace, the National Government had not yet settled on war if it could still be averted. As already demonstrated, one of the main reasons the Soviet alliance was never concluded was because the British feared it would provoke Hitler into declaring war himself. Halifax's statement to the Foreign Policy Committee on 5 May 1939, which won Chamberlain's approval, demonstrates that he had not yet given up complete hope that conflict could be avoided: 'If war was certain he would not care who helped him: But if there were a 5 per cent chance of peace, he did not wish to jeopardise it by associating with a country in whom he had no confidence.'[125]

Halifax had announced a few weeks earlier that the idea of a 'preventative war' would never find a place in British policy: 'Not only would it be the extreme of folly, not only would it lack any colour of morality, but it would be entirely foreign to the whole trend of British thought.'[126] Yet the Foreign Secretary did make a series of increasingly bellicose pronouncements on foreign affairs over the coming months. However, as usual under Chamberlain's peace-time leadership, a carrot was dangled in front of Hitler as well as a stick waved. Similarly, mounting private doubts in government about the chances of maintaining peace contrasted with public statements of sustained confidence. These were no doubt designed to both reassure the public and to let Germany know that Britain, though growing stronger and more prepared, was still open to peace. For example, on 8 June 1939, Halifax announced that 'people are apt to say these days that war is unavoidable. I do not share that view'. However, 'there must be no misunderstanding. If the issue were ever to be joined, I have no doubt at all about the ultimate outcome, whatever might be the varying fortunes of war or the duration of the struggle'.[127] At the end of this month, he addressed the Royal Institute of International Affairs at Chatham House. Here, he coupled seemingly pro-appeasement statements about possible economic concessions with more firm declarations such as 'we know that if international law and order is to be preserved we must be prepared to fight in its defence ... In the event of further aggression, we are resolved to use at once the whole of our strength in fulfilment of our pledges'.[128] Such a double line represented the government's position until the outbreak of war. As Chamberlain had said in the wake of the Munich Agreement, he hoped for the best but prepared for the worst. The Prime Minister was resolved to fight if absolutely necessary, but still clung to the hope that a war postponed might be a war avoided altogether. It was a forlorn ambition.

Conclusion

The idea of resisting the Dictators in the late 1930s appealed to a great many people in Britain and was considered on numerous occasions, both within government and outside. However, in the majority of instances, the ultimate alternative of war was rarely seriously contemplated until Nazi Germany forced Britain's hand. In a country suffering under the Great Depression, with memories of the war to end all wars still fresh, opinion was overwhelmingly opposed to even the most limited of conflicts. Open advocates of war as an alternative to appeasement at this time were few in number and the majority preferred to talk in vague terms about 'standing firm' or 'drawing a line', without following this to its obvious conclusion. It is as if people feared that uttering the word 'war' might trigger the event itself. Even when they felt this policy was the only answer, they still could not face up to the fateful choice.

Nevertheless, one or two individuals did make their feelings plain, most notably Duff Cooper, who resigned from the government because his country would not fight for the Sudetenland. While the Abyssinian and Rhineland crises of 1935 and 1936 offered the first real opportunities to consider war, or at least League military sanctions, it was the year 1938 that proved most critical. The six month period between the *Anschluss* and the Munich Agreement was dominated by the Czech crisis, where war was contemplated most of all, and only averted by a hair's breadth at the last moment. Belligerence increased throughout the country as time went on and the skies darkened. After the Prague Coup, the press and public voiced their rising anger at Hitler's actions in significant volume, though most politicians merely lapsed into the vague language of 'standing firm' once again. It is perhaps more accurate to talk of war measures now being favoured – arms and allies – rather than war itself. Indeed, many people were convinced that only the *threat* of war was needed to ensure continued peace, although this was a risky strategy based on out-bluffing Hitler.

Chamberlain had to perform a delicate balancing act between those figures such as Eden and Vansittart, who argued that the Dictators would back down if faced with a stiffer line, and his own more cautious tendencies favouring appeasement over threats. The Chiefs of Staff and other military experts played a prominent role in all these calculations and Britain's military weakness was the defining factor for the policy that was adopted. Tensions reached boiling point in September 1938, and it is fair to say that Chamberlain's persistence for peace won out with Hitler before it did with most of his Cabinet colleagues. The Munich Agreement averted war at the eleventh hour. In the final months of peace, the government prepared for the worst with grim vigour, and rearmament and alliances were pursued extensively, although Chamberlain never gave up hopes for a lasting peace.

That war was never sanctioned until September 1939 essentially boils down to widespread popular revulsion for it, so acutely felt by this most persistent of Prime Ministers, and the fact that Britain was not strong enough to protect its far-flung Imperial commitments. Appeasement, therefore, was designed to stop any war from ever occurring, rather than sanctioning even a limited conflict in the name of a lasting peace. The government greatly feared the nightmare scenario of three simultaneous opponents, acting in as many spheres against them.

Was Chamberlain right to view appeasement as a preferable alternative to war until so late in the day? Historical accounts of these years are prone to a degree of selective recollection. Almost everybody thought that Hitler should have been resisted during the Rhineland crisis in hindsight, though nobody said so at the time. Similarly, most counterfactual speculation about the merits of a 1938 war, as opposed to actual events as they occurred, seems to miss an important point. Hitler's later admission that Germany would have had to retreat from the Rhineland if opposed by Britain and France,[129] or Field Marshall von Manstein's claim at Nuremberg that a German assault against the Czechs in late 1938 might have stalled, did not help the British Cabinet in the heat of events themselves.[130]

Chamberlain heeded the military information and intelligence he was provided with in the summer of 1938, regardless of what is now known about much of its accuracy – an enduring problem for political leaders contemplating war. The fact that he is regularly criticised for not doing so during his premiership in general, or for being an autocratic leader surrounded by toadies, should cause his opponents to recognise the specific dilemma he faced before Munich with more charity than they do. Churchill, by contrast the hero of the hour, and for so long the champion of the 'war for the Sudetenland' camp, was hardly immune to military blunders and misjudgements. The leading roles he played in the Gallipoli and Norwegian campaigns, during the First and Second World Wars respectively, are testament to this. As was his constant, misplaced faith in the strength of the French Army during the later 1930s.

That said, many at the time felt that Mussolini's flight from Nyon in September 1937 provided evidence that a firm hand with the Dictators would eventually yield results. Might Hitler have retreated from the

Rhineland in 1936 with his tail between his legs if Britain and France had stood firm? Quite possibly, although the idea that his troops would have left immediately, offering minimal resistance, is highly unlikely. More probable would have been a fighting retreat at the cost of many lives, over an issue widely believed to be grossly unfair on Germany and which had no support from the British people. Either way, even if the Rhineland crisis was a missed opportunity, as the verdict of history now seems to accept, it is only with hindsight unavailable at the time that this is known. Chamberlain's personal culpability for missing the boat here, given that he was not yet Prime Minister, and he was only one of millions who did not want a war over this issue, must be slight.

Would Hitler have backed down at the last minute in September 1938, faced by the Czechs supported by Britain and France? It is doubtful, but the resulting war might have been 'better' for the Allies than the actual events following September 1939. On a purely military basis, the odds of successfully defending Poland, with Russia alongside the Nazis, were less than successfully defending Czechoslovakia one year earlier, with Russia pledged to assist if France did the same. But would Russia have fought for Czechoslovakia in late 1938? Would France, for that matter? After all, Britain would have been drawn into conflict out of its loyalty to France, more so than any genuine sympathy for the plight of the Czechs – a far away country, to paraphrase Chamberlain, to which Britain had no direct commitments.

It is known from the Anglo-French conversations just before Munich that Daladier and Bonnet were extremely reluctant for war on this issue and it remains highly probable that France could have only fought a limited, defensive struggle at this time. Thomas's recent evaluation of appeasement in the Late Third Republic concludes that France was compelled to pursue a policy similar to Britain's during September 1938 not only because of the political, social and economic instability gripping this war-weary nation, but also a chronic lack of anti-aircraft defences in many major cities, as well as limited numbers of long-range bombers ready to take the fight to Germany.[131] Alexander points out that French command was between 20 and 40 per cent short of its basic field requirements 'at every point' between

May 1938 and the outbreak of war.[132] Moreover, France would have fought only if Britain gave similar assurances, and Britain was loathe to do so unless France itself was attacked – something out of the question, at least in the short term, during September 1938.

The Soviets may have used any of these opportunities to renege on their part of the deal, as Ragsdale has suggested. Soviet troop movements in September 1938 do not necessarily mean that they would have fought in the final instance, especially given Stalin's caution and the condition of his army after the purges. The quality of assistance Russia could have rendered in this offensive war is also questionable, and the extreme reluctance of the Poles to allow Soviet troops across their borders must never be discounted. Would Hitler have been deterred or defeated in this instance?

The much-vaunted fact that Germany rearmed at a quicker pace than Britain in the year between Munich and war is also less important than the critical point that Britain made good its most vital deficiencies in that period. Europe aside, this was the difference between victory and defeat in the Battle of Britain. Admittedly, the German capacity to wage an aerial assault in any hypothetical 'other' war during 1938 may have been reduced, but London would very likely have been blitzed once areas of France had fallen, which is all but certain. The Churchill 'war for the Sudetenland' thesis is, in places, very compelling, although it is definitely open to serious questions, especially once the counterfactual analysis continues beyond immediate events, such as in Williamson Murray's 'what if' speculation. Doubtless the balance of power in central Europe shifted in Germany's favour after gaining the land, men and munitions it did from Czechoslovakia at Munich. A war against Britain and France without these gains would probably have been harder for Hitler to win and the fall of France might have been delayed. On the other hand, the extreme reluctance of the British people and Empire to go to war in September 1938 – to say nothing of France and wider opinion in America, which was ultimately so crucial – may have hindered the war effort much more than was ever the case in 1939. The cause was far from certain in 1938 over the issue of the Sudetendeutsch, whereas in 1939, over the invasion of non-German Poland, and after appeasement had been tried and failed, it was much more clear. It is interesting to speculate what historians might have made over the question of blame or guilt for a war in 1938, as opposed to the overwhelming consensus of Nazi culpability which exists today.

The truth is that it will never be known how such a conflict over the Sudetenland in 1938 would have developed, whereas it *is* certain that the Allies eventually won the war beginning in 1939. Moreover, substituting one hypothetical war for another actual conflict in no way averts the catastrophe itself and millions of lives would have been lost either way. The whole point of appeasement was to avoid such a disaster and Chamberlain was attempting, in vain, to do just that.

CONCLUSION

We were all in a muddle, and it is hard to keep track of opinion when the owners are not sure of them.[1]

(Lord Vansittart, 1958)

If it was easy to criticise Neville Chamberlain from the sidelines, it was difficult to suggest a constructive, coherent alternative that he could have pursued. No doubt affected by the confusion of the times in which they lived and the unparalleled events with which they had to grapple, critics of appeasement were frequently divided amongst themselves, though united in their general condemnation of the National Government's policy. Even those who advocated one alternative passionately to the detriment of all others bickered among themselves over the precise nature of what it meant and how it should be carried out. Furthermore, it was perfectly possible to favour more than one rival policy, evidence of the chaos of the era and the sense that people were grasping desperately at ways to avoid war and deal with an unprecedented Fascist threat. Leo Amery, for example, has featured in every chapter of this book and at one time or another advocated isolation, measures of colonial appeasement (despite apparently being a committed defender of the Empire), several kinds of alliances, a vast rearmament programme *and* the threat of war all as ways to deal with Hitler. Is this indicative of a deep thinker on foreign affairs or someone as confused and uncertain about how best to deal with the Fascist challenge as Chamberlain himself? It certainly illustrates how foreign policy opinion changed dramatically in the late 1930s, moving in response to shifting events.

Muddled thinking and hypocrisy were also prevalent. Despite advocating a series of alternatives, Chamberlain's critics regularly proclaimed that only one solution – the one they were calling for at that particular moment – could stop Hitler and should take precedence over all other strategies. Thus, within the period of a few months, Attlee claimed that economic appeasement was the issue that should be considered 'above all' and that the League of Nations route was 'the only way' to peace. Aside from the official policies of the main parties on the central issues of the day, there was a marked lack of uniformity or consistency in the suggestion of alternatives. Party loyalties frequently evaporated and an individual's own concerns and personal beliefs proved paramount. Tories could support the League, Labour MPs could back alliances, Liberals could advocate massive rearmament as well as total *dis*armament, and pacifists could call for military sanctions. Politicians from all parties could back measures of economic appeasement and yet resist the wider political appeasement. Supporters of one alternative might vehemently oppose another. Most League enthusiasts claimed to hate alliances, and *vice versa*, despite the two policies effectively merging as one in the final months of peace.

Advocates of alternatives to appeasement often contradicted themselves, undermining those occasions when criticism of Chamberlain was justified. Most obviously, Labour combined increasing calls for firmness towards the Dictators with a general opposition to the government's rearmament efforts. This glaring inconsistency was to their discredit, as was frequently pointed out at the time. Similarly, backing an alliance with the Soviet Union, as most of the opposition did in the last year of peace, did not sit easily with commitment to the League of Nations and the ideals of Geneva. Many critics of Chamberlain's conversations with the Dictators at Munich then advocated further international conferences with Hitler and Mussolini to discuss economic appeasement or disarmament initiatives. Opponents of appeasement who questioned the morality of a deal with Hitler, and then went on to advocate an alliance with Stalin, also seemed to be missing an important point.

If Chamberlain was, according to many detractors, muddled and uncertain as to how best to deal with the Fascist challenge, then so too were almost all of his contemporary critics. The notion that the so-called 'anti-appeasers' knew instinctively what sort of beast Hitler was, and that the best way to deal with him was by force, is far too simplistic and unsubstantiated by the evidence. Nevertheless, it has become ingrained in the popular understanding of appeasement, encouraged by the belief that the coming of war spelt the inevitable failure of this policy. Yet Churchill and Eden spoke positively about appeasement on many occasions before Chamberlain became Prime Minister, while Lloyd George took tea with the *Führer* in September 1936 and came back singing his praises. The fact that Churchill thought the Nazis could be deterred by the dying League of Nations, or that most of the Labour Party agreed – as well as thinking colonies and cash could buy Hitler off – is rarely noted whenever blame is apportioned in Chamberlain's direction. Few complained when the Prime Minister postponed war by flying to meet Hitler in September 1938 and the idea that Churchill or Attlee would not have taken similar steps is open to serious doubt. Even Socialist MP Rhys Davies noted in the *Glasgow Forward* that 'if Attlee had been Prime Minister at the time and had stopped war at Munich under exactly similar circumstances, he would have been hailed with sheer delight by our people'.[2] Churchill's wartime dealings with Stalin over the future of Eastern Europe show that he too was fully capable of appeasing a dictator.

Similarly, if Chamberlain was deluded about appeasement or tended to think in an overly-cautious way about how best to maintain peace, many of his political opponents seemed equally unaware of the harsh realities of Britain's position. Those who proclaimed that Britain should have stood firm on almost every occasion – often the same people who talked most about the lack of arms – seem to have been excessively confident that the country was capable of protecting the far-flung Empire from all comers with relative ease. Had they been privy to the military and strategic information at Chamberlain's disposal, it is doubtful whether they would have been so bellicose in the years before war.

All of this just goes to reiterate the uncertainty gripping Europe in the late 1930s, the overwhelming sense of crisis prevalent throughout the country, and the vagueness of many ideas about how to face the threat of war. British foreign policy debate in this decade was a complex mishmash of ideas. The confident black and white clarity with which solutions to the Fascist menace were presented by those who were wise after the event, writing to clear their names or build reputations in the emotional aftermath of war, was clearly misplaced, and swept many of the complex realities under the carpet. Instead, the popular understanding of Chamberlain and appeasement remains shrouded in myth and lazy stereotype.

* * *

In terms of government consideration of alternatives to appeasement, this study has shown that Chamberlain did explore each one as part of his wider strategy. Indeed, his foreign policy usually contained aspects of the various rival options. It is often presumed that Chamberlain dismissed the alternatives out of hand in his dogged pursuit of appeasement and this work proves that this was not the case. The Prime Minister contemplated each alternative on at least one occasion and was assailed from all sides by advocates of one or other rival course of action. These alternatives were also well represented in the views of other political and social groups, among the press and general public.

A clear timescale marks the suggestion of alternatives to appeasement, both within the government and outside. Each major event in the countdown to war sparked fresh consideration of rival strategies for the best way to maintain peace. The *Anschluss* was a clear watershed and the months between March 1938 and the Munich Agreement in September were the most feverish period for alternatives being suggested and considered. Chamberlain analysed all his options at this time and this was the period when many of his most crucial decisions were made. It was in early 1938 that the Prime Minister emphatically rejected isolation; launched his colonial appeasement scheme to repartition Central Africa and witnessed its collapse; announced the death of collective security and the League of Nations; considered and rejected both a Grand Alliance and a war over Czechoslovakia; and poured cold water on the Roosevelt Peace Initiative. The policies enshrined in Inskip's paper, *Defence Expenditure in Future Years*, were first implemented at this time. This was also the juncture when Eden resigned and Halifax replaced him, allowing the Prime Minister a freer hand to consider his various options. In the seeming absence of a viable alternative, Chamberlain reaffirmed appeasement as his favoured line which reached its zenith at Munich in September 1938.[3] Chamberlain turned to alliances and rearmament after the Prague Coup in the following year – although some opposition figures falsely attempted to present the Peace Front negotiations as his conversion to their collective security policy – and the traditional appeasement of major concessions assumed a secondary role thereafter. While he never gave up his hopes for peace, the Prime Minister increasingly prepared for war during the spring and summer of 1939.

Broadly speaking, critics of appeasement advocated policies such as the League of Nations, pacifism and varying degrees of isolation during the mid- to late 1930s and then tended towards alliances and rearmament in 1938 and 1939. After the Prague Coup, opponents overwhelmingly favoured the more belligerent, 'stand firm' policies such as arms, alliances and the threat of war. The press and general public followed suit. Economic and colonial appeasement remained a policy advocated by much of the Left all throughout Chamberlain's premiership, but died away in 1939 as Hitler's true character became more widely known. When it survived, it now had an aggressive double edge to it, increasingly taking the form of naked economic warfare against the Fascists.

There were many critics of appeasement within the government machine who either advocated its replacement by another policy or else its subtle alteration to encompass new facets, which Chamberlain himself rarely wished to impart. Even enthusiastic appeasers like Halifax came to disagree with the Prime Minister's precise conception of the policy and wanted a firmer line after events in Prague. For each of the suggested alternatives, there was usually at least one Cabinet Minister and more than one senior Foreign Office official who at one time or another strongly recommended that path. Vansittart backed alliances, intensive rearmament *and* the threat of war, as well as briefly considering colonial initiatives in the late 1930s. Eden disagreed with much of Chamberlain's foreign policy and he was not the only Cabinet Minister to resign or voice protest at appeasement and suggest other strategies as the best way forward. Ministers and officials inevitably reflected their own department's overriding aims and concerns. Naturally enough, Simon, as Chancellor of the Exchequer, resisted massively increased arms spending, whereas the Defence Ministers pushed for greater resources in preparing the army, navy and air force for war. The Foreign Office and Treasury were often at loggerheads.

The Prime Minister's opinion in Cabinet or on the strengths or weaknesses of any given final and decisive, although this also indicates broad consent for his policy, especially after Eden's resignation.[4] The minutes of the Foreign Policy Committee recall that there were usually more people in agreement with Chamberlain's line than opposing it, although the Prime Minister would have had the final say over who attended such meetings. Critics have also accused Chamberlain of not listening sufficiently to his expert advisers within the Foreign Office, but this misses an obvious point that the Foreign Office was not a body with one unified and settled consensus on any given policy. Each chapter of this study shows that Foreign Office opinions were as divided as to the best way to deal with Hitler as were those outside of it. Cadogan disagreed with Vansittart over the best course of action to take as much as Chamberlain did with Eden, Churchill or Attlee. If Chamberlain ignored or sidelined one Foreign Office official, he agreed with or took the advice of another in doing so. Similarly, the military experts and Chiefs of Staff argued amongst themselves and often changed their minds as new information became available. Intelligence was weak and contradictory. Lloyd George regularly sidelined the Foreign Office during his premiership and Churchill routinely ignored his leading military advisers in his conduct of the Second World War. Yet neither receives anywhere near as much criticism as Chamberlain for doing so.

*   *   *

With the benefit of hindsight, it is easy to accuse Chamberlain of being excessively cautious in the late 1930s. Such thinking is often born of the belief that the Second World War was both inevitable and morally justified. Critics naturally ask if the government could not have prepared for it much better. Chamberlain knew no such thing, of course, and hung on to the hope that war could be avoided longer than anyone else within his government. If this made him the best man to pursue peace, it probably also made him unsuited to prepare for war in the way that a figure like Churchill would have. Even so, Chamberlain contributed enough to allow the country to survive the opening phases of conflict.

The perceived weaknesses of the alternatives to appeasement partly explain why Chamberlain took the path he did. As he wrote in January 1938, 'in the absence of any powerful ally and until our arms are completed, we must adjust our foreign policy to the circumstances, and even bear with patience and good humour actions which we should like to treat in a very different fashion.'[5] Appeasement, however, also had its own separate impulses based upon international law and order, the inherent value of diplomacy, the concept of self-determination, a moral sense of what was right, and a popular desire to revise the harsh, post-war Versailles settlement. When Chamberlain assumed the premiership, declining British capability to protect an Empire against three simultaneous potential enemies, growing in strength and menace, acted as a sobering determinant. Even Smart's recent biography of Chamberlain, which is by no means generous in its assessment of his career, recognises that this essential strategic dilemma was 'not his fault'.[6] Without the presence of Hitler and the Nazis, appeasement might well have been the 'right' policy to pursue. Even with Hitler and the Nazis, the general ideal had considerable support in the earlier period, often from many of its later critics.

The fear of provoking Hitler and thereby prompting war was a constantly recurring feature in Chamberlain's calculations and his government's dismissal of the various alternatives. The Prime Minister was always mindful of the possible effects of provocative words and this doubtless fed into the disparity, on occasion, between his own public and private statements. In June 1937, he issued an 'earnest appeal' to politicians and the press 'to weigh their words very carefully before they utter them'. He continued, 'I have read that in high mountains there are sometimes conditions to be found when an incautious move or even a sudden loud exclamation may start an avalanche.'[7] Isolation and pacifism were rejected in part because of the fear that they would cause Hitler to attack Britain's Empire, and economic and colonial appeasement for much the same reasons. Support for the ailing League of Nations might provoke Hitler and Mussolini into further smash and grab raids in Europe. Alliances might trigger a 'Mad Dog' act or lead to the establishment of opposing blocs on the continent with the inevitability of war. Massive rearmament or the threat of war might just cause Hitler to plunge Germany into battle. In short, Chamberlain believed that all the alternatives would bring war closer than appeasement itself, which aimed at systematically removing the causes of tension. His instinct, therefore, was to treat the *Führer's* fragile temperament with kid gloves.

Chamberlain did not want war and so avoided war-like actions for as long as possible. He often did much less than his critics thought was required to prepare Britain for conflict, and that too only when Hitler's policies seemingly made such actions unavoidable. For example, his fundamental distaste for rearmament and allies influenced this tendency to do just enough to protect the country if his policy failed, while seeking not to provoke an outburst from the volatile German Chancellor. Even when Chamberlain took a much firmer line after the Prague Coup, he coupled harsh actions or words with pacific gestures, designed to convey the impression that his new strategy was purely defensive. Thus, his policy of alliances was deliberately labelled a 'Peace Front'. Indeed, in hoping until the last moment to avoid hostilities, Chamberlain subconsciously undermined many of the preparations for war so obviously needed. Perhaps this was his greatest failing – not that he tried so hard for peace, which was utterly commendable, but that he continued to delude himself that it was still possible when all about him sought intensified provisions for war. Even when making comments to the effect that Hitler was a madman or that force was the only language he understood, Chamberlain still believed that his own efforts could pacify the Nazi leader. Many have said that Chamberlain misjudged Hitler, but few at the time knew of his true nature as revealed at the end of the war in Europe and, if Chamberlain failed to understand him, so too did those who thought that the racially motivated dynamic of Nazi ideology could be soothed by colonies or dispelled by the crumbling League of Nations. The Prime Minister was under no illusions about the essential character of the man he faced, but was arrogantly deluded about his own capacity to deter him from war. As he once wrote to his sister, 'I do not trouble over criticisms which do not affect my judgement of what is right. Like Chatham, "I know that I can save this country and I do not believe that anyone else can" '.[8]

There are other striking inconsistencies in Chamberlain's character and policy that have not been afforded sufficient attention in the existing literature. The fact that he would often go out of his way to pick a quarrel with the political opposition at home, or alienate those within the government machine who most resisted appeasement, does not sit easily alongside the timid and deferential way in which he dealt with Hitler. While this suggests that Chamberlain was never the simple weakling he sometimes was presented to be, his critics would no doubt counter that similar firmness should have been applied internationally. He was, of course, playing for much higher stakes on the global scene, and on far shakier ground.

Chamberlain, by his own admission, based his rejection of alliances before 1939 on the lessons of history – particularly the origins of the Great War – and placed so little faith in the USA or Russia because of his dealings with them in the past and their foreign policy during the interwar period. It seems curious, therefore, that the lessons of history with regard to Hitler's broken promises and Nazi Germany's previous conduct should have taken so long to sink in. If he believed that his own abilities could charm Hitler into peace, then it is strange that Chamberlain never felt he could deal in a similar way with Roosevelt and persuade the President to inspire his people to take a more proactive role in European affairs. Roosevelt was, after all, a far more amenable figure than Hitler, and his country had greater cultural and historical bonds with Britain. Perhaps this can be explained by Chamberlain's short-sightedness and his belief in tackling one problem, the central problem, head-on, often to the detriment of wider issues and concerns.

However committed he was to appeasement, Chamberlain clearly could have done more to foster a Plan 'B' or back-up option. Similarly, in trying to reduce the number of Britain's enemies, he neglected to try hard enough to increase the number of its friends. Quite possibly, the fact that his critics repeatedly told him he was wrong only fortified his stubborn will to continue along the path he felt was right. Personal ego no doubt played a part in Chamberlain's policy decisions, just as it also did with Churchill a few years later. Indeed, it is only because Chamberlain's appeasement failed, whereas Churchill was the man who 'won the war', that the personal qualities which they shared – single-mindedness, arrogance, obstinacy, a dictatorial approach – are so criticised in the former yet so celebrated in the latter.

There are, however, other examples of Chamberlain's far-sightedness not shared by his contemporaries and seldom acknowledged by historians. His fears about the post-war settlement and Britain's place *vis-à-vis* the two eventual Superpowers were little recognised when so many of his critics called for alliances with Russia or the USA. Chamberlain's prescient adherence to the 'fourth arm of defence' rearmament thesis was abused by opponents urging greater arms spending, but played no small part in ensuring Britain's survival in the early stages of the war. Similarly, Chamberlain was the key figure in switching priority in aircraft production from bombers to fighters, another move that proved pivotal. If he is to be castigated for the failed policy of appeasement and the state of the British army during the war, he should at least be given credit for his many successes, not least the strength and composition of the air force and anti-aircraft defences by 1939 and 1940.

*   *   *

That appeasement was a tragic failure cannot be denied; that it had, at times, elements of weakness and shame about it is also true; that Chamberlain was an arrogant man of many faults and misjudgements is beyond doubt. When, however, one considers the alternatives open to him in the 1930s, would anything other than appeasement have necessarily been 'better' or more successful? Of this nobody can be certain. In the bleak period of history in which Chamberlain had to operate, there was a huge element of risk to whatever policy he might have undertaken, and any strategy adopted would have had a huge degree of uncertainty attached to it.

A great deal of speculation about these alternatives misses the central point that Chamberlain's policy was designed first and foremost to avoid war ever happening. He did not know that war was definitely coming and, therefore, always had to balance the risks and effects of any policy on Britain's place in the world with the possibility and hope that war could be averted. He did not, therefore, think about the 'best' war possible for Britain and its Empire, as many historians have, but rather of how he might avert the catastrophe altogether.

Would any alternative to appeasement have avoided war? Could Hitler have been deterred? Much rests upon the nature of Nazi foreign policy, an area of great debate over many years. In brief, some historians have claimed that Hitler had an 'intentionalist' long-term plan for world domination, to be carried out in a systematic way, stage by stage, as broadly mapped out in the pages of *Mein Kampf*. In this intentionalist plan, the ideological and racial elements were 'permanently binding dogmas', war and the Holocaust essential components of the bigger picture.[9] Others have countered that Nazi foreign policy emerged in a more 'structuralist', *ad hoc* way, as a by-product of the confusion and chaos resulting from the demise of central government in Germany and the establishment of various departments and ministries working more or less independently of one another.[10] In the intentionalist interpretation, 'Hitler was the master of the Third Reich'.[11] In the structuralist view, by contrast, he was a product of the system he spawned, 'in some respects a weak Dictator', exerting little control over his ambitious lieutenants and the wider party bureaucracy.[12] Thus, while D.C. Watt claimed, 'Hitler willed, wanted, craved war',[13] Tim Mason argued that Nazi foreign policy owed more to improvisation on the ground, than to any predetermined masterplan driven by one man.[14]

The rawness of this dispute has abated somewhat in recent years as scholars increasingly seek to frame the discussion in other terms more related to older questions of moral responsibility.[15] While the truth is probably found somewhere between these two poles, both intentionalist and structuralist interpretations imply that Nazi Germany could not be deterred from war, whether Hitler had a long-term policy to force conflict or whether the country stumbled into it out of the chaos of the Third Reich. Regardless of which interpretation is more accurate, neither a hell-bent madman nor a fragmented state spiralling out of control could be reasoned with or pacified by the rational, common sense arguments of Chamberlain and appeasement. For example, Kershaw talks of a Germany 'in which the regime lurched from crisis to crisis, burning its boats in a series of *ad hoc* responses to recurrent emergencies'.[16] Once Hitler's Germany began to flex its muscles on the global stage, war was perhaps inevitable, whichever path Chamberlain took. Nevile Henderson claimed during the war: 'It is probably true to say that whatever attitude we had adopted towards Hitler and the Nazi gangsters, the result today would have been the same.'[17] He went on: 'Peace was Hitler's for the asking after Munich and he alone could have ensured it.'[18]

Given this interpretation of the character of Nazi Germany – and similar things could be said of the regimes in Italy and Japan – it is probable that isolation or absolute pacifism would only have invited the enemy to converge on Britain and its vital interests once resistance on the continent had been subdued. Economic and colonial concessions would have only whet the Nazi appetite for more. The League of Nations had proved itself incapable of preventing conflict in the interwar period and its failings only encouraged Hitler to chance his arm further. A Grand Alliance in 1938 might well have postponed war or affected the precise timing of hostilities. But the fact that Germany later attacked its former Soviet ally suggests that Nazi goals for *Lebensraum* could not be easily suppressed. Moreover, dividing Europe into ideologically hostile camps would likely have made war certain, or actually provoked an outbreak earlier on. A Britain endowed with an arsenal of weapons on a par with Germany's would doubtless have caused Hitler a moment's pause, though he was not deterred from striking at Poland in 1939 despite Britain's newfound strength. Huge peace-time rearmament would, in any case, have been impossible to achieve in post-Depression Britain. The threat of an earlier war might have caused Hitler to pick his opportunity at a more favourable moment. Ultimately, however, it was impossible to out-bluff the 'greatest bluffer of modern times', a man seemingly determined to play his cards no matter what the outcome.[19]

If Hitler's Germany could not have been deterred from war, all the alternatives to appeasement were essentially as 'bad' as appeasement itself. Thus, with the hindsight unavailable to Chamberlain, we can now ask whether any of the alternatives would have led to a more preferable war for Britain. It is in speculation of this kind that rival policies become more attractive and viable than others. A combination of alternatives might have been more successful. For example, there is much that is attractive in the idea of a Grand Alliance involving a more heavily rearmed Britain, followed by a war for the Czechs in late 1938. This might have resulted in a 'better' outcome for Britain and its Allies than the course actually taken, even if it is only with knowledge of how real events progressed that this can be asserted. All of this also ignores the fact that it is extremely tenuous to speculate about the path of imaginary 'other' wars, fought on different grounds and with different participants. It is, of course, possible that a September 1938 war might have turned out worse, especially when one considers the lack of popular support in Britain and the Empire for a conflict over the Sudetenland.

At the end of the day it is the historian's primary task to base his or her conclusions on solid evidence and fact. Britain, with allies, eventually won the war that came in September 1939, which was prepared for by Chamberlain and his government, although striving so resolutely to avoid it. The so-called 'finest hour' of that war, victory in the Battle of Britain, owed a great deal to the far-sightedness of Chamberlain's rearmament programme, something ignored by most of his detractors.

Much that has been written about Chamberlain is grossly unfair to him personally, ignores or downplays the realities of the period, is steeped in an emotional, overly simplistic mythology ingrained by the Churchillian version of history, and heavily dependent on hindsight of events which Chamberlain was not able to enjoy. Despite the efforts of countless revisionist and post-revisionist historians, much of this legend still endures. Displacing it may be a losing battle, so entrenched are the *Guilty Men* myths about Chamberlain and appeasement, so popularly revered is his successor in the national memory. The alternatives available to Chamberlain all seemed deeply unattractive to him and the majority of his government, not to mention large sections of wider opinion. As David Dutton has stated, it is, in fact, 'possible that there was no good or correct policy available in the circumstances of the 1930s'.[20] Any alternative the Prime Minister might have pursued would have been dogged by great dangers. Even Eden, a supposed anti-appeaser, admitted during May 1939: 'There is no perfect course to follow, least of all with world conditions as they are today.'[21] So while R.A.C. Parker has confidently claimed that Churchill could have avoided the Second World War, David Dilks' conclusion is more compelling: 'It was hardly possible to conceive of a British government which could have confronted the continuous crises of those years without blunders and misapprehensions.'[22]

That appeasement failed did not make it wrong to try. In many ways it was a sort of necessary evil – although for the majority of the interwar period it was not seen as evil at all, it was the obvious and sensible policy to settle a continent's woes. As Paul Schroeder has commented, 'any other policy in 1938 would have been an astounding, almost inexplicable divergence from the norm' and there is much truth in this, even when applied to the decade as a whole.[23] Only by exhausting a compassionate and pacific policy based upon addressing Germany's legitimate grievances could it be finally established that it was right to stand firm against the Nazi march later on. Only in trying and failing to pacify Hitler could his true nature be revealed and it be asserted with confidence that a European war was fully justified. A war over keeping three million Germans out of Germany in September 1938 would have been deeply unpopular and fought on far less certain ground than resisting Hitler's attempt to crush the Poles a year later. The year's grace between these two points not only established the justification for the war but also allowed Britain the time to rearm and prepare sufficiently to ensure the country's survival from invasion. Chamberlain did not deliberately intend to buy a year's peace in order to fight a 'better' war at a later date – although there are many examples of him referring to the need to play for time – but, rather, to postpone war indefinitely in the hope that it might never occur: 'Peace for our time'. In his ultimate failure, his considerable achievements at least deserve acknowledgement.

Did Chamberlain have a viable alternative policy to pursue? It is difficult to believe that the Nazis could have been deterred; war was the only option against their brutal regime with its sinister aims of world domination. In failing in his mission to maintain peace, Chamberlain was at least victorious in illuminating clearly where blame for the ensuing struggle lay. History should credit him for this.

CHRONOLOGY

1918	End of Great War.
1919	Treaty of Versailles. Widely resented in Germany as a harsh 'diktat'.
1925	Treaty of Locarno. Demilitarised zone established in Rhineland.
1929	Wall Street Crash ushers in Great Depression.
1931	Chamberlain becomes Chancellor of the Exchequer.
1932	Japan invades Manchuria. War with China rages until 1945.
1933	Hitler becomes German Chancellor. Germany leaves the League.

1935

April	Stresa Conference. Britain, France and Italy unite in pledge to maintain Austrian independence.
June	Anglo-German Naval Agreement.
October	Italy invades Abyssinia. Annexation complete by the summer of 1936.
December	Hoare-Laval crisis. Britain and France acknowledge Italian conquests.

1936

March	Germany remilitarizes the Rhineland in violation of the Versailles Treaty.

June	Chamberlain announces maintenance of sanctions on Italy over Abyssinia represent 'the very midsummer of madness'.
July	Spanish Civil War begins. Conflict rages until early 1939.
November	Rome–Berlin Axis and Anti-Comintern Pact announced.
December	Abdication of Edward VIII.

1937

May	Chamberlain succeeds Baldwin as Prime Minister.
September	Nyon Conference. Diplomatic victory for the democracies over Italy.
October	Roosevelt makes 'Quarantine Speech', seemingly criticising Dictators.
November	Halifax meets Hitler in Berlin.
December	Inskip's *Defence Expenditure in Future Years* paper completed.

1938

January	Roosevelt launches secret 'Peace Initiative'.
February	Eden resigns as Foreign Secretary, to be replaced by Halifax.
March	*Anschluss* declared. Germany incorporates Austria into the Reich.
15 September	Culmination of Czech crisis: Chamberlain flies to meet Hitler at Berchtesgaden. Concedes principal of transfer of Sudetenland to Germany.
18–21 September	Anglo-French talks in London. Czechs informed of their joint decision not to fight in defence of Sudetenland. Czechs reluctantly concede to Hitler's territorial demands.
23 September	Chamberlain flies to meet Hitler at Godesberg to iron out remaining details. Hitler issues

	Godesberg Memorandum, containing the threat of war unless all territories are transferred by 1 October.
27 September	Cabinet meetings in Britain reject Hitler's new Godesberg formula. British fleet is mobilised, final preparations for war are undertaken.
28 September	Chamberlain accepts Hitler's invitation to a third meeting in Munich.
29–30 September	Munich Conference. Sudetenland transfer to Germany agreed. Signatories pledge to guarantee rump Czechoslovakia. Britain and Germany agree never to go to war with one another again.
3–6 October	Parliament debates Munich settlement.

1939

January	Rumours of imminent German invasion of Low Countries result in war scare. Chamberlain and Halifax visit Rome.
14–15 March	Prague Coup. German troops invade Czech capital in direct violation of Munich Agreement.
17 March	Chamberlain speech in Birmingham indicates significant realignment of appeasement policy.
31 March	Polish Guarantee announced by Chamberlain. Similar guarantees are extended to Greece, Romania and Turkey over coming weeks.
May	Anglo-Soviet alliance negotiations begin. Germany and Italy sign Pact of Steel.
August	Anglo-Soviet military talks begin and fail. Nazi-Soviet Pact signed.
September	Germany invades Poland. Outbreak of the Second World War.

1940

| 4 May | British forces evacuate Norway. |

7–8 May	Parliament debates Norway crisis. Government majority cut to 81.
10 May	Chamberlain resigns as Prime Minister, succeeded by Churchill.
July	'Cato' publishes *Guilty Men*.
November	Chamberlain dies of cancer.
1945	End of the Second World War.
1948	Churchill publishes *The Gathering Storm*.

NOTES

Introduction

1. H. Wilson to A. Chamberlain, 19 July 1948, Neville Chamberlain Papers (NC), NC11/1/925, Special Collections Department, University of Birmingham (BU).
2. CATO, *Guilty Men*, 21st edn. (London: 1940).
3. L. Namier, *Diplomatic Prelude, 1938–1939* (London: 1948); J. Wheeler-Bennett, *Munich: Prologue to Tragedy* (London: 1948); W.S. Churchill, *The Gathering Storm* (London: 1948).
4. D. Reynolds, *In Command of History: Churchill Fighting and Writing the Second World War* (London: 2004), pp.91–110.
5. P. Slosson, 'Review of W.S. Churchill, the gathering storm', *American Historical Review*, vol.54, 1948, pp.102–3 (p.102).
6. Churchill, p.x.
7. Viscount Simon, *Retrospect: The Memoirs of the Right Honourable Viscount Simon* (London: 1952), p.253.
8. R.J. Caputi, *Neville Chamberlain and Appeasement* (London: 2000); D.J. Dutton, *Neville Chamberlain* (London: 2001); S. Aster, 'Appeasement: Before and after revisionism', *Diplomacy and Statecraft*, vol.19(3), 2008, pp.443–80.
9. R.A.C. Parker, *Chamberlain and Appeasement: British Policy and the coming of the Second World War* (London: 1993), pp.343–47.
10. K. Neilson, *Britain, Soviet Russia and the Collapse of the Versailles Order, 1919–1939* (Cambridge: 2005); H. Ragsdale, *The Soviets, the Munich Crisis, and the Coming of World War Two* (Cambridge: 2004); M.J. Carley, *1939: The Alliance that Never Was and the Coming of World War Two* (Chicago: 1999); L.G. Shaw, *The British Political Elite and the Soviet Union, 1937–1939* (London: 2003); G. Roberts, *The Soviet Union and the Origins of the Second World War: Russo-German Relations and the Road to War, 1933–1941* (London: 1995).
11. R. Self, *Neville Chamberlain: A Biography* (London: 2006), p.2; D. Gillard, *Appeasement in Crisis: From Munich to Prague, October 1938-March 1939* (London: 2007).

12. Self, p.405; Dutton, *Neville Chamberlain*, p.218.
13. G.B. Strang, 'The spirit of Ulysses? Ideology and British appeasement in the 1930s', *Diplomacy and Statecraft*, vol.19(3), 2008, pp.481–526; Aster, 'Appeasement', p.463; K. Robbins, 'The British churches and British foreign policy', in K. Robbins, and J. Fisher (eds.), *Religion and British Foreign Policy, 1815–1941* (Dordrecht: 2010), pp.9–32; S.D. Pennybacker, *From Scottsboro to Munich: Race and Political Culture in 1930s Britain* (Princeton: 2009).
14. Churchill, p.x.
15. Ibid.
16. H. Macmillan, *The Winds of Change, 1914–1939* (London: 1966), p.382.
17. Parker, *Chamberlain*, pp.307–27.
18. R.A.C. Parker, *Churchill and Appeasement* (London: 2000), p.ix.
19. Shaw, pp.189–90.
20. J. Ruggiero, *Neville Chamberlain and British Rearmament: Pride, Prejudice, and Politics* (London: 1999), p.223.
21. J.P. Levy, *Appeasement and Rearmament: Britain, 1936–1939* (New York: 2006), p.xiv.
22. E.H. Carr and E.P. Thompson, quoted, R. Cowley (ed.), *What If? The World's Foremost Military Historians Imagine What Might Have Been* (London: 2000), p.xi; N. Ferguson (ed.), *Virtual History: Alternatives and Counterfactuals* (London: 1998), pp.4–5.
23. G. Wilson, 'PM rated worst since 1930s', *Sun*, 14 April 2008; S. Goldenberg and E. MacAskill, 'Obama warns republicans: 'lay off my wife'', *Guardian*, 20 May 2008.
24. *ITV Lunchtime News*, 27 July 2009.
25. *Glorious 39*. Dir. S. Poliakoff. Momentum Pictures. 2009.
26. R. Moorhouse, *Killing Hitler: The Plots, the Assassins, and the Dictator who Cheated Death* (New York: 2006), p.191; FO371/20475/W11340, 24 Aug. 1936, TNA. Foreign Office (FO) papers are located at The National Archives (TNA) in Kew, London.
27. FO371/20702/C8477, 8 Dec. 1937.
28. N. Chamberlain to I. Chamberlain, 4 July 1937, NC18/1/1010.
29. M. Gilbert, *The Roots of Appeasement* (London: 1966).
30. B. Porter, *The Lion's Share: A Short History of British Imperialism: 1850–1995*, 3rd edn. (London: 1996).
31. M. Gilbert, *Churchill's Political Philosophy* (Oxford: 1981), p.71.
32. *Hansard, Parliamentary Debates. Official Reports. 5th Series, House of Commons*, vol.313, col.1209, 18 June 1936.
33. P. Kennedy, *The Realities Behind Diplomacy: Background Influences on British External Policy, 1865–1980* (London: 1985), p.285.
34. Foreign Policy Committee Proceedings, 1 March 1938, CAB27/623/FP(36)/24, TNA. Cabinet (CAB) papers are located at The National Archives.

35. A. Cassels, 'Britain, Italy and the Axis: How to make friends with Mussolini and influence Hitler', in G. Johnson (ed.), *The International Context of the Spanish Civil War* (Newcastle upon Tyne: 2009), pp.19–32.
36. *The Times*, 18 March 1939.
37. N. Chamberlain to H. Chamberlain, 23 March 1935, NC18/1/910A.
38. I. Colvin, *The Chamberlain Cabinet* (New York: 1971).
39. Earl of Avon, *Facing the Dictators: The Eden Memoirs* (London: 1962), p.556.
40. Viscount Templewood, *Nine Troubled Years* (London: 1954), p.375.
41. M.L. Kenney, 'The role of the house of commons in British foreign policy during the 1937–1938 session', in N. Downs (ed.), *Essays in Honour of Conyers Read* (Chicago: 1953), pp.138–85 (p.157).
42. J. Black, *Parliament and Foreign Policy in the Eighteenth Century* (Cambridge: 2004), p.8.

Chapter 1 Isolation and Absolute Pacifism

1. HC Deb 5s, vol.313, col.1691, 18 June 1936.
2. C. Howard, 'The policy of isolation', *Historical Journal*, vol.10(1), 1967, pp.77–88; J. Charmley, *Splendid Isolation? Britain and the Balance of Power, 1874–1914* (London: 1999).
3. Lord Vansittart, *The Mist Procession* (London: 1958), pp.481–504 (p.481).
4. Macmillan, p.581.
5. A.J.P. Taylor, *Beaverbrook* (London: 1972), pp.343–50.
6. M. Ceadel, *Pacifism in Britain, 1914–1945: The Defining of a Faith* (Oxford: 1980); Parker, *Chamberlain*, pp.316–19.
7. J. Charmley, *Chamberlain and the Lost Peace* (London: 1989).
8. R. Denman, *Missed Chances: Britain and Europe in the Twentieth Century* (London: 1996), p.151.
9. *Hansard, Parliamentary Debates. Official Reports. 5th Series, House of Lords*, vol.100, cols.531–32, 24 March 1936.
10. Macmillan, p.578.
11. Parker, *Chamberlain*, p.317.
12. J. Barnes and D. Nicholson (eds.), *The Empire at Bay: The Leo Amery Diaries, vol.5, 1929–1945* (London: 1988), pp.345–46.
13. L. Amery to N. Chamberlain, 11 Nov. 1937, AMEL 2/1/27, Churchill Archives Centre (CAC), Cambridge University. The papers of Leo Amery (AMEL) are located at the Churchill Archives Centre, Cambridge University.
14. L. Amery to A. Eden, 10 Oct. 1938, AMEL 2/2/10.
15. R. Cockett, *Twilight of Truth: Chamberlain, Appeasement and the Manipulation of the Press* (London: 1989), pp.25–26.
16. *Sunday Express*, 15 July 1934.
17. *Daily Express*, 9 March 1936.

18. Ibid., 10 March 1936.
19. Ibid., 14 March 1938.
20. Lord Beaverbrook to L. Amery, 10 Nov. 1936, AMEL 2/1/26(1).
21. L. Amery to Lord Beaverbrook, 12 Nov. 1936, Ibid.
22. Lord Beaverbrook to L. Amery, 10 Nov. 1936, Ibid.
23. *Daily Express*, 14 March 1936.
24. C. Madge and T. Harrison (eds.), *Britain: By Mass Observation* (Middlesex: 1939), p.46.
25. British Union of Fascists, *Mind Britain's Business: B.U.F. Notes for Speakers* (1936).
26. HC Deb 5s, vol.333, cols.1433–34, 24 March 1938.
27. HL Deb 5s, vol.110, col.1465, 5 Oct. 1938.
28. Lord Beaverbrook to E. Grigg, 20 June 1938, quoted, Taylor, *Beaverbrook*, p.383.
29. Ceadel, *Pacifism*, pp.248–49.
30. B. Russell, *Which Way to Peace?* (London: 1936).
31. *Peace News*, 10 April 1936, quoted, Ceadel, *Pacifism*, p.249.
32. Ceadel, Pacifism; D.C. Lukowitz, 'British pacifists and appeasement: The peace pledge union', *Journal of Contemporary History*, vol.9(1), 1974, pp.115–27; E. Richards, *Pacifism: A Brief History* (London: 1981).
33. Ceadel, *Pacifism*, introduction.
34. R. Overy, 'Parting with pacifism in the 1930s', *History Today*, vol.59(8), 2009, pp.23–29.
35. A.C. Johnson, *Peace Offering* (London: 1936), pp.154–55.
36. Ceadel, *Pacifism*, pp.254–59.
37. HC Deb 5s, vol.308, cols.212–13, 5 Feb. 1936.
38. HL Deb 5s, vol.110, col.1400, 4 Oct. 1938.
39. Ibid., vol.112, cols.323–24, 20 March 1939.
40. Ibid., col.342.
41. *News Chronicle*, 11 Aug. 1939.
42. R. Griffiths, *Fellow Travellers of the Right: British Enthusiasts for Nazi Germany, 1933–1939* (Oxford: 1983).
43. HC Deb 5s, vol.339, col.65, 3 Oct. 1938.
44. Ibid., vol.320, col.1458, 17 Feb. 1937.
45. Ibid., vol.338, col.2949, 4 July 1938.
46. 'Policy Review', 14 Oct. 1938, quoted, D. Dilks (ed.), *The Diaries of Sir Alexander Cadogan, 1938–1945* (London: 1971), p.116.
47. J. Harvey (ed.), *The Diplomatic Diaries of Oliver Harvey, 1937–1940* (London: 1970), p.121.
48. M. Howard, *The Continental Commitment: The Dilemma of British Defence Policy in the Era of the Two World Wars* (London: 1971).
49. Avon, *Facing*, p.472.
50. HC Deb 5s, vol.339, col.49, 3 Oct. 1938.
51. Dilks (ed.), *The Diaries*, p.14.

52. D. Reynolds, *Summits: Six Meetings that Shaped the Twentieth Century* (New York: 2009), p.5.
53. HL Deb 5s, vol.108, col.143, 16 March 1938.
54. Ibid., vol.112, col.629, 13 April 1939.
55. Foreign Policy Committee Memoranda, 13 July 1936, CAB27/626/FP(36)/5.
56. FO371/20475/W11340, 24 Aug. 1936.
57. Conservative Research Department papers, CRD 1/24, fol.2, Bodleian Library (BL), Oxford University. Conservative Research Department papers (CRD) are located at the Bodleian Library, Oxford University.
58. N. Chamberlain to L. Amery, 6 Oct. 1936, AMEL 2/1/26(1).
59. FO371/20735/C3621, 10 May 1937.
60. K. Feiling, *The Life of Neville Chamberlain* (London: 1946), p.322.
61. HC Deb 5s, vol.270, cols.632–38, 10 Nov. 1932; U. Bialer, *The Shadow of the Bomber: The Fear of Air Attack and British Politics, 1932–1939* (London: 1980).
62. CRD 1/78/1, fol.96, p.3.
63. HC Deb 5s, vol.309, col.85, 24 Feb. 1936.
64. CAB27/623/FP(36)/22, 3 Feb. 1938, pp.12–17.
65. Ibid., p.15.
66. FO371/21659/C14471, 10 Oct. 1938.
67. Parker, *Chamberlain*, p.318.
68. 'British Foreign Policy', 17 July 1936, DRAX 2/18, CAC.
69. 'Relations with Germany', 24 Oct. 1937, Ibid.
70. HC Deb 5s, vol.309, col.160, 24 Feb. 1936.
71. Ibid., vol.313, col.1646, 23 June 1936.
72. Ibid., cols.1613–15.
73. Ibid., vol.330, col.1829, 21 Dec. 1937.
74. *Daily Herald*, 3 Oct. 1938.
75. Ibid., 14 March 1938.
76. *News Chronicle*, 11 March 1938.
77. *Manchester Guardian*, 16 March 1938.
78. *News Chronicle*, 15 March 1939.
79. 'Statement of Policy', 31 March 1938, Gilbert Murray papers, MS Gilbert Murray 232, fol.214, BL.
80. Overy, 'Parting'.
81. G.L. Weinberg, *The Foreign Policy of Hitler's Germany: Starting World War Two, 1937–1939* (Chicago: 1980), pp.462–63.
82. K.P. Fischer, *Nazi Germany: A New History* (London: 1995), p.171.
83. Charmley, *Chamberlain*.

Chapter 2   Economic and Colonial Appeasement

1. HC Deb 5s, vol.310, cols.1459–60, 26 March 1936.
2. T. Jones, *A Diary with Letters, 1931–1950* (Oxford: 1954), p.177.

3. R. Boothby, *I Fight to Live* (London: 1947), pp.229–30.
4. F. Williams, *A Prime Minister Remembers* (London: 1961), pp.15–16.
5. A.J. Crozier, *Appeasement and Germany's Last Bid for Colonies* (London: 1988), p.269.
6. B.J. Wendt, *Economic Appeasement: Handel und Finanz in der Britischen Deutschland Politik, 1933–1939* (Düsseldorf: 1971), p.616.
7. G. Schmidt, *The Politics and Economics of Appeasement: British Foreign Policy in the 1930s*, trans. by J. Bennett-Ruete (Oxford: 1986), p.386.
8. Ibid., p.147.
9. N. Forbes, *Doing Business with the Nazis: Britain's Economic and Financial Relations with Germany, 1931–1939* (London: 2000), pp.225–28.
10. S. Newton, *Profits of Peace: The Political Economy of Anglo-German Appeasement* (Oxford: 1996), pp.76–77.
11. R. Grayson, 'Leo Amery's imperialist alternative to appeasement in the 1930s', *Twentieth Century British History*, vol.17(4), 2006, pp.489–515 (pp.499–500).
12. Schmidt, pp.33–37.
13. A.D. Stedman, 'Reassessing economic appeasement during Chamberlain's peace-time premiership: A two-headed beast?', *Working Papers in Military and International History: University of Salford European Studies Research Institute*, vol.7, 2009, pp.5–31.
14. CAB27/626/FP(36)/18, Annex G, 15 March 1937.
15. HC Deb 5s, vol.308, col.244, 5 Feb. 1936.
16. Ibid., vol.309, cols.87–88, 24 Feb. 1936.
17. Ibid., col.2000, 10 March 1936.
18. *The Times*, 11 Feb. 1936.
19. HC Deb 5s, vol.313, col.1690, 23 June 1936.
20. Ibid., col.1696.
21. Ibid., vol.318, cols.2841–47, 18 Dec. 1936.
22. Labour Party, *Labour's Immediate Programme* (1937).
23. HC Deb 5s, vol.321, col.205, 2 March 1937.
24. Liberal Party, *Freedom and Peace* (1937), p.3.
25. HC Deb 5s, vol.330, col.1802, 21 Dec. 1937.
26. Ibid., cols.1834–35.
27. Ibid., col.1821.
28. Ibid., cols.1818–22.
29. L. Amery to N. Chamberlain, 11 Nov. 1937, AMEL 2/1/27; Barnes and Nicholson (eds.), 22 Oct. 1937, p.449.
30. P. van Zeeland, *Report to the Governments of the United Kingdom and France on the Possibility of Obtaining a General Reduction of the Obstacles to International Trade*, Presented by the Prime Minister to Parliament by Command of His Majesty, 26 January 1938 (London: 1938).
31. HC Deb 5s, vol.333, col.1420, 24 March 1938.
32. Ibid., col.1432.

33. Ibid., vol.338, col.3028, 4 July 1938.
34. Ibid., col.3025.
35. Ibid., col.3037.
36. Ibid., vol.330, col.181, 21 Dec. 1937.
37. Avon, *Facing*, p.324.
38. HC Deb 5s, vol.339, col.66, 3 Oct. 1938.
39. HL Deb 5s, vol.110, col.1381, 4 Oct. 1938.
40. Ibid., col.1460, 5 Oct. 1938.
41. HC Deb 5s, vol.342, cols.1199–1211, 7 Dec. 1938.
42. Ibid., cols.1236–37.
43. Communist Party, *Colonies, Mandates and Peace* (1936).
44. Independent Labour Party, *The Socialist Challenge to Poverty, Fascism, Imperialism, War: The Basic Policy of the I.L.P.* (1939).
45. FO371/21780/C9990, 17 Sept. 1938.
46. FO371/20704/C1588, 18 Feb. 1937.
47. Women's International League for Peace and Freedom, *Opening the Empire Door: A Positive Policy for Peace* (1937), p.6.
48. League of Nations Union, *Economic Steps Towards World Peace* (1937), pp.2–6.
49. G. Murray to L. Amery, 8 Oct. 1937, MS Gilbert Murray 83, fol.9.
50. 'Resolutions Adopted on 10 Dec. 1938', quoted, FO371/24029/W323, 2 Jan. 1939.
51. G. Dawson to H.G. Daniels, 11 May 1937, MS Dawson 79, fols.129–30, BL.
52. *Daily Herald*, 14 March 1938.
53. Ibid., 3 Oct. 1938.
54. *Manchester Guardian*, 3 Oct. 1938.
55. Gallup, p.10.
56. *Daily Herald*, 16 March 1938.
57. *Manchester Guardian*, 19 March 1938.
58. *Daily Telegraph and Morning Post*, 21 March 1939.
59. HC Deb 5s, vol.345, col.448, 15 March 1939.
60. Ibid., col.2517, 3 April 1939.
61. HL Deb 5s, vol.112, col.343, 20 March 1939.
62. HC Deb 5s, vol.347, cols.1827–28, 19 May 1939.
63. Ibid., vol.350, cols.2003–4, 31 July 1939.
64. Ibid., vol.345, cols.2014–17.
65. Ibid., col.544, 15 March 1939.
66. Stedman, 'Reassessing', pp.10–13.
67. HC Deb 5s, vol.350, cols.2042–44.
68. Parker, *Chamberlain*, chapters four and thirteen.
69. HC Deb 5s, vol.310, cols.2557–58, 6 April 1936.
70. N. Chamberlain to L. Amery, 2 Dec. 1938, AMEL 2/1/28(1).
71. N. Chamberlain to I. Chamberlain, 13 April 1936, NC18/1/956.
72. CAB27/622/FP(36)/4, 27 July 1936.
73. CAB27/626/FP(36)/8, 20 Aug. 1936.

74. FO371/20472/W3851, 15 April 1936.
75. FO371/19884/C807, 31 Jan. 1936.
76. CAB27/626/FP(36)/23, 2 April 1937.
77. CAB27/626/FP(36)/34, 7 June 1937.
78. FO371/21247/W11812, 11 June 1937.
79. CAB27/622/FP(36)/13, 16 June 1937.
80. N. Chamberlain to I. Chamberlain, 26 Nov. 1937, NC18/1/1030.
81. HC Deb 5s, vol.330, col.1806, 21 Dec. 1937.
82. CAB27/623/FP(36)/21, 24 Jan. 1938.
83. CAB27/623/FP(36)/22, 3 Feb. 1938.
84. Parker, *Chamberlain*, p.131.
85. Forbes, p.203.
86. D. Kaiser, *Economic Diplomacy and the Origins of the Second World War: Germany, Britain, France and Eastern Europe, 1930–1939* (Princeton: 1980).
87. Newton, p.98.
88. FO371/21247/W11812, 11 June 1937.
89. C.A. MacDonald, 'Economic appeasement and the German 'moderates', 1937–1939: An introductory essay', *Past and Present*, vol.56(3), 1972, pp.105–35 (p.123).
90. Ibid., pp.111–13.
91. Schmidt, p.105.
92. FO371/19806/A1159, 7 Feb. 1936.
93. FO371/20660/A4165, 11 June 1937.
94. FO371/22517/R3279, 1 March 1938.
95. J. Smuts to L. Amery, 9 Dec. 1937, AMEL 2/1/27(2).
96. FO371/21674/C1866, 17 March 1938.
97. Kaiser, p.249.
98. CAB27/627/FP(36)/54, 26 Oct. 1938.
99. Newton, p.88.
100. FO371/21659/C14471, 9 Nov. 1938.
101. FO371/23818/R6506, 21 July 1939.
102. HC Deb 5s, vol.347, cols.1827–29, 19 May 1939.
103. HL Deb 5s, vol.113, col.361, 8 June 1939.
104. Parker, *Chamberlain*, pp.264–70.
105. HC Deb 5s, vol.330, col.1806, 21 Dec. 1937.
106. FO371/20475/W10243, 25 Aug. 1936.
107. FO371/19934/C6145, 3 Sept. 1936.
108. FO371/20483/W1331, 13 Feb. 1936.
109. CAB27/626/FP(36)/4.
110. E. Phipps to A. Eden, 13 April 1937, PHPP 1/18/3, CAC.
111. FO371/20731/C6216, 1 Sept. 1937.
112. 'Relations with Germany', 24 Oct. 1937, DRAX 2/18.
113. CAB27/623/FP(36)/21, 24 Jan. 1938.
114. CAB27/622/FP(36)/12, 11 June 1937.

115. FO371/20483/W195, 8 Jan. 1936.
116. D. Meredith, 'British trade diversion policy and the colonial issue in the 1930s', *Journal of European Economic History*, vol.25(1), 1996, pp.33–68 (p.56).
117. FO371/19886/C1180, 19 Feb. 1936.
118. CAB27/623/FP(36)/21, 24 Jan. 1938.
119. Ibid.
120. CAB27/622/FP(36)/12, 11 June 1937.
121. CAB27/623/FP(36)/30, 1 June 1938.
122. Ibid.
123. CAB27/627/FP(36)/54, 26 Oct. 1938.
124. CAB27/624/FP(36)/33, 21 Nov. 1938.
125. Feiling, pp.316–19.
126. Ruggiero, p.90.
127. A. Best, 'Economic appeasement or economic nationalism? A political perspective on the British empire, Japan, and the rise of intra-Asian trade, 1933–1937', *Journal of Imperial and Commonwealth History*, vol.30(2), 2002, pp.77–101 (pp.81–83).
128. Schmidt, p.147.
129. CAB27/623/FP(36)/30, 1 June 1938.
130. CAB27/626/FP(36)/4, pp.16–17.
131. CAB27/622/FP(36)/7, 18 March 1937.
132. CAB27/626/FP(36)/37.
133. A.A. Offner, *American Appeasement: United States Foreign Policy and Germany, 1933–1938* (Cambridge, MA: 1969); C.A. MacDonald, *The United States, Britain and Appeasement, 1936–1939* (London: 1981); W.R. Rock, *Chamberlain and Roosevelt: British Foreign Policy and the United States, 1937–1940* (Ohio: 1988).
134. FO371/21501/A5662, 6 July 1938.
135. Schmidt, p.127.
136. HC Deb 5s, vol.308, cols.246–48, 5 Feb. 1936.
137. Ibid., vol.310, col.1507, 26 March 1936.
138. N. Nicolson (ed.), *Harold Nicolson: Diaries and Letters, 1930–1939* (London: 1966), pp.345–46.
139. HC Deb 5s, vol.339, col.126, 3 Oct. 1938.
140. Ibid., vol.342, cols.1203–6, 7 Dec. 1938.
141. Ibid., cols.1218–20.
142. Ibid., cols.1252–53.
143. Colonial Defence League, *German Colonial Demands* (1938), p.3.
144. *News Chronicle*, 21 March 1939.
145. Gallup, p.10.
146. Ibid., p.21.
147. FO371/19933/C5021, 23 June 1936.
148. N. Henderson to N. Chamberlain, 23 Feb. 1939, FO800/315/8.

149. Newton, pp.76–77.
150. Forbes, p.xii.

Chapter 3   League of Nations

1. HC Deb 5s, vol.321, cols.645–46, 4 March 1937.
2. Churchill, p.16.
3. Ibid., p.168.
4. Ibid., pp.171–82.
5. Macmillan, p.438.
6. Ibid., p.524.
7. G. Murray, *From the League of Nations to United Nations* (Oxford: 1948), pp.71–76.
8. Williams, p.12.
9. Earl of Halifax, *Fullness of Days*, 2nd edn. (London: 1957), p.227.
10. Simon, p.244.
11. Vansittart, p.506.
12. Lord Strang, *Home and Abroad* (London: 1956), p.65.
13. Templewood, p.187.
14. L.S. Amery, *My Political Life, vol.3, The Unforgiving Years, 1929–1940* (London: 1955), p.175.
15. A. Duff Cooper, *Old Men Forget* (London: 1953), p.205.
16. A. Duff Cooper, *The Funeral of the League of Nations* (1940), quoted, DUFC 8/1/9, CAC.
17. Avon, *Facing*, pp.317–18.
18. Williams, p.12.
19. E.H. Carr, *The Twenty Year Crisis, 1919–1939* (London: 1946), pp.25–26.
20. F.S. Northedge, *The Troubled Giant: Britain Among the Great Powers, 1916–1939* (Suffolk: 1966), p.123.
21. F.S. Northedge, *The League of Nations: Its Life and Times, 1920–1946* (Leicester: 1986), p.252.
22. Ibid., pp.276–77.
23. P. Kennedy, *The Realities*, p.244.
24. D.S. Birn, *The League of Nations Union, 1918–1945* (Oxford: 1981), p.229.
25. P.J. Beck, 'Britain and appeasement in the late 1930s: Was there a league of nations alternative?', in D. Richardson and G. Stone (eds.), *Decisions and Diplomacy: Essays in Twentieth-Century International History* (London: 1995), pp.153–73 (p.153).
26. S. Pederson, 'Back to the league of nations'. *American History Review*, vol.112(4), 2007, pp.1091–1117.
27. A.D. Stedman, '"A most dishonest argument"?: Chamberlain's government, anti-appeasers, and the persistence of league of nations language before the second world war', *Contemporary British History, Special Issue:*

Politics, Power and Diplomacy in the Twentieth Century: Essays in Honour of David Dutton, vol.25(1), 2011.

28. N. Smart (ed.), *The Diaries and Letters of Robert Bernays, 1932–1939: An Insider's Account of the House of Commons* (New York: 1996), p.274.
29. HC Deb 5s, vol.309, col.97, 24 Feb. 1936.
30. Ibid., col.153.
31. Ibid., vol.310, col.1450, 26 March 1936.
32. Ibid., cols.1499–1500.
33. Ibid., cols.1527–28.
34. Ibid., col.2487, 6 April 1936.
35. Ibid., vol.311, col.106, 21 April 1936.
36. HL Deb 5s, vol.100, col.537, 8 April 1936.
37. Ibid., col.577.
38. *The Times*, 11 June 1936.
39. HC Deb 5s, vol.313, col.1216, 18 June 1936.
40. Ibid., col.1240.
41. Macmillan, p.479.
42. FO371/21240/W250, 3 Jan. 1937.
43. HC Deb 5s, vol.321, col.218, 2 March 1937.
44. Ibid., vol.325, col.1556, 25 June 1937.
45. Ibid., vol.330, col.1877, 21 Dec. 1937.
46. Ibid., col.1838.
47. Ibid.
48. Macmillan, p.465.
49. H. Macmillan to G. Dawson, 28 March 1936, MS Macmillan 101, fol.36, BL.
50. HC Deb 5s, vol.333, cols.99–100, 14 March 1938.
51. Ibid.
52. HC Deb 5s, vol.333, col.111.
53. Ibid., cols.55–56.
54. Ibid., cols.58–62.
55. Ibid., col.1432, 24 March 1938.
56. Ibid., col.1504.
57. HL Deb 5s, vol.108, col.436, 29 March 1938.
58. Ibid., col.172, 16 March 1938.
59. HC Deb 5s, vol.339, cols.56–64, 3 Oct. 1938.
60. Ibid., cols.172–73, 4 Oct. 1938.
61. Ibid., cols.359–73, 5 Oct. 1938.
62. Ibid., cols.149–50, 3 Oct. 1938.
63. Ibid., col.358, 5 Oct. 1938.
64. Ibid., col.213, 4 Oct. 1938.
65. Ibid., col.257.
66. HL Deb 5s, vol.110, cols.1427–28, 4 Oct. 1938.
67. HC Deb 5s, vol.339, cols.534–38, 6 Oct. 1938.
68. HL Deb 5s, vol.110, col.1341, 3 Oct. 1938.

69. Ibid., col.1451, 6 Oct. 1938.
70. Ceadel, *Pacifism*, Appendix 1.
71. FO371/20181/J5088, 4 June 1936.
72. G. Murray to Lord Ponsonby, 9 March 1936, MS Gilbert Murray 224, fol.143.
73. G. Murray to E. Lyttelton, 14 April 1938, MS Gilbert Murray 232, fols.113–14.
74. HL Deb 5s, vol.110, cols.1333–34, 3 Oct. 1938.
75. FO371/24029/W323, 2 Jan. 1939.
76. Macmillan, p.525.
77. FO371/20704/C1588, 18 Feb. 1937.
78. HC Deb 5s, vol.310, col.2495, 6 April 1936.
79. Communist Party, *Labour and Armaments* (1937), p.2.
80. *Daily Herald*, 12 March 1938.
81. Ibid., 3 Oct. 1938.
82. *News Chronicle*, 11 March 1938.
83. Ibid., 14 March 1938.
84. HC Deb 5s, vol.320, col.1442, 18 Feb. 1937.
85. *News Chronicle*, 5 Oct. 1938.
86. Gallup, p.2.
87. Ibid., p.4.
88. Ibid., pp.12–17.
89. HC Deb 5s, vol.345, col.2499, 3 April 1939.
90. Ibid., col.2489.
91. HL Deb 5s, vol.112, col.616, 13 April 1939.
92. HC Deb 5s, vol.345, cols.2475–2578, 3 April 1939.
93. *Daily Herald*, 21 March 1939.
94. Ibid., 22 March 1939.
95. HL Deb 5s, vol.112, col.668, 19 April 1939.
96. Ibid., cols.336–37, 20 March 1939.
97. Ibid., vol.113, cols.390–91, 12 June 1939.
98. B. Pimlott (ed.), *The Political Diary of Hugh Dalton, 1918–1940, 1945–1960* (London: 1986), pp.197–98.
99. HL Deb 5s, vol.108, cols.153–55, 16 March 1938.
100. A. Moore, *The Necessity for a British League of Nations* (1938), pp.3–11.
101. H. Gillet to Lord Halifax, 6 April 1939, FO800/315/H/XV/146, Public Opinion 10.
102. HC Deb 5s, vol.310, col.1540, 26 March 1936.
103. N. Chamberlain to I. Chamberlain, 13 April 1936, NC18/1/956.
104. FO371/20472/W3851, 15 April 1936.
105. Feiling, p.295.
106. CAB27/626/FP(36)/5, 13 July 1936.
107. FO371/20474/W6346, 16 July 1936; FO371/20475/W11340, 24 Aug. 1936.

108. CAB27/626/FP(36)/12, 21 Aug. 1936.
109. CAB27/622/FP(36)/5, 25 Aug. 1936.
110. FO371/19914/C7936, 5 Nov. 1936.
111. Kenney, p.162.
112. FO371/21659/C14471, 14 Nov. 1938.
113. CAB27/623/FP(36)/26, 18 March 1938, Appendix 1.
114. FO371/24038/W5267, 22 March 1939.
115. FO371/23063/C5524, April 1939.
116. Dilks (ed.), *The Diaries*, p.182.
117. HL Deb 5s, vol.100, col.515, 8 April 1936.
118. HC Deb 5s, vol.311, col.126, 21 April 1936.
119. Ibid., vol.310, col.1484, 26 March 1936.
120. Ibid., col.1549.
121. N. Chamberlain to H. Chamberlain, 4 April 1936, NC18/1/955.
122. HC Deb 5s, vol.313, col.1725, 23 June 1936.
123. FO371/20472/W3851, 15 April 1936.
124. FO371/19884/C614, 29 Jan. 1936.
125. Avon, *Facing*, p.366.
126. Northedge, *The League*, pp.288–89; M.S. Alexander, *The Republic in Danger: General Maurice Gamelin and the Politics of French Defence, 1933–1940* (Cambridge: 1992), p.239.
127. FO371/20473/W5075, 22 June 1936.
128. 'British Foreign Policy', 17 July 1936, DRAX 2/18.
129. FO371/20475/W 9131, 11 Aug. 1936.
130. HC Deb 5s, vol.321, col.215, 2 March 1937.
131. Ibid., vol.327, col.166, 21 Oct. 1937.
132. N. Chamberlain to L. Amery, 15 Nov. 1937, AMEL 2/1/27(1).
133. CAB27/626/FP(36)/40, 1 Jan. 1938.
134. HC Deb 5s, vol.332, cols.226–29, 22 Feb. 1938.
135. HL Deb 5s, vol.108, col.481, 29 March 1938.
136. N. Chamberlain to H. Chamberlain, 13 March 1938, NC18/1/1041.
137. FO371/21624/C1704, 1 March 1938.
138. P.J. Beck, 'Searching for peace in Munich, not Geneva: The British government, the league of nations and the Sudeten question', *Diplomacy and Statecraft*, vol.10(2), 1999, pp.236–57 (p.251).
139. HC Deb 5s, vol.339, col.549, 6 Oct. 1938.
140. FO371/23063/C5524, April 1939.
141. FO371/20475/W11340, 24 Aug. 1936; E.J. Tarr *After Munich: Where do we go from here?* (1938).
142. HC Deb 5s, vol.332, col.116, 21 Feb. 1938.
143. Ibid., col.263, 22 Feb. 1938.
144. Lord Lothian to G. Murray, 24 Feb. 1938, MS Gilbert Murray 232, fol.5.
145. F. McDonough, *Neville Chamberlain, Appeasement and the British Road to War* (Manchester: 1998), p.96.

146. AMEL 1/5/24, 19 Sept. 1936.
147. L. Amery to N. Chamberlain, 11 Nov. 1937, AMEL 2/1/27.
148. British Union of Fascists, *Mind Britain's Business*, p.4.
149. McDonough, *Neville Chamberlain*, p.105.
150. HC Deb 5s, vol.332, col.267, 21 Feb. 1938.
151. Lukowitz, p.119.
152. G. Murray to Lady Howard of Penrith, 16 May 1938, MS Gilbert Murray 232, fol.177.
153. Nicolson (ed.), p.378.
154. H. Morgenthau, *The Problem of Neutrality* (1938), pp.118–23.
155. G.W. Egerton, 'Collective security as political myth: Liberal internationalism and the league of nations in politics and history', *International History Review*, vol.5(4), 1983, pp.496–524 (p.511).
156. *Daily Express*, 11 March 1936.
157. Ibid., 1 Oct. 1938.
158. *Manchester Guardian*, 5 Oct. 1938.
159. *Daily Herald*, 17 March 1939.
160. Gallup, pp.16–17.
161. *Daily Telegraph and Morning Post*, 1 Oct. 1938.
162. 'The Gap in the Bridge', *Punch*, 10 Dec. 1919.
163. B. Porter, *Britain, Europe and the World, 1850–1982: Delusions of Grandeur* (London: 1983), p.98.
164. Northedge, *The League*, pp.253–54.
165. Avon, *Facing*, p.366.

Chapter 4   Alliances

1. HC Deb 5s, vol.333, cols.99–100, 14 March 1938.
2. Churchill, p.239.
3. Ibid., p.223.
4. Ibid., p.229.
5. Ibid., p.246.
6. Ibid., pp.325–27.
7. Avon, *Facing*, p.317.
8. Ibid., pp.569–602.
9. Duff Cooper, *Old Men*, p.191.
10. Ibid., p.210.
11. Amery, *My Political*, p.163.
12. Ibid., p.227.
13. Ibid., pp.189–93.
14. Vansittart, pp.481–82.
15. Strang, *Home*, pp.194–98.
16. Templewood, p.262.

17. Ibid., pp.342–70.
18. N. Henderson, *Failure of a Mission: Berlin 1937–1939* (London: 1940), pp.238–39; Lord Home, *The Way the Wind Blows* (London: 1976), p.68.
19. Simon, p.253.
20. Halifax, p.194.
21. Namier, p.ix.
22. A.L. Rowse, *Appeasement: A Study in Political Decline, 1933–1939* (New York: 1961), p.63.
23. A.J.P. Taylor, *The Origins of the Second World War*, 1961 edn. (London: 1961), pp.243–44.
24. F.S. Northedge, *The International Political System* (London: 1976), p.323.
25. Kennedy, *The Realities*, pp.245–46.
26. Charmley, *Chamberlain*, p.64.
27. Ibid., p.212.
28. P. Neville, *Neville Chamberlain: A Study in Failure?* (Kent: 1992), p.92.
29. Parker, *Chamberlain*, pp.324–44.
30. Parker, *Churchill*, p.ix.
31. Denman, pp.85–98.
32. Dutton, *Neville Chamberlain*, pp.164–65.
33. Kaiser, pp.313–14.
34. G. Roberts, 'The Soviet decision for a pact with Nazi Germany', *Soviet Studies*, vol.44(1) 1992, pp.57–78 (p.58).
35. Carley, *1939*.
36. Shaw, p.4.
37. Ibid., p.16.
38. Ibid., p.190.
39. HC Deb 5s, vol.308, col.546, 10 Feb. 1936.
40. Ibid., vol.310, col.1469, 26 March 1936.
41. Ibid., vol.311, col.115, 21 April 1936.
42. Ibid., vol.310, cols.1522–23, 26 March 1936.
43. Ibid., vol.320, col.1459, 18 Feb. 1937.
44. Ibid., col.2270, 25 Feb. 1937.
45. Ibid., vol.321, col.581, 4 March 1937.
46. Ibid., cols.621–22.
47. Ibid., vol.320, col.1484, 18 Feb. 1937.
48. Boothby, pp.141–42.
49. Smart (ed.), p.273.
50. Barnes and Nicholson (eds.), 17 March 1936, p.411.
51. L. Amery to N. Chamberlain, 11 Nov. 1937, AMEL 2/1/27.
52. HC Deb 5s, vol.325, col.1599, 25 June 1937.
53. Ibid., col.1538.
54. Churchill, p.222.
55. HC Deb 5s, vol.327, cols.87–89, 21 Oct. 1937.
56. FO371/21626/C1935, 17 March 1938.

57. HC Deb 5s, vol.333, cols.1503–4, 24 March 1938.
58. Ibid., col.62, 14 March 1938.
59. *Manchester Guardian*, 30 April 1938.
60. HC Deb 5s, vol.333, col.78, 14 March 1938.
61. Ibid., cols.1470–74, 24 March 1938.
62. 'Notes on the European Situation', March 1938, quoted, MS Macmillan 119, fol.168.
63. HC Deb 5s, vol.333, col.147, 14 March 1938.
64. *News of the World*, 15 May 1938.
65. HC Deb 5s, vol.338, cols.2949–59, 4 July 1938.
66. Ibid., col.3030.
67. Ibid., col.3004.
68. Independent Labour Party, *The Socialist*.
69. Communist Party, *Labour*.
70. League of Nations Union, *Policy Manifesto* (1936).
71. G. Murray to Lady Howard of Penrith, 16 May 1938, MS Gilbert Murray 232, fol.177.
72. League of Nations Union, *Resolutions of the Executive Committee* (1939).
73. International Peace Campaign to H. Macmillan, Sept. 1938, quoted, MS Macmillan 123, fol.288.
74. *Manchester Guardian*, 15 March 1938.
75. *News Chronicle*, 16 March 1938.
76. Ibid., 7 Oct. 1938.
77. A. Mann to Lord Halifax, 31 Aug. 1938, Arthur Mann papers, MS Eng. c. 5236, fol.10, BL.
78. A. Mann to Lord Halifax, 30 June 1939, MS Eng. c. 5236, fol.42.
79. *Daily Express*, 20 March 1939.
80. *Daily Herald*, 20 March 1939.
81. *News Chronicle*, 18–21 March 1939.
82. *The Times*, 16 March 1939.
83. F.W. Balch to H. Macmillan, 22 March 1938, MS Macmillan 131, fol.51.
84. *Daily Telegraph and Morning Post*, 20 March 1939.
85. Gallup, p.17.
86. Ibid., pp.2–4.
87. HC Deb 5s, vol.345, col.2482, 3 April 1939.
88. Ibid., vol.339, col.356, 5 Oct. 1938.
89. Ibid., vol.345, cols.2475–80, 3 April 1939.
90. Ibid., cols.2486–93.
91. HL Deb 5s, vol.112, col.615, 13 April 1939.
92. Ibid., col.619.
93. HC Deb 5s, vol.347, cols.1823–24, 19 May 1939.
94. HL Deb 5s, vol.113, cols.421–23, 12 June 1939.
95. HC Deb 5s, vol.347, col.1847, 19 May 1939.
96. Ibid., vol.350, col.1996, 31 July 1939.

97. Ibid., col.2037.
98. Ibid., vol.309, cols.160–61, 24 Feb. 1936.
99. E. Phipps to A. Eden, 29 Feb. 1936, PHPP 1/16/27.
100. FO371/20412/R6694, 4 Nov. 1936.
101. Vansittart, pp.481–521.
102. Templewood, pp.191–200.
103. FO371/20702/C8477, 8 Dec. 1937.
104. HC Deb 5s, vol.338, col.2963, 4 July 1938.
105. FO371/23818/R6506, 21 July 1939.
106. HC Deb 5s, vol.327, col.58, 21 Oct. 1937.
107. A. Adamthwaite, *France and the Coming of the Second World War, 1936–1939* (London: 1977), p.358.
108. B. Bond, *British Military Policy Between the Two World Wars* (Oxford: 1980), p.286.
109. M. Thomas, *Britain, France and Appeasement: Anglo-French Relations in the Popular Front Era* (Oxford: 1996), pp.7–11.
110. G. Stone, 'Britain, France and the Spanish problem, 1936–1939', in Richardson and Stone (eds.), *Decisions*, pp.129–52.
111. Avon, *Facing*, p.486.
112. HL Deb 5s, vol.100, cols.546–52, 24 March 1936.
113. Lord Halifax to E. Phipps, 1 Nov. 1938, PHPP 1/21/59.
114. Adamthwaite, *France*, p.xv.
115. J. Herman, *The Paris Embassy of Sir Eric Phipps: Anglo-French Relations and the Foreign Office, 1937–1939* (Sussex: 1998), p.51.
116. E. Phipps to Lord Halifax, 26 March 1938, PHPP 1/20/5.
117. CAB27/627/FP(36)/56, 21 March 1938.
118. FO371/21600/C11641, 4 Oct. 1938.
119. Herman, p.54.
120. Harvey (ed.), p.71.
121. N. Chamberlain to I. Chamberlain, 27 Oct. 1934, NC18/1/893.
122. W.R. Rock, *Chamberlain and Roosevelt: British Foreign Policy and the United States* (Ohio: 1988), pp.293–314 (p.314).
123. I. Cowman, *Dominion or Decline: Anglo-American Naval Relations on the Pacific, 1937–1941* (Oxford: 1996).
124. D. Reynolds, *The Creation of the Anglo-American Alliance, 1937–1941: A Study in Competitive Cooperation* (London: 1981), pp.11–15.
125. Rock, *Chamberlain*, p.12.
126. FO371/20473/W5075, 3 June 1936, pp.202–3.
127. FO115/3411/410, 15 Sept. 1936.
128. 'The World Situation and British Rearmament', 31 Dec. 1936, quoted, VNST 1/1/19, CAC.
129. FO115/3413/506, 16 March 1937, pp.31–35.
130. S. Welles to F.D. Roosevelt, 27 May 1937, quoted, Offner, p.180.
131. N. Chamberlain to H. Chamberlain, 17 Dec. 1937, NC18/1/1032.

132. N. Chamberlain to Lord Tweedsmuir, 19 Nov. 1937, quoted, R. Ovendale, *Appeasement and the English Speaking World: Britain, the USA, the Dominions, and the Policy of 'Appeasement', 1937–1939* (Cardiff: 1975), p.318.
133. FO371/21041/F11265, 12 Nov. 1937.
134. FO371/20665/A9142, 17 Dec. 1937.
135. Avon, p.552.
136. Ibid., p.560.
137. FO371/21526/A2127, 12 Jan. 1938.
138. Ibid.
139. Rock, *Chamberlain*, p.297.
140. A. Eden to F.S. Northedge, 18 Aug. 1966, quoted, STRN 2/12, CAC.
141. N. Chamberlain to M. Prince, 16 Jan. 1938, quoted, Feiling, p.322.
142. Ibid.
143. Home, p.66.
144. FO115/3415/35, 3 Nov. 1938.
145. CAB27/624/FP(36)/35, 23 Jan. 1939.
146. CAB27/627/FP(36)/80, 20 April 1939.
147. FO371/20731/C6212, 1 Sept. 1937.
148. 9 Sept. 1937, ACAD 1/6, CAC.
149. Avon, *Facing*, p.571.
150. Dilks (ed.), *The Diaries*, p.61.
151. FO371/21626/C1935, 17 March 1938.
152. N. Chamberlain to I. Chamberlain, 20 March 1938, NC18/1/1042.
153. CAB27/623/FP(36)/26, 18 March 1938, Appendix 1.
154. CAB27/627/FP(36)/56, 21 March 1938, pp.15–16.
155. HC Deb 5s, vol.333, col.1403, 24 March 1938.
156. CAB27/624/FP(36)/35, 23 Jan. 1939.
157. Pimlott (ed.), p.239.
158. A. Eden to E. Phipps, 28 Feb. 1936, PHPP 1/16/26.
159. A. Howard, *The life of R.A. Butler* (London: 1987), p.85.
160. HC Deb 5s, vol.339, cols.298–304, 4 Oct. 1938.
161. Ibid., vol.345, cols.2485–2586, 31 March 1939.
162. FO371/22944/C4311, 23 March 1939.
163. Churchill, p.259.
164. Templewood, p.343; Ragsdale, p.156.
165. FO371/21104/N4148, 7 Aug. 1937.
166. FO371/21102/N6137, 14 Dec. 1937.
167. K. Neilson, '"Pursued by a bear": British estimates of Soviet military strength and Anglo-Soviet relations, 1922–1939', *Canadian Journal of History*, vol.28(2), 1993, pp.189–221.
168. Ragsdale, pp.156–66.
169. M. Thomas, 'France and the Czechoslovak crisis', in I. Lukes and E. Goldstein (eds.), *The Munich Crisis, 1938: Prelude to World War Two* (London: 1999), pp.122–59 (pp.129–30).

170. N. Chamberlain to H. Chamberlain, NC18/1/1091, 26 March 1939.

171. Parker, *Chamberlain*, p.223.

172. N. Chamberlain to I. Chamberlain, 9 April 1939, NC18/1/1093.

173. Ragsdale, pp.208–11.

174. CAB27/625/FP(36)/47, 16 May 1939, Appendix 2.

175. CAB27/624/FP(36)/38, 27 March 1939, p.2.

176. Ibid., pp.4–6.

177. Ibid., p.8.

178. HL Deb 5s, vol.112, col.646, 13 April 1939 (my emphasis).

179. 'Account of the August 1939 Moscow Mission', 4 Aug. 1966, DRAX 6/5.

180. CAB27/625/FP(36)/45–49, 5–19 May 1939.

181. CAB27/625/FP(36)/50–54, 9–26 June 1939; CAB27/625/FP(36)/57–58, 10–19 July 1939.

182. Dilks (ed.), *The Diaries*, p.189.

183. CAB27/625/FP(36)/54, 26 June 1939.

184. CAB27/625/FP(36)/56–57, 10–19 July 1939.

185. HC Deb 5s, vol.339, col.406, 5 Oct. 1938.

186. HL Deb 5s, vol.112, cols.636–37, 13 April 1939.

187. Barnes and Nicholson (eds.), p.426.

188. L. Amery to N. Chamberlain, 11 Nov. 1937, AMEL 2/1/27.

189. L. Amery to D. Lloyd George, 25 Aug. 1939, AMEL 2/1/28.

190. *Glasgow Forward*, 26 Nov. 1938.

191. G. Murray to E. Lyttelton, 14 April 1938, MS Gilbert Murray 232, fol.115.

192. Pimlott (ed.), p.275.

193. *Daily Express*, 1 Oct. 1938.

194. Gallup, p.2.

195. Ibid., p.22.

196. D. Dilks, ' "We must hope for the best and prepare for the worst": The prime minister, the cabinet and Hitler's Germany, 1937–39', *Proceedings of the British Academy*, vol.73, 1987, pp.309–52.

197. Kennedy, *The Realities*, p.322.

198. Dutton, *Neville Chamberlain*, p.191.

199. Reynolds, *The Creation*, p.286.

200. N. Chamberlain to I. Chamberlain, 27 Jan. 1940, NC18/1/1140.

201. Rock, *Chamberlain*, p.293.

202. J.V. Compton, *The Swastika and the Eagle: Hitler, the United States and the Origins of World War Two* (Boston: 1968), p.32.

203. Kaiser, p.314.

Chapter 5   Armaments and Defences

1. HC Deb 5s, vol.313, col.1243, 18 June 1936.

2. 'Article on Neville Chamberlain', pp.9–10, quoted, DUFC 8/1/14.

3. CATO, p.14.
4. Ibid., p.76.
5. Ibid., p.99.
6. Churchill, p.x.
7. Ibid., p.16.
8. Ibid., p.214.
9. Avon, *Facing*, p.318.
10. Williams, p.18.
11. Ibid., p.11.
12. Home, pp.62–63.
13. Templewood, p.340.
14. R.J. Minney (ed.), *The Private Papers of Hore-Belisha* (London: 1960), p.33.
15. Feiling, p.312.
16. Ibid., p.316.
17. R.P. Shay, *British Rearmament in the Thirties: Politics and Profits* (Princeton: 1977), pp.285–86.
18. G. Peden, *British Rearmament and the Treasury, 1932–1939* (Edinburgh: 1979), p.184.
19. G. Peden, 'A matter of timing: The economic background to British foreign policy, 1937–1939', *History*, vol.69(225), 1984, pp.15–28 (p.26).
20. P. Kennedy, *The Rise and Fall of the Great Powers: Economic Change and Military Conflict from 1500 to 2000* (London: 1988), pp.xxiii-iv.
21. Kennedy, *The Realities*, p.230.
22. J.P.D. Dunbabin, 'British rearmament in the 1930s: A chronology and review', *Historical Journal*, vol.18(3), 1975, pp.587–609 (p.609).
23. Ruggiero, p.8.
24. Ibid., p.228.
25. Ibid., p.223.
26. Newton, p.69.
27. Levy, p.xiv.
28. C. Andrew, *Secret Service: The Making of the British Intelligence Community* (London: 1985); W. Wark, *The Ultimate Enemy: British Intelligence and Nazi Germany* (New York: 1985).
29. HC Deb 5s, vol.310, col.1528, 26 March 1936.
30. Ibid., vol.308, col.1853, 9 March 1936.
31. Ibid., col.2011.
32. Ibid., vol.310, col.3040, 9 April 1936.
33. Ibid., vol.313, col.1241, 18 June 1936.
34. Ibid., col.1654.
35. D.M. Roberts, 'Hugh Dalton and the Labour Party in the 1930s', unpublished PhD thesis, University of Kingston upon Thames (1978).
36. HC Deb 5s, vol.313, cols.1707–14, 18 June 1936.
37. Ibid., vol.321, col.580, 4 March 1937.
38. Ibid., col.647.

39. Boothby, pp.141–42.
40. HC Deb 5s, vol.320, cols.1443–49, 18 Feb. 1937.
41. Ibid., vol.327, cols.133–34, 21 Oct. 1937.
42. Ibid., vol.333, col.64, 14 March 1938.
43. Ibid., col.85.
44. Ibid., col.1455, 24 March 1938.
45. HL Deb 5s, vol.108, col.450, 29 March 1938.
46. HC Deb 5s, vol.333, cols.60–61, 14 March 1938.
47. Ibid., col.1419, 24 March 1938.
48. HL Deb 5s, vol.108, cols.131–32, 16 March 1938.
49. Ibid., cols.135–37.
50. HC Deb 5s, vol.333, cols.112–14, 14 March 1938.
51. Pimlott (ed.), pp.229–32.
52. R. Bernays to L. Brereton, 27 May 1938, quoted, Smart (ed.), p.355.
53. N.J. Crowson, 'The conservative party and the call for national service, 1937–1939: Compulsion versus voluntarism', *Journal of Contemporary British History*, vol.9(3), 1995, pp.507–28 (pp.514–16).
54. R. Bernays to L. Brereton, 21 Oct. 1938, quoted, Smart (ed.), p.377.
55. HC Deb 5s, vol.339, cols.87–88, 3 Oct. 1938.
56. Ibid., cols.372–73, 5 Oct. 1938.
57. Nicolson (ed.), p.366–67.
58. HC Deb 5s, vol.339, cols.205–7, 4 Oct. 1938.
59. Barnes and Nicholson (eds.), p.528.
60. HC Deb 5s, vol.339, col.245, 4 Oct. 1938.
61. Ibid., col.407, 5 Oct. 1938.
62. HL Deb 5s, vol.110, cols.1381–86, 4 Oct. 1938.
63. HC Deb 5s, vol.339, col.180, 4 Oct. 1938.
64. Ibid., vol.341, cols.1130–45, 17 Nov. 1938.
65. Ibid., cols.1187–89.
66. Ibid., cols.1116–21.
67. Ibid., col.1098.
68. FO371/21240/W2920, Dec. 1936.
69. 'Statement of Policy', 31 May 1938, MS Gilbert Murray 232, fol.215.
70. G. Murray to N. Davies, 22 Sept. 1938, MS Gilbert Murray 233, fols.140–41.
71. FO371/24029/W323, 8–10 Dec. 1938.
72. J.L. Garvin to L. Amery, 28 Sept. 1938, AMEL 2/1/28(1).
73. *Daily Express*, 9 March 1937.
74. Ibid., 14 March 1938.
75. *Daily Telegraph and Morning Post*, 15 March 1938.
76. *Manchester Guardian*, 15 Feb. 1937.
77. *News Chronicle*, 14–15 March 1938.
78. Ibid., 17 March 1938.
79. Ibid., 3 Oct. 1938.
80. *Daily Herald*, 3 Oct. 1938.

81. Ibid., 16 Feb. 1939.
82. *News Chronicle*, 18 March 1939.
83. AMEL 1/5/24, 19 Sept. 1936.
84. CAB27/623/FP(36)/27, 21 March 1938.
85. F. McDonough, 'Why appeasement?', *Modern History Review*, vol.5(4), 1994, pp.6–9 (p.7).
86. Gallup, p.1.
87. Ibid., p.4.
88. Ibid., p.10.
89. Ibid., p.13.
90. Ibid., p.17.
91. HC Deb 5s, vol.345, cols.3118–19, 6 April 1939.
92. Ibid., col.2510, 3 April 1939.
93. HL Deb 5s, vol.112, col.626, 13 April 1939.
94. HC Deb 5s, vol.347, col.1847, 19 May 1939.
95. Ibid., col.1812.
96. HL Deb 5s, vol.113, col.412, 12 June 1939.
97. HC Deb 5s, vol.350, col.2067, 31 July 1939.
98. C.R. Attlee, *As It Happened* (London: 1954), p.509.
99. Dutton, *Neville Chamberlain*, p.172.
100. McDonough, 'Why appeasement?', p.9.
101. Feiling, pp.314–15.
102. Newton, p.69.
103. Parker, *Chamberlain*, p.283.
104. Newton, p.69.
105. Harvey (ed.), p.292.
106. McDonough, 'Why appeasement?', p.9.
107. N. Chamberlain to I. Chamberlain, 8 Dec. 1935, NC18/1/940.
108. 'England's Last Chance', *Naval Review*, 10 Oct. 1938, DRAX 2/18.
109. McDonough, 'Why appeasement?', p.7.
110. VNST 1/2/35(3).
111. Ruggiero, p.67.
112. N. Chamberlain to I. Chamberlain, 25 April 1937, NC18/1/1003.
113. 'The World Situation and British Rearmament', 31 Dec. 1936, quoted, VNST 1/1/19, pp.15–16.
114. Harvey (ed.), p.19.
115. FO371/21160/R4854, 14 July 1937.
116. FO371/20735/C3621, 10 May 1937.
117. ACAD 1/6, 24 May 1937.
118. FO371/20701/C1586, 22 Feb. 1937.
119. Air Cabinet Papers, Oct. 1937, quoted, SWIN 1/2/7, CAC.
120. Caputi, p.138.
121. N. Chamberlain to I. Chamberlain, 23 July 1939, NC/18/1/1108.
122. FO371/22341/R2184, 3 March 1938.

123. Newton, pp.70–72.
124. Harvey (ed.), p.416.
125. Feiling, p.322.
126. CAB27/623/FP(36)/26, 18 March 1938, p.187.
127. HC Deb 5s, vol.333, cols.1402–10, 24 March 1938.
128. CAB27/627/FP(36)/56, 21 March 1938, p.10.
129. Newton, p.72.
130. Dilks (ed.), *The Diaries*, p.71.
131. HC Deb 5s, vol.339, col.348, 5 Oct. 1938.
132. Ibid., col.551.
133. FO371/21659/C14471, Oct. and Nov. 1938, pp.44–78.
134. Ibid., 14 Nov. 1938, p.43.
135. HC Deb 5s, vol.339, col.236, 4 Oct. 1938.
136. Dutton, *Neville Chamberlain*, p.176.
137. N. Chamberlain to H. Chamberlain, 15 Oct. 1938, NC/18/1/1072.
138. CAB27/624/FP(36)/32, 14 Nov. 1938, pp.5–19.
139. Ibid., pp.15–16.
140. Ibid., p.18.
141. Ibid., p.19.
142. HC Deb 5s, vol.341, cols.1115–1203, 17 Nov. 1938.
143. Ibid., cols.1198–1203.
144. Ibid., col.1105.
145. CAB27/624/FP(36)/35, 23 Jan. 1939, pp.18–20.
146. FO371/22922/C940, 30 Jan. 1939.
147. L. Hore-Belisha to T. Inskip, 30 Jan. 1939, HOBE 7/19, CAC.
148. N. Chamberlain to Major E.O. Kellett, 29 April, 1939, CRD 1/24/3.
149. Dilks (ed.), *The Diaries*, p.150.
150. HC Deb 5s, vol.350, col.2020, 31 July 1939.
151. Macmillan, p.433.
152. HC Deb 5s, vol.320, col.1462, 18 Feb. 1937.
153. Ibid., col.1501.
154. Ibid., vol.332, col.281, 22 Feb. 1938.
155. Ibid., vol.333, col.1438, 24 March 1938.
156. Ibid., vol.339, col.409, 5 Oct. 1938.
157. Ibid., vol.345, col.2545, 3 April 1939.
158. HL Deb 5s, vol.112, col.705, 19 April 1939.
159. Ibid., vol.113, col.372, 8 June 1939.
160. Communist Party, *Colonies*, p.15.
161. Communist Party, *Can Conscription Save Peace?* (1939), pp.13–16.

Chapter 6   War and the Threat of War

1. HC Deb 5s, vol.339, col.34, 3 Oct. 1938.
2. Churchill, p.159.

3. Ibid., p.288.
4. Ibid., pp.274–75.
5. Ibid., pp.301–4.
6. Avon, *Facing*, pp.338–66 (p.338).
7. Duff Cooper, *Old Men*, p.196.
8. Ibid., p.244.
9. Macmillan, p.462.
10. Ibid., pp.574–79.
11. Ibid., p.579.
12. Halifax, p.197; Simon, p.214.
13. Halifax, p.198.
14. Simon, p.242.
15. Ibid., p.253.
16. Vansittart, p.545.
17. Lord Balfour, *Wings over Westminster* (London: 1973), pp.110–11.
18. Strang, pp.149–55.
19. Ibid., p.155.
20. K. Robbins, *Munich 1938* (London: 1968), pp.329–55.
21. Ibid., p.355.
22. Offner, p.276.
23. P. Calvocoressi and G. Wint (eds.), *Total War: Causes and Courses of the Second World War* (London: 1972), pp.92–96.
24. R. Kee, *Munich: The Eleventh Hour* (London: 1988), pp.210–11.
25. R. Lamb, *The Drift to War, 1922–1939* (London: 1989), p.269.
26. W. Murray, 'The war of 1938: Chamberlain fails to sway Hitler at Munich', in Cowley (ed.) *More What If?*, pp.255–78.
27. Denman, pp.101–10.
28. Dutton, *Neville Chamberlain*, pp.208–16 (p.208).
29. Ibid., p.137.
30. Ragsdale, pp.156–66 (p.156); I. Lukes, *Czechoslovakia Between Stalin and Hitler: The Diplomacy of Edvard Benes in the 1930s* (Oxford: 1996).
31. R. Bernays to L. Brereton, 23 Aug. 1935, quoted, Smart (ed.), p.220.
32. HC Deb 5s, vol.310, col.1498, 26 March 1936.
33. *The Times*, 28 March 1936.
34. HC Deb 5s, vol.310, col.2495, 6 April 1936.
35. HL Deb 5s, vol.100, col.577, 8 April 1936.
36. HC Deb 5s, vol.313, cols.1242–43, 18 June 1936.
37. Ibid., vol.332, col.47, 21 Feb. 1938.
38. Ibid., col.79.
39. Ibid., col.246, 22 Feb. 1938.
40. Ibid., vol.333, col.55, 14 March 1938.
41. Ibid., col.133.
42. Ibid., vol.338, col.2960, 4 July 1938.
43. Ibid., col.2991.

44. Ibid., col.3005.
45. Ibid., vol.333, cols.107–51, 14 March 1938.
46. Ibid., col.86.
47. Barnes and Nicholson (eds.), 20 March 1938, p.498.
48. HL Deb 5s, vol.108, col.152, 16 March 1938.
49. HC Deb 5s, vol.333, col.1446, 24 March 1938.
50. Churchill, pp.262–63.
51. Nicolson (ed.), pp.366–67.
52. J. Wedgwood to A. Duff Cooper, 2 Oct. 1938, DUFC 2/14.
53. HC Deb 5s, vol.339, col.260, 4 Oct. 1938.
54. Ibid., col.40, 3 Oct. 1938.
55. Ibid., cols.361–64, 5 Oct. 1938.
56. Ibid., cols.430–31.
57. Ibid., col.212, 4 Oct. 1938.
58. HL Deb 5s, vol.110, col.1369, 4 Oct. 1938.
59. Nicolson (ed.), p.376.
60. MS Gilbert Murray 233, fol.156, 7 Oct. 1938.
61. International Peace Campaign to H. Macmillan, Sept. 1938, MS Macmillan 123, fol.289.
62. *News Chronicle*, 14 March 1938.
63. Ibid., 4 Oct. 1938.
64. *Daily Telegraph and Morning Post*, 17 March 1939.
65. *The Times*, 16 March 1939.
66. *Daily Herald*, 16 March 1938.
67. Madge and Harrison (eds.), p.87.
68. Gallup, p.21.
69. HC Deb 5s, vol.345, col.545, 15 March 1939.
70. HL Deb 5s, vol.112, col.307, 20 March 1939.
71. Ibid., col.321.
72. Ibid., cols.617–25, 13 April 1939.
73. Nicolson (ed.), p.401.
74. HL Deb 5s, vol.113, col.403, 12 June 1939.
75. HC Deb 5s, vol.350, cols.2071–72, 31 July 1939.
76. Nicolson (ed.), p.421.
77. Diary, 5 July 1935, quoted, Feiling, p.265.
78. Ibid., p.272.
79. HC Deb 5s, vol.308, col.2081, 10 March 1936.
80. E. Phipps to A. Eden, 13 March 1936, PHPP 1/16/41.
81. VNST 1/2/35(3).
82. Denman, p.149.
83. 'The World Situation and British Rearmament', 31 Dec. 1936, VNST. 1/1/19.
84. FO371/21119/R3302, 15 May 1937.
85. FO371/20731/C6212, 1 Sept. 1937.

86. Avon, *Facing*, p.470.
87. FO371/20704/C8961, 10 Nov. 1937.
88. Dilks (ed.), *The Diaries*, p.15.
89. FO371/20702/C8477, 8 Dec. 1937.
90. HC Deb 5s, vol.330, col.1883, 21 Dec. 1937.
91. R. Vansittart to A. Eden, 4 March 1938, VNST 1/2/35(1).
92. Harvey (ed.), 15 March 1938, p.117.
93. N. Chamberlain to H. Chamberlain, 13 March 1938, NC18/1/1041.
94. Dilks (ed.), *The Diaries*, p.60.
95. HL Deb 5s, vol.108, cols.179–80, 16 March 1938.
96. CAB27/623/FP(36)/26, 18 March 1938.
97. Ibid., Appendix 1, pp.5–12 (p.12).
98. CAB27/627/FP(36)/56, 21 March 1938.
99. HC Deb 5s, vol.333, cols.1399–1405, 24 March 1938.
100. O. Harvey to Lord Halifax, 30 June 1936, quoted, Harvey (ed.), pp.426–27.
101. FO800/314, H/XV/60, Central Europe 26, 5 Aug. 1938.
102. SIS to R. Vansittart, 10 Aug. 1938, VNST 2/2/18.
103. Parker, *Chamberlain*, pp.156–57.
104. R.H. Haigh and P.W. Turner, *The Tilted Scales: The Military Balance of Power at the Time of the Munich Crisis, Autumn 1938* (Sheffield: 1978), p.7.
105. FO371/21737/C9704, 13 Sept. 1938.
106. N. Chamberlain to H. Chamberlain, 11 Sept. 1938, NC18/1/1068.
107. Minney (ed.), p.138.
108. Ibid., p.146.
109. Dilks (ed.), *The Diaries*, pp.103–4.
110. Ibid., p.123.
111. CAB27/624/FP(36)/32, 14 Nov. 1938, pp.4–9.
112. N. Chamberlain to H. Chamberlain, 15 Oct. 1938, NC18/1/1072; N. Chamberlain to I. Chamberlain, 26 Feb. 1939, NC18/1/1087.
113. CRD 1/24, fol.3, 13 Dec. 1938.
114. Ibid.
115. CAB27/627/FP(36)/74, 17 Jan. 1939, pp.3–31.
116. CAB27/624/FP(36)/35, 23 Jan. 1939, pp.10–15.
117. CAB27/624/FP(36)/36, 26 Jan. 1939, pp.2–4.
118. Halifax, p.198.
119. Harvey (ed.), p.256.
120. N. Chamberlain to H. Chamberlain, 19 March 1939, NC18/1/1090.
121. Dilks (ed.), *The Diaries*, p.161.
122. CAB27/624/FP(36)/38, 27 March 1939, p.15.
123. Dilks (ed.), *The Diaries*, p.167.
124. HC Deb 5s, vol.345, col.2486, 3 April 1939.
125. CAB27/624/FP(36)/45, 5 May 1939, p.13.
126. HL Deb 5s, vol.112, col.691, 19 April 1939.
127. Ibid., vol.113, col.363, 8 June 1939.

128. *The Times*, 30 June 1939.
129. Denman, p.83.
130. Haigh and Turner, *The Tilted Scales*, p.14.
131. M. Thomas, 'Appeasement in the late third republic', *Diplomacy and Statecraft*, vol.19(3), 2008, pp.566–607 (pp.574–86).
132. Alexander, p.118.

Conclusion

1. Vansittart, p.544.
2. *Glasgow Forward*, 26 Nov. 1938.
3. CAB27/623/FP(36)/25, 15 March 1938.
4. Templewood, pp.260–91.
5. Feiling, p.324.
6. N. Smart, *Neville Chamberlain* (London: 2010), p.202.
7. HC Deb 5s, vol.325, col.1549, 25 June 1937.
8. N. Chamberlain to I. Chamberlain, 12 March 1939, NC18/1/1089.
9. K. Hildebrand, *The Foreign Policy of the Third Reich*, trans. by B.T. Batsford (London: 1973), p.139.
10. H. Mommsen, 'Hitler's stellung im nationalsozialistchen herrschaftsystem', in G. Hirschfeld and L. Kettenacker (eds.) *Der Führerstaat: Mythos und Realitat* (Stuttgart: 1981), pp.43–72.
11. N. Rich, *Hitler's War Aims: Ideology, the Nazi State, and the Course of Expansion* (London: 1974), p.11; L.S. Dawidowicz, *The War Against the Jews, 1933–1945* (London: 1986), pp.xvii–xxxiii.
12. Mommsen, col.702; G. Aly, *Final Solution: Nazi Population Policy and the Murder of the European Jews* (London: 1999), pp.252–60.
13. D.C. Watt, *How War Came: The Immediate Origins of the Second World War, 1938–1939* (London: 1989), p.623.
14. T. Mason, 'Intention and explanation: A current controversy about the interpretation of national socialism', in Hirschfeld and Kettenacker (eds.), pp.23–42.
15. M. Burleigh, *The Third Reich: A New History* (New York: 2000).
16. I. Kershaw, *The Nazi Dictatorship: Problems and Perspectives of Interpretation* (London: 1985), p.68.
17. Henderson, p.35.
18. Ibid., p.196.
19. G. Murray to N. Davies, 22 Sept. 1938, MS Gilbert Murray 233, fol.141.
20. Dutton, *Neville Chamberlain*, p.218.
21. HC Deb 5s, vol.347, col.1860, 19 May 1939.
22. Dilks, ' "We must hope" ', p.350.
23. P.W. Schroeder, 'Munich and the British tradition', *Historical Journal*, vol.19(1) 1976, pp.223–43 (p.242).

BIBLIOGRAPHY

Primary Sources: Unpublished

Official Documents

The National Archives (formerly Public Record Office), Kew, London (TNA):
Committee of Imperial Defence Papers (CAB2).
Cabinet Minutes (CAB23).
Cabinet Memoranda (CAB24).
Foreign Policy Committee Papers (CAB27).
Imperial Conference Papers (CAB32).
Chiefs of Staff Committee Papers (CAB53).

Prime Minister's Papers (PREM1).

Foreign Office Washington Embassy Correspondence (FO115).
Foreign Office General Political Correspondence (FO371).
Private Papers of the Foreign Secretary (FO800).
Lord Avon's Papers (FO954).

Treasury – Leith-Ross Papers (T188).
Board of Trade – Department of Overseas Trade Papers (BT61).

Private Papers

University of Birmingham: Special Collections Department, Library (BU):
Neville Chamberlain Papers (NC).

Cambridge University: Churchill Archives Centre, Churchill College (CAC):
Alexander Cadogan (ACAD).
Leo Amery (AMEL).
Alfred Duff Cooper (DUFC).
Admiral Drax (DRAX).
Leslie Hore-Belisha (HOBE).

Sir Thomas Inskip (INKP).
Lord Margesson (MRGN).
Sir Eric Phipps (PHPP).
Lord Strang (STRN).
Lord Swinton (SWIN).
Sir Robert Vansittart (VNST).

Oxford University: Modern Papers Room, Bodleian Library (BL):

Conservative Research Department Papers (CRD).
Lord Attlee Papers (MS Attlee).
Geoffrey Dawson Papers (MS Dawson).
Arthur Mann Papers (MS Eng.).
Lord Ponsonby Papers (MS Eng. Hist.).
Gilbert Murray Papers (MS Gilbert Murray).
Harold Macmillan Papers (MS Macmillan).
Viscount Simon Papers (MS Simon).

Primary Sources: Published

Official Documents

Gallup, G.H., *The Gallup International Public Opinion Polls: Great Britain, 1937–1975*, vol.1 (New York: 1976).
Hansard, *Parliamentary Debates. Official Reports. 5th Series, House of Commons,* 1935–1939.
Hansard, *Parliamentary Debates. Official Reports. 5th Series, House of Lords,* 1935–1939.
Madge, C. and Harrison T., *Britain: By Mass Observation* (Middlesex: 1939).
Van Zeeland, P., *Report to the Governments of the United Kingdom and France on the Possibility of Obtaining a General Reduction of the Obstacles to International Trade,* (London: 1938).
Woodward, E.L. and Butler, R. (eds.), *Documents on British Foreign Policy: 1919–1939. 3rd Series,* vol.2 (London: 1949).
——, (eds.), *Documents on British Foreign Policy 1919–1939. 3rd Series,* vol.3 (London: 1949).

Newspapers and Periodicals

Daily Express.
Daily Herald.
Daily Mail.
Daily Telegraph and Morning Post.
Daily Worker.
Economist.

Glasgow Forward.
Guardian.
Headway.
Independent.
Independent on Sunday.
Listener.
Manchester Guardian.
Naval Review.
New York Times.
News Chronicle.
News of the World.
Observer.
Peace News.
Punch.
Socialist Leader.
Spectator.
Sun.
The Sunday Times.
The Times.
Tribune.
Yorkshire Post.

Diaries and Memoirs

Amery, L.S., *My Political Life, vol.3, The Unforgiving Years, 1929–1940* (London: 1955).
Attlee, C.R., *As It Happened* (London: 1954).
Avon, Earl of, *Facing the Dictators: The Eden Memoirs* (London: 1962).
———, *The Reckoning: The Eden Memoirs* (London: 1965).
Balfour, Lord, *Wings over Westminster* (London: 1973).
Barnes, J. and Nicholson, D. (eds.), *The Empire at Bay: The Leo Amery Diaries, vol.5, 1929–1945* (London: 1988).
Bond, B. (ed.), *Chief of Staff: The Diaries of Lieutenant-General Sir Henry Pownall, vol.1, 1933–1940* (London: 1972).
Boothby, R., *I Fight to Live* (London: 1947).
Cecil, Viscount, *All the Way* (London: 1949).
Churchill, W.S., *The Gathering Storm* (London: 1948).
Colville, J., *The Fringes of Power: Downing Street Diaries, 1939–1955* (London: 1985).
Cook, R., *The Point of Departure* (London: 2003).
Crowson, N.J. (ed.), *Fleet Street, Press Barons and Politics: The Journals of Collin Brooks, 1932–1940* (London: 1998).
Dalton, H., *The Fateful Years: Memoirs, 1931–1945* (London: 1957).
Dilks, D. (ed.), *The Diaries of Sir Alexander Cadogan: 1938–1945* (London: 1971).
Duff Cooper, A., *Old Men Forget* (London: 1953).

Halifax, Earl of, *Fullness of Days*, 2nd edn. (London: 1957).
Harvey, J. (ed.), *The Diplomatic Diaries of Oliver Harvey: 1937–1940* (London: 1970).
Henderson, N., *Failure of a Mission: Berlin 1937–1939* (London: 1940).
Home, Lord, *The Way the Wind Blows* (London: 1976).
Jones, T., *A Diary with Letters, 1931–1950* (Oxford: 1954).
Macmillan, H., *The Winds of Change, 1914–1939* (London: 1966).
Minney, R.J. (ed.), *The Private Papers of Hore-Belisha* (London: 1960).
Nicolson, N. (ed.), *Harold Nicolson: Diaries and Letters, 1930–1939* (London: 1966).
Pimlott, B. (ed.), *The Political Diary of Hugh Dalton, 1918–1940, 1945–1960* (London: 1986).
Rhodes, J.R. (ed.), *Chips: The Diaries of Sir Henry Channon* (London: 1967).
Roskill, S. (ed.), *Hankey: Man of Secrets, vol.3, 1931–1963* (London: 1974).
Simon, Viscount, *Retrospect: The Memoirs of the Right Honourable Viscount Simon* (London: 1952).
Smart, N. (ed.), *The Diaries and Letters of Robert Bernays, 1932–1939: An Insider's Account of the House of Commons* (New York: 1996).
Strang, Lord, *Home and Abroad* (London: 1956).
Templewood, Viscount, *Nine Troubled Years* (London: 1954).
Vansittart, Lord, *The Mist Procession* (London: 1958).
Williams, F., *A Prime Minister Remembers* (London: 1961).

Contemporary Political Pamphlets

Anti-Slavery Committee, *Letter to the Prime Minister on the Transfer of Colonial Territories* (1938).
British Union of Fascists, *Mind Britain's Business: B.U.F. Notes for Speakers* (1936).
Colonial League, *German Colonial Demands* (1938).
Communist Party, *A.R.P.: The Practical Air Raid Protection Britain Needs* (1938).
——, *Can Conscription Save Peace?* (1939).
——, *Colonies, Mandates and Peace* (1936).
——, *Labour and Armaments* (1937).
Debb, D.N., *World Peace and How to Establish it* (1938).
Gollancz, V., *Is Mr Chamberlain Saving Peace?* (1939).
Hall, N.F., *Economic Appeasement* (1937).
Hathaway, C.A., *Collective Security: The Road to Peace* (1938).
Independent Labour Party, *The Socialist Challenge to Poverty, Fascism, Imperialism, War: Basic Policy of the I.L.P.* (1939).
Labour Party, *The Full Facts of the Czech Crisis* (1938).
——, *Labour's Immediate Programme* (1937).
——, *'National' Government's Disarmament Record* (1935).
Lansbury, G., *Peace Through Economic Cooperation* (1937).
League of Nations Union, *Economic Steps Towards World Peace* (1937).
——, *Memorandum on Policy* (1938).
——, *Policy Manifesto* (1936).

——, *Resolutions of the Executive Committee* (1939).

Liberal Party, *For Peace and Democracy: The Liberal Party and 'Popular Front'* (1937).

——, *Freedom and Peace* (1937).

——, *Liberal Policy for Today's Needs* (1937).

Militant Labour League, *'Peace Alliance' and the Road to War* (1938).

Moore, A., *The Necessity for a British League of Nations* (1938).

Morgenthau, H.J., *The Problem of Neutrality* (1938).

National Labour Party, *To Peace: Which Way Now?* (1938).

National Peace Council, *Peace and Colonial Policy* (1936).

National Unemployed Workers' Movement, *Chamberlain! Face the Facts* (1939).

Pacifist Research Bureau, *New Tendencies in Colonial Policy* (1939).

Public Economy League, *Armaments and their Cost: High Taxes and High Prices* (1937).

Socialist Party, *Peace Alliance or Worker's Front?* (1938).

Tarr, E.J., *After Munich: Where do we go from here?* (1938).

Witte, S., *Background for Chamberlain: A Turn of the Century Plan for European Peace* (1938).

Women's International League for Peace and Freedom, *Opening the Empire Door: A Positive Policy for Peace* (1937).

World Peace Foundation, *Raw Materials, Population Pressure and War* (1936).

Secondary Sources

Books

Adamthwaite, A., *France and the Coming of the Second World War, 1936–1939* (London: 1977).

——, *The Lost Peace: International Relations in Europe, 1918–1939* (London: 1980).

Albig, W., *Modern Public Opinion* (New York: 1956).

Alexander, M.S., *The Republic in Danger: General Maurice Gamelin and the Politics of French Defence, 1933–1940* (Cambridge: 1992).

Aly, G., *Final Solution: Nazi Population Policy and the Murder of the European Jews* (London: 1999).

Amery, L.S., *The Forward View* (London: 1935).

Andrew, C., *Secret Service: The Making of the British Intelligence Community* (London: 1985).

Aster, S., *Appeasement and All Souls: A Portrait with Documents, 1937–1939* (Cambridge: 2004).

Barnett, C., *The Collapse of British Power* (Gloucester: 1972).

Beasley, W.G., *Japanese Imperialism, 1894–1945* (Oxford: 1991).

Bell, P., *The Origins of the Second World War in Europe*, 2nd edn. (Harlow: 1997).

Bialer, U., *The Shadow of the Bomber: The Fear of Air Attack in British Politics, 1932–1939* (London: 1980).

Billington, D., *Lothian: Phillip Kerr and the Quest for World Order* (London: 2006).

Birn, D.S., *The League of Nations Union, 1918–1945* (Oxford: 1981).

Black, J., *Parliament and Foreign Policy in the Eighteenth Century* (Cambridge: 2004).

Bond, B., *British Military Policy Between the Two World Wars* (Oxford: 1980).

Booth, W.C., *The Rhetoric of Rhetoric: The Quest for Effective Communication.* (Oxford: 2004).

Bourne, K., *The Foreign Policy of Victorian England, 1830–1902* (London: 1970).

Broszat, M., *Der Staat Hitlers* (Munich: 1969).

Browning, C.R., *The Origins of the Final Solution: The Evolution of Nazi Jewish Policy: September 1939–March 1942* (Lincoln, NB: 2004).

Burleigh, M., *The Third Reich: A New History* (New York: 2000).

Burridge, T., *Clement Attlee: A Political Biography* (London: 1985).

Calvocoressi, P. and Wint, G. (eds.), *Total War: Causes and Courses of the Second World War* (London: 1972).

Caputi, R.J., *Neville Chamberlain and Appeasement* (London: 2000).

Carley, M.J., *1939: The Alliance that Never Was and the Coming of World War Two* (Chicago: 1999).

Carr, E.H., *The Twenty Years Crisis, 1919–1939* (London: 1946).

Carstairs, C. and Ware, R. (eds.), *Parliament and International Relations* (Milton Keynes: 1991).

CATO, *Guilty Men*, 21st edn. (London: 1940).

Ceadel, M., *Pacifism in Britain, 1914–1945: The Defining of a Faith* (Oxford: 1980).

Charmley, J., *Chamberlain and the Lost Peace* (London: 1989).

——, *Splendid Isolation: Britain and the Balance of Power, 1874–1914* (London: 1999).

Cockett, R., *Twilight of Truth: Chamberlain, Appeasement and the Manipulation of the Press* (London: 1989).

Colvin, I., *The Chamberlain Cabinet* (New York: 1971).

Compton, J.V., *The Swastika and the Eagle: Hitler, the United States, and the Origins of World War Two* (Boston: 1968).

Cowley, R. (ed.), *More What If? Eminent Historians Imagine What Might Have Been* (London: 2003).

——, (ed.), *What If? The World's Foremost Military Historians Imagine What Might Have Been* (London: 2000).

Cowman, I., *Dominion or Decline: Anglo-American Naval Relations on the Pacific, 1937–1941* (Oxford: 1996).

Crowson, N.J., *Facing Fascism: The Conservative Party and the European Dictators, 1935–1940* (London: 1997).

Crozier, A.J., *Appeasement and Germany's Last Bid for Colonies* (London: 1988).

Dawidowicz, L.S., *The War Against the Jews, 1933–1945* (London: 1986).

De Groot, G.J., *Liberal Crusader: The Life of Sir Archibald Sinclair* (London: 1993).

Denman, R., *Missed Chances: Britain and Europe in the Twentieth Century* (London: 1996).

Dennis, P., *Decision by Default: Peacetime Conscription and British Defence, 1919–1939* (Durham, NC: 1972).

Dutton, D.J, *Liberals in Schism: A History of the National Liberal Party* (London: 2008).
——, *Neville Chamberlain* (London: 2001).
Eubank, K., *Munich* (Oklahoma: 1963).
Faber, D., *Munich: The 1938 Appeasement Crisis* (London: 2008).
Feiling, K., *The Life of Neville Chamberlain* (London: 1946).
Ferguson, N. (ed.), *Virtual History: Alternatives and Counterfactuals* (London: 1998).
Fischer, K.P., *Nazi Germany: A New History* (London: 1995).
Forbes, N., *Doing Business with the Nazis: Britain's Economic and Financial Relations with Germany, 1931–1939* (London: 2000).
Fuchser, L.W., *Neville Chamberlain and Appeasement: A Study in the Politics of History* (London: 1982).
Gannon, F.R., *The British Press and Nazi Germany, 1936–1939* (Oxford: 1971).
George, M., *The Warped Vision: British Foreign Policy, 1933–1939* (Pittsburgh: 1965).
Gibbs, N., *Grand Strategy: vol.1, Rearmament Policy* (London: 1976).
Gilbert, M., *Churchill and America* (London: 2005).
——, *Churchill's Political Philosophy* (Oxford: 1981).
——, *The Roots of Appeasement* (London: 1966).
Gilbert, M. and Gott R. (eds.), *The Appeasers* (London: 1963).
Gill, G., *The League of Nations from 1929–1946* (New York: 1996).
Gillard, D., *Appeasement in Crisis: From Munich to Prague, October 1938–March 1939* (London: 2007).
Griffiths, R., *Fellow Travellers of the Right: British Enthusiasts for Nazi Germany, 1933–1939* (Oxford: 1983).
Haigh, R.H., Morris, D.S. and Peters, A.R., *European Rearmament Policies and their Effect on the Balance of Military Power from Munich 1938 to the Outbreak of War 1939* (Sheffield: 1981).
Haigh, R.H. and Turner, P.W., *The Military and Diplomatic Effects of the Munich Agreement* (Sheffield: 1978).
——, *The Tilted Scales: The Military Balance of Power at the Time of the Munich Crisis, Autumn 1938* (Sheffield: 1978).
Harris, K., *Attlee* (London: 1982).
Harrison, M. (ed.), *The Economics of World War Two: Six Great Powers in International Comparison* (Cambridge: 1998).
Herman, J., *The Paris Embassy of Sir Eric Phipps: Anglo-French Relations and the Foreign Office, 1937–1939* (Sussex: 1998).
Hildebrand, K., *The Foreign Policy of the Third Reich*, trans. by Batsford, B.T. (London: 1973).
——, *The Third Reich* (London: 1984).
Hill, C., *Cabinet Decisions on Foreign Policy: The British Experience, October 1938–June 1941* (Cambridge: 1991).
Hillgruber, A., *Germany and the Two World Wars*, trans. by Kirby, W.C. (Cambridge: 1981).
Hinsley, F.H., *British Intelligence in the Second World War*, vol.1 (London: 1990).
Hobsbawm, E., *Age of Extremes: The Short Twentieth Century* (London: 1994).

————, *On History* (London: 1998).

Howard, A., *The Life of R.A. Butler* (London: 1987).

Howard, M., *The Continental Commitment: The Dilemma of British Defence Policy in the Era of the Two World Wars* (London: 1971).

Johnson, A.C., *Peace Offering* (London: 1936).

Johnson, F.A., *Defence by Committee: The British Committee of Imperial Defence, 1885–1959* (Oxford: 1960).

Joll, J., *Europe Since 1870: An International History*, 4th edn. (London: 1990).

Kaiser, D.E., *Economic Diplomacy and the Origins of the Second World War: Germany, Britain, France, and Eastern Europe, 1930–1939* (Princeton: 1980).

Kee, R., *Munich: The Eleventh Hour* (London: 1988).

Keith-Shaw, D., *Prime Minister Neville Chamberlain* (London: 1939).

Kennedy, J.F., *Why England Slept* (New York: 1940).

Kennedy, P., *The Realities Behind Diplomacy: Background Influences on British External Policy, 1865–1980* (London: 1985).

————, *The Rise and Fall of the Great Powers: Economic Change and Military Conflict from 1500 to 2000* (London: 1988).

Kershaw, I., *The Nazi Dictatorship: Problems and Perspectives of Interpretation* (London: 1985).

Keylor, W.R., *The Twentieth Century World: An International History*, 3rd edn. (Oxford: 1996).

Lamb, R., *The Drift to War, 1922–1939* (London: 1989).

Levy, J.P., *Appeasement and Rearmament: Britain, 1936–1939* (New York: 2006).

Lukacs, J., *Churchill: Visionary, Statesman, Historian* (New Haven: 2002).

Lukes, I., *Czechoslovakia Between Stalin and Hitler: The Diplomacy of Edvard Benes in the 1930s* (Oxford: 1996).

Macleod, I., *Neville Chamberlain* (London: 1961).

Mangold, P., *Success and Failure in British Foreign Policy: Evaluating the Record, 1900–2000* (Basingstoke: 2001).

Mazower, M., *Dark Continent: Europe's Twentieth Century* (London: 1998).

McDonough, F., *Neville Chamberlain, Appeasement and the British Road to War* (Manchester: 1998).

McLachlan, D., *In the Chair: Barrington-Ward of The Times, 1927–1948* (London: 1971).

McLaine, I., *Ministry of Morale: Home Front Morale and the Ministry of Information in World War Two* (London: 1979).

Middlemas, K., *Diplomacy of Illusion: The British Government and Germany, 1937–1939* (London: 1972).

Mommsen, W.J. and Kettenacker, L. (eds.), *The Fascist Challenge and the Policy of Appeasement* (London: 1993).

Moorhouse, R., *Killing Hitler: The Plots, the Assassins, and the Dictator who Cheated Death* (New York: 2006).

Morris, B., *The Roots of Appeasement: The British Weekly Press and Nazi Germany During the 1930s* (London: 1991).

Murray, G., *From the League of Nations to United Nations* (Oxford: 1948).

Murray, W. and Millett, A.R., *A War to be Won: Fighting the Second World War* (Cambridge, MA: 2000).

Namier, L., *Diplomatic Prelude, 1938–1939* (London: 1948).

Neilson, K., *Britain, Soviet Russia and the Collapse of the Versailles Order, 1919–1939* (Cambridge: 2005).

Neville, P., *Appeasing Hitler: The Diplomacy of Sir Nevile Henderson, 1937–1939* (London: 1999).

——, *Hitler and Appeasement: The British Attempt to Prevent the Second World War* (London: 2006).

——, *Neville Chamberlain: A Study in Failure?* (Kent: 1992).

Newton, S., *Profits of Peace: The Political Economy of Anglo-German Appeasement* (Oxford: 1996).

Northedge, F.S., *The International Political System* (London: 1976).

——, *The League of Nations: Its Life and Times, 1920–1946* (Leicester: 1986).

——, *The Troubled Giant: Britain Among the Great Powers, 1916–1939* (Suffolk: 1966).

Offner, A.A., *American Appeasement: United States Foreign Policy and Germany, 1933–1938* (Cambridge, MA: 1969).

Olson, L., *Troublesome Young Men: The Rebels Who Brought Churchill to Power and Helped Save England* (London: 2007).

Ostrower, G.B., *Collective Insecurity: The United States and the League of Nations in the Early 1930s*, (London: 1976).

——, *The League of Nations from 1919–1929* (New York: 1996).

Ovendale, R., *Appeasement and the English Speaking World: Britain, the USA, the Dominions, and the Policy of 'Appeasement', 1937–1939* (Cardiff: 1975).

Parker, R.A.C., *Chamberlain and Appeasement: British Policy and the Coming of the Second World War* (London: 1993).

——, *Churchill and Appeasement* (London: 2000).

Parkinson, R., *Peace for our Time: Munich to Dunkirk – The Inside Story* (London: 1971).

Peden, G., *British Rearmament and the Treasury, 1932–1939* (Edinburgh: 1979).

Pennybacker, S.D., *From Scottsboro to Munich: Race and Political Culture in 1930s Britain* (Princeton: 2009).

Peters, A.R., *Anthony Eden at the Foreign Office, 1931–1938* (New York: 1986).

Porter, B., *Britain, Europe and the World, 1850–1982: Delusions of Grandeur* (London: 1983).

——, *The Lion's Share: A Short History of British Imperialism, 1850–1995*, 3rd edn. (London: 1996).

Pyper, C.B., *Chamberlain and his Critics: A Statesman Vindicated* (Hounslow: 1962).

Raffo, P., *The League of Nations*, (London: 1974).

Ragsdale, H., *The Soviets, the Munich Crisis, and the Coming of World War Two* (Cambridge: 2004).

Reynolds, D., *In Command of History: Churchill Fighting and Writing the Second World War* (London: 2004).

——, *The Creation of the Anglo-American Alliance, 1937–1941: A Study in Competitive Cooperation* (London: 1981).

——, *Summits: Six Meetings that Shaped the Twentieth Century* (New York: 2009).

Rich, N., *Hitler's War Aims: Ideology, the Nazi State and the Course of Expansion* (London: 1974).

Richards, E., *Pacifism: A Brief History* (London: 1981).

Robbins, K., *Munich 1938* (London: 1968).

Roberts, A. (ed.), *What Might Have Been? Imaginary History from Twelve Leading Historians* (London: 2003).

Roberts, G., *The Soviet Union and the Origins of the Second World War: Russo-German Relations and the Road to War, 1933–1941* (London: 1995).

——, *Stalin's Wars: From World War to Cold War, 1939–1953* (New Haven: 2006).

Rock, W.R., *Appeasement on Trial: British Foreign Policy and its Critics, 1938–1939* (Washington: 1966).

——, *British Appeasement in the 1930s* (London: 1977).

——, *Chamberlain and Roosevelt: British Foreign Policy and the United States, 1937–1940* (Ohio: 1988).

Roi, M.L., *Alternative to Appeasement, Sir Robert Vansittart and Alliance Diplomacy, 1934–1937* (London: 1997).

Rose, N., *The Cliveden Set: Portrait of an Exclusive Fraternity* (London: 2000).

——, *Vansittart: Study of a Diplomat* (London: 1978).

Rowse, A.L., *All Souls and Appeasement* (London: 1961).

——, *Appeasement: A Study in Political Decline, 1933–1939* (New York: 1961).

Ruggiero, J., *Neville Chamberlain and British Rearmament: Pride, Prejudice, and Politics* (London: 1999).

Russel, B., *Which Way to Peace?* (London: 1936).

Rzheshevsky, O., *Europe 1939: Was War Inevitable?* (Moscow: 1989).

Schmidt, G., *The Politics and Economics of Appeasement: British Foreign Policy in the 1930s*, trans. by Bennett-Ruete, J. (Oxford: 1986).

Self, R., *Neville Chamberlain: A Biography* (London: 2006).

——, (ed.), *The Neville Chamberlain Diary Letters. vol.1: The Making of a Politician, 1915–1920* (London: 2000).

——, (ed.), *The Neville Chamberlain Diary Letters. vol.2: The Reform Years, 1921–1927* (London: 2000).

——, (ed.), *The Neville Chamberlain Diary Letters. vol.3: The Heir Apparent, 1928–1933* (London: 2002).

——, (ed.), *The Neville Chamberlain Diary Letters. vol.4: The Downing Street Years, 1934–1940* (London: 2005).

Shaw, L.G., *The British Political Elite and the Soviet Union, 1937–1939* (London: 2003).

Shay, R., *British Rearmament in the Thirties: Politics and Profits* (Princeton: 1977).

Shepherd, R., *A Class Divided: Appeasement and the Road to Munich 1938* (London: 1988).

Smart, N., *Neville Chamberlain* (London: 2010).

Stewart, G., *Burying Caesar: Churchill, Chamberlain and the Battle for the Tory Party* (London: 1999).

Stone, D., *Responses to Nazism in Britain, 1933–1939: Before War and Holocaust* (London: 2003).

Strang, Lord, *The Diplomatic Career* (London: 1962).

Taylor, A.J.P., *Beaverbrook* (London: 1972).

——, *Europe: Grandeur and Decline*, 1974 edn. (Middlesex: 1974).

——, *The Origins of the Second World War*, 1961 edn. (London: 1961).

Taylor, T., *Munich: The Price of Peace* (London: 1979).

Thomas, M., *Britain, France and Appeasement: Anglo-French Relations in the Popular Front Era* (Oxford: 1996).

Thompson, N., *The Anti-Appeasers: Conservative Opposition to Appeasement in the 1930s* (Oxford: 1971).

Thurlow, R., *Fascism in Britain: From Oswald Mosley's Blackshirts to the National Front* (London: 1998).

Watt, D.C. (ed.), *Hitler's Mein Kampf* (London: 1990).

——, *How War Came: The Immediate Origins of the Second World War, 1938–1939* (London: 1989).

Wark, W., *The Ultimate Enemy: British Intelligence and Nazi Germany*, (New York: 1985).

Weinberg, G.L., *The Foreign Policy of Hitler's Germany: Diplomatic Revolution in Europe, 1933–1936* (Chicago: 1970).

——, *The Foreign Policy of Hitler's Germany: Starting World War Two, 1937–1939* (Chicago: 1980).

Weindling, P. (ed.), *International Health Organisations and Movements, 1918–1939* (Cambridge: 1995).

Wendt, B.J., *Economic Appeasement. Handel und Finanz in der Britischen Deutschland Politik, 1933–1939* (Düsseldorf: 1971).

Wheeler-Bennett, J., *Munich: Prologue to Tragedy* (London: 1948).

Wrench, J.E., *Geoffrey Dawson and Our Times* (London: 1955).

Wybrow, R.J., *Britain Speaks Out, 1937–1987: A Social History as Seen Through the Gallup Data* (London: 1989).

Young, R.J., *France and the Origins of the Second World War* (London: 1996).

Articles in Journals and Newspapers

Adamthwaite, A., 'The British government and the media, 1937–1939', *Journal of Contemporary History*, vol.18(2), 1983, pp.281–98.

Aster, S., 'Appeasement: Before and after revisionism', *Diplomacy and Statecraft*, vol.19(3), 2008, pp.443–80.

Aulach, H., 'Britain and the Sudeten issue, 1938: The evolution of a policy', *Journal of Contemporary History*, vol.18(2), 1983, pp.233–60.

Beck, P.J., 'The league of nations and the great powers, 1936–1940', *World Affairs*, vol.157(4), 1995, pp.175–90.

———, 'Politicians verses historians: Lord Avon's "appeasement battle" against "lamentably, appeasement-minded historians"', *Twentieth Century British History*, vol.9(3), 1998, pp.396–419.

———, 'Searching for peace in Munich, not Geneva: The British government, the league of nations and the Sudeten question', *Diplomacy and Statecraft*, vol.10(2), 1999, pp.236–57.

———, 'Was the league of nations really a failure?: The 'new diplomacy' in a period of appeasement', *The Yearbook of the Scottish Association of Teachers of History*, vol.9, 1995, pp.32–38.

Bell, P., 'The foreign office and the 1939 royal visit to america: Courting the USA in an era of isolationism', *Journal of Contemporary History*, vol.37(4), 2002, pp.599–616.

Bessel, R., 'Functionalists vs. intentionalists: The debate twenty years on *or* whatever happened to functionalism and intentionalism?', *German Studies Review*, vol.26(1), 2003, pp.15–20.

Best, A., 'Economic appeasement or economic nationalism? A political perspective on the British empire, Japan, and the rise of intra-Asian trade, 1933–1937', *Journal of Imperial and Commonwealth History*, vol.30(2), 2002, pp.77–101.

Blakeway, D., 'Umbrella in the works', *Listener*, 22 Sept. 1988.

Brien, A., 'A peace of paper', *Listener*, 12 May 1988.

Chandler, A., 'Munich and morality: The bishops of the church of England and appeasement', *Twentieth Century British History*, vol.5(1), 1994, pp.77–99.

Charmley, J., 'The men who would have kept peace with Hitler', *The Times*, 29 Aug. 1989.

Coghlan, F., 'Armaments, economic policy and appeasement: Background to British foreign policy, 1931–1937', *History*, vol.57(190), 1972, pp.205–16.

Coleman, T., 'Peace on a wing and a prayer', *Guardian*, 23 Sept. 1988.

Crowson, N.J., 'Conservative parliamentary dissent over foreign policy during the premiership of Neville Chamberlain: Myth or reality?', *Parliamentary History*, vol.14(3), 1995, pp.315–36.

———, 'The conservative party and the call for national service, 1937–1939: Compulsion versus voluntarism', *Journal of Contemporary British History*, vol.9(3), 1995, pp.507–28.

Crozier, A.J., 'Prelude to Munich: British foreign policy and Germany, 1935–1938', *European Studies Review*, vol.6(3), 1976, pp.357–82.

Dilks, D., 'New perspectives on Chamberlain', *Listener*, 11 Nov. 1976.

———, 'A question of intelligence', *Listener*, 12 Oct. 1978.

———, '"We must hope for the best and prepare for the worst": The prime minister, the cabinet and Hitler's Germany, 1937–1939', *Proceedings of the British Academy*, vol.73, 1987, pp.309–52.

Dunbabin, J.P.D., 'British rearmament in the 1930s: A chronology and review', *Historical Journal*, vol.18(3), 1975, pp.587–609.

Dutton, D.J., 'Power brokers or just 'glamour boys'? The Eden group, September 1939–May 1940', *English Historical Review*, vol.118(476), 2003, pp.412–24.

Eatwell, R., 'Munich, public opinion, and popular front', *Journal of Contemporary History*, vol.6(4), 1971, pp.122–40.

Ekoko, A.E, 'The British attitude towards Germany's colonial irredentism in Africa in the inter-war years', *Journal of Contemporary History*, vol.14(2), 1979, pp.287–308.

Egerton, G.W., 'Collective security as political myth: Liberal internationalism and the league of nations in politics and history', *International History Review*, vol.5(4), 1983, pp.496–524.

Ferris, J.R., ' "Now that the milk is spilt": Appeasement and the archive on intelligence', *Diplomacy and Statecraft*, vol.19(3), 2008, pp.527–65.

Foster, A., 'The times and appeasement: The second phase', *Journal of Contemporary History*, vol.16(3), 1981, pp.441–66.

Goldenberg, S. and MacAskill, E., 'Obama warns republicans: 'Lay off my wife'', *Guardian*, 20 May 2008.

Goldman, A.L., 'Sir Robert Vansittart's search for Italian cooperation against Hitler, 1933–1936', *Journal of Contemporary History*, vol.9(3), 1974, pp.93–130.

Goodlad, G.D., 'Appeasement', *Modern History Review*, vol.12(4), pp.14–15.

Grayson, R., 'Leo Amery's imperialist alternative to appeasement in the 1930s', *Twentieth Century British History*, vol.17(4), 2006, pp.489–515.

Hill, L., 'Three crises, 1938–1939', *Journal of Contemporary History*, vol.3(1), 1988, pp.113–44.

Howard, C., 'The policy of isolation', *Historical Journal*, vol.10(1), 1967, pp.77–88.

Hucker, D., 'The unending debate: Appeasement, Chamberlain and the origins of the second world war', *Intelligence and National Security*, vol.23(4), 2008, pp.536–51.

Hughes, M.J., 'The peripatetic career structure of the British diplomatic establishment', *Diplomacy and Statecraft*, vol.14(1), 2003, pp.29–48.

Kee, R., 'Peace with dishonour?', *Independent*, 23 Sept. 1988.

Kennedy, G., 'Becoming dependant on the kindness of strangers: Britain's secret foreign policy, naval arms limitation and the Soviet factor, 1935–1937', *War in History*, vol.2(1), 2004, pp.34–60.

Lammers, D., 'From Whitehall after Munich: The foreign office and the future control of British policy', *Historical Journal*, vol.16(4), 1973, pp.831–56.

Lukowitz, D.C., 'British pacifists and appeasement: The peace pledge union', *Journal of Contemporary History*, vol.9(1), 1974, pp.115–27.

MacDonald, C.A., 'Economic appeasement and the German 'moderates', 1937–1939: An introductory essay', *Past and Present*, vol.56, 1972, pp.105–35.

McDonough, F., 'Why appeasement?', *Modern History Review*, vol.5(4), 1994, pp.6–9.

McKercher, B.J.C., 'National security and imperial defence: British grand strategy and appeasement, 1930–1939', *Diplomacy and Statecraft*, vol.19(3), 2008, pp.391–442.

Meredith, D., 'The British government and colonial economic policy, 1919–1939', *Economic History Review*, vol.28, 1975, pp.484–99.

——, 'British trade diversion policy and the colonial issue in the 1930s', *Journal of European Economic History*, vol.25(1), 1996, pp.38–68.

Mills, W.C., 'The nyon conference: Neville Chamberlain, Anthony Eden, and the appeasement of Italy in 1937', *International History Review*, vol.15(1), 1993, pp.1–22.

Moradiellos, E., 'The origins of British non-intervention in the Spanish civil war: Anglo-Spanish relations in early 1936', *European History Quarterly*, vol.21(3), 1991, pp.339–64.

Murray, W., 'Neither navy was ready', *United States Naval Institute Proceedings*, vol.107(4), 1981, pp.38–47.

Neilson, K., 'Orme Sargent, appeasement and British policy in Europe, 1933–1939', *Twentieth Century British History*, vol.21(1), 2010, pp.1–28.

——, ' "Pursued by a bear": British estimates of Soviet military strength and Anglo-Soviet relations, 1922–1939', *Canadian Journal of History*, vol.28(2), 1993, pp.189–221.

Neville, P., 'Lord Vansittart, Sir Welford Selby and the debate about treasury interference in the conduct of British foreign policy in the 1930s', *Journal of Contemporary History*, vol.36(4), 2001, pp.623–33.

——, 'A prophet scorned? Ralph Wigram, the foreign office and the German threat, 1933–1936', *Journal of Contemporary History*, vol.40(1), 2005, pp.41–54.

Nicolson, H., 'The commos and the 1938 crisis', *Listener*, 25 Nov. 1948.

Overy, R., 'Parting with pacifism in the 1930s', *History Today*, vol.59(8), 2009, pp.23–29.

Peden, G., 'A matter of timing: The economic background to British foreign policy, 1937–1939', *History*, vol.69(225), 1984, pp.15–28.

Pederson, S., 'Back to the league of nations', *American History Review*, vol.112(4), 2007, pp.1091–1117.

Pemberton, J., 'New worlds for old: The league of nations in the age of electricity', *Review of International Studies*, vol.28(2), 2002, pp.311–36.

Powers, R.H., 'Winston Churchill's parliamentary commentary on British foreign policy, 1935–1938', *Journal of Modern History*, vol.26(3), 1954, pp.179–82.

Robbins, K., 'Konrad Henlein, the Sudeten question and British foreign policy', *Historical Journal*, vol.12(4), 1969, pp.674–97.

Roberts, G., 'The foreign office and the failure of Anglo-Soviet rapprochement', *Journal of Contemporary History*, vol.16(4), 1981, pp.725–55.

——, 'The Soviet decision for a pact with Nazi Germany', *Soviet Studies*, vol.44(1), 1992, pp.57–78.

Roi, M.L., 'Appeasement: Rethinking the policy and the policy makers', *Diplomacy and Statecraft*, vol.19(3), 2008, pp.383–90.

Schroeder, P.W., 'Munich and the British tradition', *Historical Journal*, vol.19(1), 1976, pp.223–43.

Sheridan, D., 'Mass observing the British', *History Today*, vol.34(3), 1984, pp.42–46.

Slosson, P., 'Review of W.S. Churchill, the gathering storm', *American Historical Review*, vol.54, 1948, pp.102–3.

Smith, M.S., 'Rearmament and deterrence in Britain in the 1930s', *Journal of Strategic Studies*, vol.1(3), 1978, pp.313–37.

Stedman, A.D., '"A most dishonest argument"?: Chamberlain's government, anti-appeasers, and the persistence of league of nations language before the second world war', *Contemporary British History, Special Issue: Politics, Power and Diplomacy in the Twentieth Century: Essays in Honour of David Dutton*, vol.25(1), 2011.

——, 'Reassessing economic appeasement during Chamberlain's peace-time premiership: A two-headed beast?', *Working Papers in Military and International History: University of Salford European Studies Research Institute*, vol.7, 2009, pp.5–31.

Strang, G.B., 'The spirit of ulysses? Ideology and British appeasement in the 1930s', *Diplomacy and Statecraft*, vol.19(3), 2008, pp.481–526.

Sylvest, C., 'Interwar internationalism, the British labour party and the historiography of international relations', *International Studies Quarterly*, vol.48(2), 2004, pp.409–32.

Taylor, P.M., 'Appeasement: Guilty men or guilty conscience?', *Modern History Review*, vol.1(2), 1989, pp.23–25.

Thomas, M., 'Appeasement in the late third republic', *Diplomacy and Statecraft*, vol.19(3), 2008, pp.566–607.

Thompson, J.A., 'Lord cecil and the pacifists in the league of nations union', *Historical Journal*, vol.20(4), 1977, pp.949–59.

Vital, D., 'Czechoslovakia and the powers: September 1938', *Journal of Contemporary History*, vol.1(4), 1966, pp.37–68.

Watt, D.C., 'Appeasement: The rise of a 'revisionist' school?', *Political Quarterly*, vol.36(2), 1965, pp.191–213.

Weinberg, G.L., 'The Munich crisis revisited', *International History Review*, vol.11(4), 1989, pp.668–88.

Wheatcroft, G., 'The great appeasers', *Independent on Sunday*, 20 Sept. 1988.

Wilkinson, A., 'Thanking god for Neville Chamberlain: Appeasement and the English churches', *Modern History Review*, vol.1(2), 1989, pp.26–27.

Williamson, P., 'Christian conservatives and the totalitarian challenge, 1933–1940', *English Historical Review*, vol.115(462), 2000, pp.607–42.

Wilson, G., 'PM rated worst since 1930s', *Sun*, 14 April 2008.

Witherell, L.L., 'Lord Salisbury's "watching committee" and the fall of Neville Chamberlain, may 1940', *English Historical Review*, vol.116(469), 2001, pp.1134–66.

Chapters in Edited Collections

Aster, S., '"Guilty men": The case of Neville Chamberlain', in Boyce, R. and Robertson, E.M. (eds.), *Paths to War: New Essays on the Origins of the Second World War* (London: 1989), pp.233–68.

Beck, P.J., 'Britain and appeasement in the late 1930s: Was there a league of nations alternative?', in Richardson, D. and Stone G. (eds.), *Decisions and*

Diplomacy: Essays in Twentieth Century International History (London: 1995), pp.153–73.

Carley, M.J., 'Caught in a cleft stick: Soviet diplomacy and the Spanish civil war', in Johnson, G. (ed.), *The International Context of the Spanish Civil War* (Newcastle upon Tyne: 2009), pp.151–82.

Cassels, A., 'Britain, Italy and the Axis: How to make friends with Mussolini and influence Hitler', in Johnson, G. (ed.), *The International Context of the Spanish Civil War* (Newcastle upon Tyne: 2009), pp.19–32.

Ceadel, M., 'The peace movements between the wars: Problems of definition', in Taylor, R. and Young, N. (eds.), *Campaigns for Peace: British Peace Movements in the Twentieth Century* (Manchester: 1987), pp.73–99.

Dilks, D., ' "The unnecessary war"? Military advice and foreign policy in Great Britain, 1931–1939', in Preston, A. (ed.), *General Staffs and Diplomacy Before the Second World War* (London: 1978), pp.98–132.

Johnson, G., 'Lord Robert Cecil and Europe's fascist dictators: Three case studies, 1935–1939', in Johnson, G. (ed.) *The International Context of the Spanish Civil War* (Newcastle upon Tyne: 2009), pp.57–74.

Kenney, M.L., 'The role of the house of commons in British foreign policy during the 1937–1938 session', in Downs, N. (ed.), *Essays in Honour of Conyers Read* (Chicago: 1953), pp.138–85.

Keylor, W.R., 'Franklin D. Roosevelt in Europe: Responding to German revisionism, 1935–1938', in Johnson, G. (ed.), *The International Context of the Spanish Civil War* (Newcastle upon Tyne: 2009), pp.117–30.

Lacaze, Y., 'Daladier, Bonnet and the decision-making process during the Munich crisis, 1938', in Boyce, R. (ed.), *French Foreign and Defence Policy, 1918–1940: The Decline and Fall of a Great Power* (London: 1999), pp.215–33.

Mason, T., 'Intention and explanation: A current controversy about the interpretation of national socialism', in Hirschfeld, G. and Kettenacker, L. (eds.), *Der Führerstaat: Mythos und Realität* (Stuttgart: 1981), pp.23–42.

Mommsen, H., 'Hitler's stellung im nationalsozialistchen herrschaftsystem', in Hirschfeld, G. and Kettenacker, L. (eds.), *Der Führerstaat: Mythos und Realität* (Stuttgart: 1981), pp.43–72.

Murray, W., 'The war of 1938: Chamberlain fails to sway Hitler at Munich', in Cowley, R. (ed.), *More What If? Eminent Historians Imagine What Might Have Been* (London: 2003), pp.255–78.

Neville, P., 'Sir Alexander Cadogan, the foreign office and British involvement in the Spanish civil war', in Johnson, G. (ed.), *The International Context of the Spanish Civil War* (Newcastle upon Tyne: 2009), pp.75–86.

Robbins, K., 'The British churches and British foreign policy', in Robbins, K. and Fisher, J. (eds.), *Religion and British Foreign Policy, 1815–1941* (Dordrecht: 2010), pp.9–32.

Roberts, A., 'Prime minister Halifax: Great Britain makes peace with Germany, 1940', in Cowley, R. (ed.), *More What If? Eminent Historians Imagine What Might Have Been* (London: 2003), pp.279–90.

Searle, A., 'The German military contribution to the Spanish civil war', in Johnson, G. (ed.), *The International Context of the Spanish Civil War* (Newcastle upon Tyne: 2009), pp.131–50.

Shaw, M., 'War, peace and British marxism, 1895–1945', in Taylor, R. and Young, N. (eds.), *Campaigns for Peace: British Peace Movements in the Twentieth Century* (Manchester: 1987), pp.49–72.

Stead, P, 'The people and the pictures: The British working-class and film in the 1930s', in Pronay, N. and Spring, D.W. (eds.), *Propaganda, Politics and Film, 1918–1945* (London: 1982), pp.77–97.

Stedman, A.D., ' "Then what could Chamberlain do other than what Chamberlain did?" the enduring need for a more nuanced understanding of British policy and alternatives to appeasement, 1937–1939', in Johnson, G. (ed.), *The International Context of the Spanish Civil War* (Newcastle upon Tyne: 2009), pp.87–116.

Stone, G., 'Britain, France and the Spanish problem, 1936–1939', in Richardson, D. and Stone, G. (eds.), *Decisions and Diplomacy: Essays in Twentieth Century International History* (London: 1995), pp.129–52.

——, 'From entente to alliance: Anglo-French relations, 1935–1939', in Sharp, A. and Stone, G. (eds.), *Anglo-French Relations in the Twentieth Century* (London: 2000), pp.180–204.

——, 'Italo-German-Portuguese collaboration in the Spanish civil war, 1936–1939', in Johnson, G. (ed.), *The International Context of the Spanish Civil War* (Newcastle upon Tyne: 2009), pp.33–56.

Taylor, P.M., 'British official attitudes towards propaganda abroad, 1918–1938', in Pronay, N. and Spring, D.W. (eds.), *Propaganda, Politics and Film, 1918–1945* (London: 1982), pp.23–49.

Thomas, M., 'France and the Czechoslovak crisis', in Lukes, I. and Goldstein, E. (eds.), *The Munich Crisis, 1938: Prelude to World War Two* (London: 1999), pp.122–59.

Van den Dungen, P., 'Critics and criticism of the British peace movement', in Taylor, R. and Young, N. (eds.), *Campaigns for Peace: British Peace Movements in the Twentieth Century* (Manchester: 1987), pp.260–86.

Watt, D.C., 'European military leadership and the breakdown of Europe, 1919–1939', in Preston, A. (ed.), *General Staffs and Diplomacy Before the Second World War* (London: 1978), pp.9–23.

——, 'The historiography of appeasement', in Sked, A. and Cook, C. (eds.), *Crisis and Controversy: Essays in Honour of A.J.P. Taylor* (London: 1976), pp.110–29.

Young, N., 'Tradition and innovation in the British peace movement: Towards an analytical framework', in Taylor, R. and Young, N. (eds.), *Campaigns for Peace: British Peace Movements in the Twentieth Century* (Manchester: 1987), pp.5–22.

——, 'War resistance and the British peace movement since 1914', in Taylor, R. and Young, N. (eds.), *Campaigns for Peace: British Peace Movements in the Twentieth Century* (Manchester: 1987), pp.23–48.

Unpublished Theses

Burzan, B.G., 'The British Peace Movement, 1919–1931', unpublished PhD thesis, London University (1973).

Roberts, D.M., 'Hugh Dalton and the Labour Party in the 1930s', unpublished PhD thesis, University of Kingston upon Thames (1978).

Archive Reference Works

Aster, S. (ed.), *British Foreign Policy, 1918–1945: A Guide to Research and Research Materials* (Wilmington, DE: 1984).

Cook, C., *Sources in British Political History, 1900–1951: A Guide to the Private Papers of Members of Parliament* (London: 1977).

Ford, G. and Ford, P. (eds.), *A Guide to Parliamentary Papers: What they are, How to find them, How to use them*, 3rd edn. (Shannon: 1972).

Snow, P. (ed.), *The United States: A Guide to Library Holdings in the United Kingdom* (Boston Spa: 1982).

Wilson, S.S., *The Cabinet Office to 1945* (London: 1975).

TV and Films

Glorious 39. Dir. S. Poliakoff. Momentum Pictures. 2009.

ITV Lunchtime News, 27 July 2009.

INDEX

308   Alternatives to Appeasement

USSR
  See Soviet Union

Vansittart, Sir Robert   15, 27, 70, 86,
  121, 137, 141, 172, 183, 184,
  186, 187, 189–90, 199–200,
  214–215, 216, 217, 219, 227,
  232, 236, 237
Van Zeeland Report   49–51, 55, 59
Versailles Settlement   10, 41, 45–46,
  84, 91, 96, 107, 112, 117, 138,
  168, 200, 214, 238
Von Manstein, Field Marshall
  Erich   228

Walker, James   127
Wall Street Crash
  See Great Depression
War, the threat of (in British
  diplomacy and as an alternative to
  appeasement)   8, 204, 226–231
  Government consideration and
    practice   9, 213–226
  Historical writing on   2, 196–203
  Non-government political
    consideration   204–210, 212–213
  Press and public opinion on
    210–212

See also Great War; Second World
  War; Spanish Civil War
War scare (January 1939)   68,
  144–145, 147, 173, 189, 223–224
Watt, D.C.   242
Wedgwood, Josiah   96, 100, 131–132,
  170, 180, 206, 208, 209, 213
Welles, Sumner   141–142
Wellock, Wilfred   23
Wendt, Berndt   42–43
Wheeler-Bennett, Sir John   2
Williams, Francis   41–42, 87
Wilson, Sir Arnold   17, 57
Wilson, Sir Horace   1–2, 4, 7, 220
Wilson, Woodrow   84, 114, 116
Wint, Guy   201
Wise, Alfred   111
Wohlthat, Helmuth   68
Wolmer, Viscount   130, 161,
  169, 205
Women's International League for Peace
  and Freedom   54
World Economic Conference   55, 140

Yalta Conference   203, 234
Yorkshire Post   133
Yugoslavia   134, 147, 150